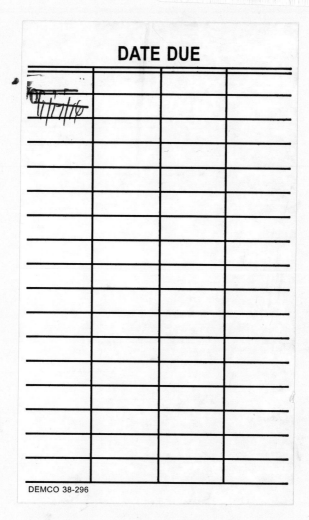

DATE DUE

The Craft of the Media Interview

Also by Dennis Barker

The Craft
of the
Media Interview

DENNIS BARKER

ROBERT HALE · LONDON

© *Dennis Barker 1998*
First published in Great Britain 1998

131 5

mited
louse
reen
0HT

The right of Dennis Barker to be identified as
author of this work has been asserted by him
in accordance with the Copyright, Designs and
Patents Act 1988.

Typeset in North Wales by
Derek Doyle & Associates, Mold, Flintshire
Printed in Great Britain by
St Edmundsbury Press Limited, Bury St Edmunds
and bound by
WBC Book Manufacturers Limited, Bridgend

For George and Gertrude Barker in the past, Sarah and Eleanor in the present, and all those who honestly and perceptively practise or appreciate the craft of the media interview in the present and future.

Contents

Part Three: How Not to Interview

Part Four: In Conclusion

Acknowledgements

I am grateful to all those who have helped or advised in the development and publication of this book.

John Hale, a publisher who can discuss books as well as money, took from the first a close interest in the book and its ideas, his comments always challenging and helpful. My editor Neville Gomes expressed valuable views on the concision and usefulness of the material and may have helped postpone, if not my dotage, at least my anecdotage. Susan Hale has kept a close eye on the production of the book in the latter stages.

Interviews conducted by the author and referred to in this book were meant for, or first appeared in, as follows:

The Guardian: Lord Attenborough (Richard Attenborough), Tony Benn, Edward de Bono, Sir Adrian Boult, Lord Callaghan (James Callaghan), Prince Charles, Jackie Collins, Benny Goodman, Lord Hailsham (Quintin Hogg), Illtyd Harrington, Alger Hiss, Alfred Hitchcock, Roger Moore, Lord Olivier (Laurence Olivier), Joseph Papp, David Rappaport, Cliff Richard, Sir Ralph Richardson, Harry Saltzman, Margaret Thatcher, Sir Peter Ustinov, John Wayne.

Express and Star, Wolverhampton: Agatha Christie, Cicely Courtneidge, David Frost, Jack Hulbert, Cliff Richard.

East Anglian Daily Times: Randolph Churchill.

Suffolk Chronicle and Mercury: Benjamin Britten.

Stop the Week With Robert Robinson, BBC Radio 4: Sir John Gielgud.

Author's book, *One Man's Estate*: the eighth Marquess of Hertford.

Author's book, *Guarding the Skies*: Royal Air Force women personnel in Cyprus.

Interviews conducted by others appeared, were seen or heard as follows:

BBC1: John Humphrys *On the Record* interview of John Major.

BBC1: David Frost *Breakfast With Frost* interviews of Martin Bell, Michael Howard, John Prescott.

BBC2: Jeremy Paxman *Newsnight* interviews of Ann Widdecombe, Michael Howard.

(Extracts from *On the Record* (8/12/96), *Breakfast with Frost* (4 & 11/5/97) and *Newsnight* (5/97) reproduced by permission of the BBC.)

London Evening Standard: Tony Blair, privatized railways Vox Pop by Sally Pook.

The Spectator: Simon Sebag Montefiore interview with The Spice Girls.

The Times: Valerie Grove interview of John Mortimer © Times Newspapers Limited, 1997.

British Film Institute book, *Talking Pictures* by Graham Jones, edited by Lucy Johnson – interviews of various film makers.

Introduction

Partly because of the infusion of entertainment values from show business into the electronic media, the concept of a media interview has changed and not necessarily for the better.

At the same time it has never been more socially necessary, because of the increasing pressures applied by spin-doctors – public relations people, lobbyists and other paid advocates of specific points of view – that interviewers of competence, flair and integrity should do their job of revealing to the public what interviewees are, think and intend to do. This applies not only to the interviewing of politicians, important as that undoubtedly is, but also to interviews with writers, artists, actors, pop singers, sportsmen and other figures of influence.

In one sense interviewing has to be an assertive craft. It involves thrusting yourself on strangers and asking them questions you might not like to ask your own mother. It should also be a humble (but not mock-humble) craft, in which the interviewer does not indulge his own vanity but subordinates himself to the public's right to know. It is in some ways easier for print journalists to remember this than for radio and (especially) television journalists. Television can be a great inflator of reputations and egos.

But for all three media, there is really no such thing as a brilliant question, only a question that produces a brilliantly revealing answer. In the print media a humble, fumbling question can often produce a revelation. In the electronic media, a question has to be a 'performance' question because it is indeed part of the performance seen by the public. It is therefore easy for a television interviewer to spend more time on straightening his hair and rehearsing his profound questions than he does thinking how to dig the most out of the interviewee, particularly if he has to efface himself to do so. Some interviewers on television find it expedient to put their streamlined and re-thought questions straight to camera *after* the interview is over and the interviewee has left; whether this is more narcissistic than fair is a matter for debate.

What is less open to debate is that the function of the electronic media interview is precisely the same as that in any other medium: to elicit revelation which is fair and relevant and at the same time arresting enough to hold the public's attention.

Sometimes in any job it is necessary to go back to first principles and the underlying techniques. I have tried in this book to deal with interviewing techniques by drawing on interviews conducted by myself and by other people and by creating a series of fictional but not entirely untypical badly or even atrociously conducted interviews whose inadequacy I subsequently analyse.

My aim is to be instructional at a practical level and also to interest all those who have views on what interviewing consists of, be they politicians, other 'celebrities', media students or interested members of the general public. The television interview in which two showbiz personalities give a rehearsed performance of unrevealing trivialities cannot be the peak of the craft; some might say it is not a real interview at all and that its influence on the craft of interviewing has encouraged more shallowness than should be tolerated by any intelligent society. Neither should an interview be the verbal equivalent of the visceral attentions of the paparazzi at the time they were pursuing Diana, Princess of Wales, to her death.

At the opposite pole to such attentions should be the journalistic interviewer who does his homework, is both sensitive and firm in handling the interviewee, manages to extract far more of interest than either interviewer or interviewee expected at the outset, and presents the result without distortion, misrepresentation or other dishonesty.

That is truly candid and interesting interviewing – which this book, I hope, will encourage.

Part One:
How to Interview

Chapter 1
The Starting Line

The object of any media interview is quite simple, yet often forgotten. The increased influence of television and radio and their technological marvels, to some extent overshadowing more traditional print journalism, does not alter that fact one jot. It is to put one intelligence and sensibility (the interviewer's) in touch with another (the interviewee's) for the benefit of a third (the reader, listener or viewer's).

What is *not* the object of an interview? It is *not* to enable the interviewer to show off in front of the reader, listener or viewer while paying the words of the interviewee scant attention. It is *not* to enable the interviewer to show off in front of the interviewee in a way that excludes the reader, listener or viewer. It is *not* to enable the interviewee, unchecked, to inundate the reader, listener or viewer with unchallenged propaganda. It is *not* to enable the interviewer to suck up to the interviewee for his or her own purposes, such as getting his or her coming book well reviewed, without regard to the fraud perpetrated on the reader, listener or viewer. It is *not* to enable the interviewer to settle personal old scores with the interviewee at the expense of puzzling or boring the reader, listener or viewer.

If the interview has become too close to a threadbare or corrupted form, it is because these criteria are not kept in mind by interviewers or enforced by editors. However clever, simple, friendly or hostile an interview may seem, it must perform the rudimentary task of putting together the three crucial intelligences and sensibilities. Other things may be attached by way of decoration to this need, but they remain decoration: the need itself is paramount.

All this is best borne firmly in mind be it the interviewer's first or 1001st interview. If it is kept in mind from the very first, that state of mind will in itself tend to make for a satisfactory interview – or for a satisfactory bid for the interview in the first place, because the interviewee with something to say will feel confident he will be able to say it, not unchecked, but not superciliously insulted or mishandled either.

Journalists who work for news organizations as staff members or contract journalists may have interviews set up for them or even have them arranged over their heads and then farmed out to them. But it is best to assume that even staff men and women have to set up their own first interviews; freelances will almost certainly have to.

How do you start? You may well start because you have special access to a particular potential interviewee and have seen a news peg on which you could hang an interview with him. In local or regional journalism it is often easier to get access to national celebrities of whatever sort who happen to live in the locality or region.

My first such 'celebrity' interview, conducted when I was a very raw eighteen, illustrated how inexperience and diffidence need not be insoluble problems provided that the interviewer is prepared to do two things: to *use* his true feelings if need be and to slant his questions so that the interviewee is tempted to answer them – in the first instance, asking those questions which interest the interviewee rather than those that interest the interviewer.

The composer Benjamin Britten had just written the opera *Peter Grimes* and was hailed as the first great British composer of opera since Purcell. He was an attractive target for interviewers who were, however, almost always unsuccessful in gaining access. As is better known now than it was then, he was reclusive partly to protect his life with the tenor Peter Pears at The Crag House, 4 Crabbe Street, Aldeburgh, Suffolk – a location which was within the circulation area of the local weekly for which I then worked, the *Suffolk Chronicle and Mercury*.

I was in Aldeburgh on other business and no interview had been pre-arranged. I was not in any sense qualified to be part of Britten's musical or emotional life. In such a position, the interviewer must ask himself what he *does* have going for him. Britten had been born in Lowestoft, that small Suffolk fishing port and holiday resort; so had I. He had got out in favour of more stimulating climates as soon as he could; so had I. His family and mine had mutual acquaintances in the cultural life of the town. I believe his father had been my grandfather's dentist. In other words, it was not an imposing list of things going for me.

Any interviewer should aim to be determined, which is useful, rather than thick-skinned, which can be off-putting. Sitting in the lych-gate of the nearby local church, I determinedly lectured myself for at least half an hour on why I should somehow overcome my inhibiting shyness and ring the doorbell of The Crag House. While such inner pep talks go on, it is advisable to use the time by also planning and noting down at least your initial questions. This I did. There was a non-musical news-peg I could address; something even he might conceivably want to talk about. He had just returned from the Continent, where he had attended a conference of the European Peace Movement. He was a keen pacifist, having left Britain for the USA as the second world war broke out, in company with the writers W.H. Auden, Christopher Isherwood and others.

Every interviewer afflicted with hesitancy must know when to draw a line under it and ring the bell, however attractively self-deceiving it may be to spend another five minutes 'planning'. I rang the bell. The door was opened by Imogen Holst, daughter of the British composer Gustav Holst and a friend of Britten's, some said the original of the village schoolmistress in *Peter Grimes*, almost the only villager to sympathize with Grimes in his tortured relationships with ships' boys. She asked me to wait a moment while she consulted Britten. Left alone I grew even more nervous. At such a point the interviewer should absorb and use the energy of the nervousness in observation of the venue: wallpaper, furniture, ornaments, books, anything and everything.

A minute later I was shown into the living room where Britten, wearing a while cellular shirt, stood uneasily by the mantelpiece. I photographed all this in my mind, at that stage thankful that I had the sort of face to which apprehension gave a look closely resembling that of brassy confidence. It can be useful to an interviewer to develop such a face, but not in every case.

In this case, as I sat down on the sofa with my notebook on my knee, facing the still standing Britten, I put my first question. It seemed as if Britten wanted to answer it, but he was hesitant. He played with the front of his shirt, looked at the floor, looked at Peter Pears, who sat in an armchair, and at Imogen Holst. He hardly ever looked at me. Questions two and three fared no better. I thought his knuckles were going to crack even more loudly than my own. I realized he was possibly more nervous than I was.

Half intuitively, I did the right thing. I blurted out an apology (sincere but intended to be disarming) for disturbing him without warning and for my nervousness – indeed, I said, I had been so nervous that I had nearly gone away without ringing the bell.

Immediately, Britten's attitude changed. He seemed suddenly at ease and in control. He sat down, and asked me to put the first three questions again. Cups of tea were summoned. I then had quite a long interview about the European Peace Movement and his present and future work. I do not think I would have got any of this material had I not been genuinely nervous and, in the end, seen the potential advantage in admitting it. In this respect, as in others, honesty can be the most effective policy.

If you wish to get access to any celebrity who may have local or other connections which might suggest a direct approach, you can afford to seem human, not a mechanical news-ferret. A human being, however inexperienced, is more likely to endear himself or herself to a celebrity who is used to dealing with soaring egos among his colleagues, and insensitive questions from the media, than a mechanical question-asker. This is a sphere of interviewing in which the general dictum – 'Be human as an interviewer and find the humanity in the interviewee' – is especially applicable.

But here, as in any other area of interviewing activity, being human is not the same thing as being incompetent. I had carefully prepared my questions to Britten, even if by themselves they might not have loosened his tongue. Had I not prepared questions and given some impression of thought processes going on, I doubt whether my confession of nervousness would itself have loosened his tongue either. Approaching an interviewee 'cold' without an appointment or notice, requires both thought and humanity in as large a measure as possible and even then may not always be successful.

In any case, you cannot rely on 'special connections' of any sort, local or otherwise. With most interviewees, you will have no special access. You will have to take pot-luck along, possibly, with many other would-be interviewers. Generally it is better to have any interview set up in advance, with as much notice as possible. There is a courteous drill for doing this, which may not be as daunting as a beginner may imagine. Most public figures of any type now have individuals, organizations or press offices through which they can be approached.

In the first place, look up the potential interviewee in the appropriate reference books. Debrett's *People of Today* has a very comprehensive list of the sort of people you are likely to want to interview, from politicians and bishops to writers and popular entertainers, and *Who's Who* can be of help across a somewhat narrower range. Many trades and professions have their own reference books. Actors and actresses may be looked up in *Spotlight*, which will have the address and telephone numbers of their agents, and is produced periodically. (The trade union Actors' Equity may also assist in providing names and telephone numbers of members' agents though it is sensitive about otherwise discussing its individual members.) Musicians can be looked up in the *International Who's Who In Music* or *Who's Who In Music*; writers in the *International Authors and Writers Who's Who* or *The Writers' Directory*; politicians in the four-volume *Parliamentary Profiles*; doctors in *The Medical Directory*; businessmen in the

Directory of Directors; churchmen in *Crockford's*. If you are employed by a media concern, its library should have such books; if you are a freelance you should be able to find them in your local public library.

It is highly desirable, even perhaps absolutely essential, to consult all the reference books you can before you make even the first exploratory call – even if a public relations person has intimated that your subject is too little-known for your research to bear fruit. A cuttings library, which your target market may have even if you are a freelance, should be consulted.

Here, however, a word of warning. Good interviewing does *not* consist of recycling all past cuttings. Glance over the cuttings by all means and make a mental or very, very short written note of anything of interest. But do not fill your notebook up with so much advance material from the cuttings library that you are tempted to rely on it when you come to write the interview. There is something makeshift and dead about an interview which is all cuttings and no question and answer: it smacks of laziness. It suggests the interviewer is not sufficiently interested in his interviewee, or has insufficient general human understanding to be a worthwhile interviewer. Interviewees often complain that something they said as a joke thirty years previously finds its way, minus the tongue-in-cheek inflection, into successive contemporary interviews. This is annoying for them. If a man aged twenty-five is asked his opinion of his life in advertising and says ironically, 'I can't bear to be sober very long after breakfast', he is naturally disconcerted when some cuttings-addicted interviewer, thirty years later, when he has acquired a wife and two children and long abandoned advertising for charity organization, suggests that his recipe for a happy life is to be drunk as soon as possible after breakfast. If you want to know your interviewee's views on any subject at all, it is best to ask him yourself. That, at very least, is the best way of keeping yourself up to date.

Ideally, do all your preliminary research yourself. Avoid leaving it to a researcher. Some people in television may regard themselves as far too grand to do such basic donkey work. They are mistaken. An interviewer who has not done the research himself is a hostage to fortune and is certainly a hostage to the interviewee. If you say to the interviewee, 'Ten years ago you were convicted of possession of drugs', the interviewee could very well look at you askance and say, 'You haven't done your homework, have you?' You then make yourself appear even more stupid by looking blank. Eventually, having played with you like a cat playing with a mouse, the interviewee can add, 'I thought everyone knew the conviction was quashed on appeal.' You are left cursing a poor underpaid researcher on the grounds that he or she has not done your homework properly – homework you should have done for yourself.

Elementary errors like that are not the only reason for doing all research yourself. Faced with a thick wad of newspaper cuttings, a researcher will tend to go for the 'important', which in practice will mean the obvious. He will single out big profiles of the subject, and not get bogged down in studying small clippings. A mistake. The big profiles will tend to recycle the same facts that have appeared in earlier profiles. They shouldn't, but they often do. If you do the research yourself, go back in time further than a researcher might be prepared to do; in particular, do not despise short clippings about the interviewee before he became well known. In the 1980s and 1990s I have often found small cuttings dating back to the 1940s and 1950s of considerable help in building up a picture of an interviewee on the basis of which he can be questioned.

Public people, as they get more well known, tend to edit themselves: they reveal only what they want to reveal. The big film star may not want to remember he once kept an antiques stall in the Portobello Road. A bishop may not want to remember that as a very young clergyman he was once arrested on a CND march for obstructing the police. A successful playwright may not want to remember that his first performed play brought him 75 pence as his first week's royalties. They may be prepared to discuss these things if you raise them, but they themselves are not likely to volunteer them.

But the real essence of the reason why you should do your research yourself is that you do not want to have your mind and wishes filtered through the mind and wishes of another human being, however competent that human being may be. Something that might have struck you as significant may not strike the researcher as significant; his mind is different from yours and he cannot infallibly second-guess you, even if over a long period of time he has gained some insight into how your mind and interests work. All research is a rather blunt instrument. Researching at second hand is a very blunt instrument indeed.

But, before you can deploy your first or second hand research, you have to get your interview lined up. Do not be cast down at the thought of approaching the highest in your geographical area or in the land. You will find the Cabinet Office in the telephone directory, and its press office is open to you as a bona fide journalist, which in practice means staff man or woman or commissioned freelance. You will similarly find Buckingham Palace in the telephone directory, all the government ministries, Scotland Yard and the virtual headquarters of the Church of England, Diocesan House. All have press offices stocked with mostly experienced and helpful professionals.

A few are dedicated to stonewalling or glib obstruction; I will always vividly remember one Whitehall press officer who could transform the most determined enquirer into a baffled wreck in a quarter of an hour; his usual habitat was the Home Office but I suspected that when any particular ministry was up against it, he was quickly seconded to it in order to put off enquirers with the mere sound of his voice on the telephone. Interview his minister? Now that might be a little difficult. Could you put it in writing? Oh, you had put it in writing? It must have gone astray! Certainly the minister couldn't do it this week, and next week he was off abroad. Could you perhaps call again in two weeks time? That wouldn't do at all? Oh! Well, there was really no need to take that tone! What did you mean, there was every reason to take that tone? The man was worth ten times his salary as an impregnable concrete wall between ministers and the press. He was just as 'good' at handling day-to-day enquiries.

Fortunately, most press officers today are more helpful. They believe that a journalist snubbed is a journalist alienated, and that such a journalist will write on the subject he wants to write about anyway, probably with less credit to the 'protected' interviewee.

How should you approach any agents, press officers and so on in pursuit of an interview? Answer: with confidence, but in a manner which suggests you are an interested human being rather than a news hawk from some moronically melodramatic television series. Tone of voice can count. It helps if you sound like an observer rather than a hanging judge. An educated voice may not be absolutely essential, but it helps to build confidence: it also helps the intermediary (and later the interviewee) to understand what you are saying.

The intermediary will almost certainly, especially if you are an unknown quantity to him, not give an immediate decision. He will say he will speak to the potential interviewee and get back to you. You should have left him, not necessarily overtly, with several reasons why the interview should be granted. You represent a newspaper, magazine or programme which is sympathetic to his point of view on a certain topical subject or one which is not normally sympathetic but wants to hear more about his point of view. You are personally interested in music/films/novels or whatever. You have noticed that there is no major interview with the interviewee on file and you think there ought to be.

State how you intend to carry out the interview, and be prepared to switch from notebook to tape recorder or from tape recorder to notebook if the interviewee has any strong feelings on the matter. You don't have shorthand? Acquire it as quickly as you can. (No! I person-

ally do not want to hear any plausible reasons from would-be interviewers for not doing so and would dismiss all reasons for not having
shorthand as mere rationalizations: recording machines sometimes
break down, to put it no more strongly. Get to grips with shorthand,
then you won't have to make plausible excuses.)

Don't be too discouraged if the original attitude of the potential
interviewee is rather negative. Find other reasons why the interviewee
should grant the interview and why you are the ideal person to
conduct it. Keep a dialogue going with the intermediary and see if you
can persuade him to let you have a few words with the interviewee
himself. If this is granted, your manner is even more important. One
news editor, a cynic with a lot of sense behind the flip exterior, used
to say, 'For God's sake don't behave like a bloody journalist!' There is
a lot of truth in this: approach the interviewee as a genuinely interested person rather than as a newsroom or features department ferret.

Sometimes you will be asked by the intermediary or the interviewee
what your attitude to the interviewee and his views is. It is unwise, in
your anxiety to get the interview, to say something like, 'I admire
him/you greatly and agree with his/your views.' It may well make you
suspect as being too glib and, if the published interview turns out to be
less than favourable, you can be accused of deception and hypocrisy.
This can be used against not only you but also the organization which
publishes it, which will not endear you to it and promote future
opportunities.

A friendly neutrality, if this position is sincerely held, is the best attitude. I have said hundreds of times, 'I am not actively hostile. I don't
have any preconceived notions and the result will be determined by
the way the interview itself goes.' This covers you if you have to
reverse your own first opinion in the light of the interview itself. Of
course, if you represent a newspaper which is known to be against the
political views of a politician, it will be difficult to persuade the interviewee that your position is neutral. It is still open to you to say that
your employers' views are known, but that you personally will not
distort nor misrepresent anything the interviewee says. If despite this
the resultant interview is rewritten in the office or given a misleading
headline, you will know that, for you, that particular section of the
media is a wrongly chosen one.

Often you will discover that the prospective interviewee who is
initially against the whole idea of an interview will eventually take on
board the whole prospect and be among the most keen to go ahead. It
is a matter of being patient and putting out as many positive signals as
you can and minimizing the negative ones. Once the interviewee's
mind has begun to take in the prospect of being able to talk for publi-

cation, and begun to compose the things he would want to say, he will probably resist any attempt to be cheated of his opportunity. People who at first refuse interviews almost by definition do it because they take themselves more seriously than the average. That being so, once your patient foot-slogging is over, the idea of having a public platform, albeit an imperfect one, will be more attractive to them than the average.

Once you have reassured the intermediary that you are interested in more than sexual and mercenary tittle-tattle and are concerned with more than the interviewee's divorces and the value to the nearest five thousand of his house and motor car, you will tend to get the interview. Once you have got the interview set up and then started, you can use the same techniques, and many others to be discussed later, to make sure you get the material you want.

If you constantly find that people you want to talk to don't want to talk to the medium you are representing, the only solution is to change the medium; you are working for the wrong employer. If on the other hand the medium – as much or more than yourself – can inspire confidence in the potential interviewee, then you are well on the road to a successful interview.

Chapter 2

The Handshake and Beyond

You are about to enter the room where the interviewee is.

You have agreed the terms of the interview, or are about to do so as the first priority. The forms an interview can take are time-honoured and should be, as far as possible among fallible human beings, crystal clear.

At best, you will want the interview to be attributable, which means that you can use as direct quotes anything the interviewee may say to you. A government minister might say, 'I am going to impose higher taxes in this area', and you could quote him direct.

Unattributable means that you can use any facts you may glean in the interview, but not attribute them to the interviewee or write them up in such a way that by inference he will be seen as the provider of the facts. You could write after seeing the government minister that higher taxes are expected in this area, but not suggest that the news came from the minister himself.

Off the record is the least satisfactory arrangement to the interviewer: it means that what is said may be used as guidance but not quoted as fact, and certainly not from a source. You could not suggest that you had even seen the minister, or that he was about to introduce higher taxes, but you could set out, in a more informed way than you would otherwise have been able to manage, the reasons why higher taxes in this area would make sense.

In practice, an interviewee may seek to vary the terms from one category to another as the interview progresses. You may have to play along with this if the stakes are high enough, but the result can be confusing if an attributable interview suddenly becomes non-attributable or off the record.

What is not acceptable is for an interviewee to speak attributably, get cold feet *afterwards,* ring you up and try to insist that everything said was non-attributable or off the record. This is like trying to move the goalposts after the match is over. Such a suggestion should either be declined or, if the issues are complex, be referred to higher editorial levels for a decision. It is permissible after a non-attributable or off the record interview for the interviewer to ask if the interview or certain parts of it can be attributable or on the record, but if the request is declined, the interviewer is morally obliged to honour the original arrangement.

It is best, if you can, to get a clear undertaking about the status of the interview when setting it up or as the first item on the agenda after you have shaken hands.

Other things you will also already have done before you present yourself at the interviewee's door. If a freelance, you will have telephoned the news or features editor of your market and got their commission, verbal or written authorization – preferably written – for the resultant piece.

You will certainly already have made sure that you appear in the most promising light from the moment he or she sees you. This means several things.

First, you will have dressed appropriately. This is a difficult issue. Some interviewers take the view that to change the style of attire because they are going to meet any particular person is fundamentally dishonest. Ask yourself whether this is self-righteous, finnicky puritanism. If you think it is, decide what mode of attire would be most suitable – that is, the most likely to convey the most friendly, least disruptive message. Obviously it would be absurd, if you were going to meet a bishop, to wear a dog collar or cassock; but you would possibly not wear a Hell's Angels leather jacket either. The aim is, without wearing anything totally out of character for you, to reassure the interviewee and put him at his ease. You may feel yourself to be on trial: so will he.

Keep your mind on the central and long-lasting point. Your style of dress for an interview should be something you are comfortable with that your interviewee will also be comfortable with. Do not give the impression that you are trying to ape him: he will mistrust you. Do not give the impression that you are trying to defy him, such as wearing an open-necked shirt on a cold day in Downing Street: that will either anger or bore him. You should look like a reputable journalist, possibly one with a style sense, but not one so narcissistic that he spends more time looking at himself in a mirror than at other people. Convey the fact that you respect yourself and your style of dress and are therefore prepared to respect him and his.

You will of course have had no alcohol whatever to drink before the interview, even if the interviewee is chairman of a brewing company.

This is a controversial point of view. On the whole and other than in exceptional circumstances (such as that you and the interviewee have both been guests at the same public dinner) I stand by it. You may be nowhere near drunk, but how is the interviewee to be certain of that? It indicates that you may have a slovenly attitude to your job as a whole and to your approach to him. Can he be happy about the accuracy of your shorthand note if alcohol fumes are wafting into his face? Mayn't it reinforce the stereotype of journalists he may have in his mind as boozy, unreliable, insensitive and not overly intelligent riff-raff? Better not to take the risk of alcohol on your breath, especially as there is no need for it: there is plenty of time to drink other than before or during an interview.

If you drink in the hope that it will inspire your own confidence, you are acting both weakly and foolishly. As Napoleon said about something else entirely, it is worse than a crime; it is a blunder. Confidence will come when you are more sure of what you are doing and sure that you are doing it well. There is no short cut to this sort of confidence, certainly not through alcohol. Until you acquire it, your excessive nervousness will be part of your stock in trade, forcing you to take special pains to get the results you want. As a matter of fact, I have never divested myself of feelings of nervousness before any inter-view, and rather believe that it is vital to the job: you are probably not functioning in a fully tuned way unless you have it. Even a minor inter-view usually leaves me with a mouth so dry that I can scarcely swal-low, however confident I may have appeared on the surface. (There is no reason why you shouldn't have a drink after a particularly gruelling interview if you want to, though decoding notes or transcribing tapes tends to be easier if you are stone cold sober.) Lack of nervousness suggests you are temperamentally wooden rather than acutely percep-tive, and therefore unlikely to make an insightful interviewer.

I said that even drinking during rather than before an interview was undesirable. Admittedly, this is a far more puritanical assertion than my contention that you should not drink before an interview. Alcohol will not enable you keep a better grip on the interview, nor will it enable the interviewee to keep a better grip on his own part in the proceedings. Alcohol may, however, encourage someone to talk less guardedly. Perhaps the ideal interview is one in which the interviewee is pleasantly lubricated and the interviewer stone cold sober. In prac-tice, this will be difficult to arrange.

The interviewee may be the sort of person who regards joining him or her in a drink as a necessary sign of comradeship. I once conducted a long interview with the lugubrious, tragic comedian Tony Hancock, a broadcasting icon of the 1950s and early 1960s with his radio and television versions of *Hancock's Half Hour*. I did it while he was on a down-beat theatre tour by sitting in his dressing room in a provincial theatre all evening and questioning him when he came off-stage and returned to the dressing room. At this sad point in his career, he had parted company with the scriptwriters who had helped make his name, Ray Galton and Alan Simpson, under the illusion that the material he had written himself was better. His broadcast shows had been discontinued. A theatre tour was his only way of staying before the public and paying his bills.

At the outset of the interview, he said: 'I must have a drink. You'd like one?' In the circumstances, since he was known to be fond of the booze as well as being sensitive and touchy, I said I'd like a whisky. He phoned to the theatre staff: 'One vodka and one whisky, please.' It arrived almost immediately – one bottle of vodka and one bottle of whisky. The staff knew their man. Much of my bottle and all of his had been consumed by the time the interview ended. Though I got some good material it was not always as easy for me to focus on it as usual. It was in the easy alcohol era, when journalists were on the whole used to imbibing vast quantities without losing their grip on what they were doing. I managed to decipher my notes. Nevertheless, it is not a method of conducting an interview that I can recommend.

If you decide that you will not drink, even during the interview to keep the interviewee company, there are a number of polite ways of declining. One is, when offered a drink at the outset of the interview, to say, 'Not just yet, thank you.' Then, if offered a drink again towards the end of the interview, you say, 'It's a bit late now.' Say anything you like, as long as your tone is not moralistic. It isn't a moral issue: it's a functional issue. If you function best without alcohol, find ways of evading it partly or entirely. Work all this out in advance.

Very well, so much for the preplanning of your attitudes. Before that interviewee's door opens, you have resolved all these issues in your mind. What do you do when the door opens?

The handshake is important. I have tended to regard a limp, lifeless handshake in others as a mild insult, a sign of apathy about the meeting, perhaps an indication of a lack of feeling for one's fellows as a whole. I fail to see why any interviewee should not share at least part of that instinctive feeling. I do not see why an interviewee shouldn't regard a limp handshake as thoroughly off-putting. Even in a woman, a too-delicate handshake can be a turn-off. The only exception may be for royalty or top level politicians who are doomed to shake hundreds of hands a day and have to be fairly limp about it or suffer repetitive strain injury.

The best handshake for an interviewer is one which is positive, friendly without being presumptuous (you are not greeting an old friend) and above all, dry. If your palms are subject to sweating, wipe them inconspicuously on a clean handkerchief before walking through the interviewee's door.

Any suggestion of either servility or presumptuousness is best avoided. By conventional codes the interviewee, as the senior of the two (you want to interview him, he does not want to interview you) should extend his hand first. Only when he does that do you extend yours and take it. The danger of proceeding on this basis is that a shy or inexperienced interviewee, not quite certain how to proceed in the circumstances, may not extend his hand at all or be so slow to do so that your own failure to extend your hand to him may be taken as a sign of hostility or reserve. Leaving aside meeting royalty or similar interviewees whose social or intellectual status is plainly and perhaps touchily above one's own, my own inclination has been to extend my own hand whether there is any sign of a reciprocal move or not. Your hand can hardly be refused (mine never has been) and the nature of your handshake can establish you from the start as a briskly businesslike but not personally hostile presence.

The handshake over, where do you sit? This can be important. It can be uncomfortably hard going conducting an interview across a wide desk, especially if the interviewee has a high chair and has given you a low one. Even this is better than the reverse: you will never get an interviewee to open up if you loom above him. Your heads should ideally be more or less on the same level; neither should dominate, and especially not yours.

Many interviewees who receive you in their offices have a low table with surrounding chairs somewhere in the room and will come out from behind their desks and shepherd you towards this configuration. This is an arrangement ostensibly to promote informality. In such a case I have found it better to sit at right angles to the interviewee, rather than facing him. You might think an eyeball-to-eyeball confrontation would enable you to bring to bear the full force of your personality. You may be overestimating the force of your personality. Even if you are not, its eyeball-to-eyeball deployment is likely to be psychologically inhibiting rather than encouraging, perhaps to both parties.

There is a further disadvantage in the face-to-face arrangement. If you are using a notebook and bending down over it, the interviewee will be permanently looking at the top of your head. This will constantly suggest to him that you are mentally elsewhere, whereas if he is at right angles to you, he can always see the side of your face, which reminds him that you are a human being more vividly than the top of your head could ever do. He will also be comfortably free to look away from you as he gets his thoughts in order.

However, if your interviewee places you firmly in a chair on the other side of his wide desk, facing him, you must not allow this to intimidate you. People vary in their reaction to a psychological put-down: some succumb, some over-compensate with steely assertiveness or bluster, some remain simply unflurried. A born interviewer will automatically find it a challenge and step up his own morale accordingly. Others need consciously to crank up their attack, working on the strength of their voice, the pithiness of their questions, the determination with which they come back to a question only half answered or not answered at all.

Interviews in the interviewee's own home are probably easier and more profitable to conduct; the seating problem will certainly be easier, because it is not easy as in an office for the interviewee to direct you where to sit, whereas it is easier for you to ask to sit elsewhere. Interviewing from an armchair facing the interviewee's armchair in front of the grate is in any case easier than facing the same individual across his desk; both parties are more likely to be at ease, the interviewee because he is in the safety of his own home, the interviewer because he has a better guide to the interviewee's private personality.

One warning about the choice of seat if you see an interviewee at home. I once interviewed a female novelist at her London flat. I made the mistake of sitting where I could see a large number of her collection of Art Nouveau. Since I was also a collector in a minor way, I had to fight hard to prevent my attention wandering to them. In such circumstances it is politic to try to convert a negative into a plus. I admitted the distraction and explained why, which gave us a human bridge irrespective of the subject in hand. She was no longer talking to 'a journalist' but a fellow collector. But in any interview it is better to sit where there are no distractions either to the interviewer or the interviewee.

Earlier I mentioned eye levels. Physical height can have a bearing on interviewing. You can't alter the height you were doomed to by your genes. You will remain tall however much you would prefer to be inconspicuous or short however much you feel your personality would be more suited to a dominant height. Inside some tall men there is a short man trembling with apprehension and in some short men there is a tall man fuming to get out.

Except in the case of showbiz television 'interviewers' who are really stars of their shows, using their human fodder merely as unpaid straight men or women, height is not an advantage to an interviewer. It belittles, unless you are careful, the ego of the interviewee and will make him more reticent. It must be consciously stage-managed.

Interviewees do not like being dominated by a looming presence; would you? If you doubt this, watch a crowd of men grouped at a bar and notice how they pull themselves up to their full height every so often, especially when they start to speak. They do not like talking uphill, as it were. Neither do interviewees. Come come, you say, are people really as petty as that? Yes they are. Nor is it really as 'petty' as it might seem. We are all very conscious of the figure we cut in the world, and height is part of it.

Even at the simplest, purely physical level it is uncomfortable to talk for long with one's head bent backwards so that one can meet someone else's eyes. If you are tall and doubt this, test it some time by sitting on a chair and talking to someone standing up. You will want to bring this state of affairs to an end as soon as possible, as will an interviewee put into a comparable situation. It will not help you get a long and interesting interview.

It is the same for women interviewers; perhaps more so. Tall women interviewers run the risk of affronting sensitive male vanity if they loom too long and too obviously, and not every woman interviewee will appeciate being loomed over either, especially if she is in a position where she is accustomed to being dominant. Such observations may or may not be politically correct, but as an interviewer you are there to do the job as efficiently as you can, not to act out your own opinions and attitudes. Always put these into the background.

I said that commanding height in an interviewer had to be stage-managed. This can be done in a number of ways. Do not carry yourself at your full height, as a short person with a dominant temperament will tend to do; stoop diffidently in such a way that the interviewee may comfortably view your height as an embarrassment to you rather than him. Do not continue to stand too close to the interviewee in such a way that he is too immediately conscious of your height and has to bend his neck backwards to meet your eyes. If the interviewee indicates a low chair for you to sit on (as he may well do if he is short in stature) take it as soon as possible, even if it is not ideal from your point of view. If you are facing the interviewer from a chair of similar height, inconspicuously slump in it more than you would do normally. In all ways project diffidence.

If you lack height, you have few problems except perhaps your own feelings of inadequacy. These, like other personal feelings, should be put and kept firmly in the background. Your lack of height, though it may detract from your feelings of adequacy, will add to the interviewee's feelings of adequacy, which is all you should be concerned about.

There is only one proviso: in some cases the interviewee must be discouraged from patronizing you in his mind as 'that little man'. The first time I interviewed the distinguished and pleasantly irreverent actor Peter O'Toole on a film set, I was scribbling furiously, my head bent over my notebook when I, from my moderate height, looked up at his face and his six feet three, and caught an amused, derisory grin. I did not begrudge him this, but I instantly asked him a pointed question which indicated in the nicest possible way that I was intelligent and to be taken seriously professionally even if the sight of my bowed head miles below his own eye level was slightly risible. Instantly his manner went into a different and more rewarding gear.

Your method of note-taking deserves serious consideration. You must take notes, even in the shortest interview. The only exception I can think of is in the case of news reporting when you do not immediately want to indicate to an unsophisticated and perhaps dodgy person that what is being said is to be reported. The obverse of this is that a notebook or recorder indicates quite plainly that an interview for media use is being conducted, warding off any possible future complaint that the interviewee did not know you were a journalist interviewing him for publication.

If you are using a tape recorder (and there is something to be said for using an inconspicuous one, even if only as a back up to your notes), the seating rules are more or less unaffected. Just be sure to point the microphone towards the interviewee; your own questions, even if fainter on the playback, will almost certainly be more easily remembered than the answers, especially if you have drafted them out in your notebook.

You are seated to your interviewee's satisfaction and yours. If you haven't done so already, give a thought to your voice.

Regional accents are more acceptable than they were half a century ago. They still have one disadvantage: they are more difficult to understand when used outside their areas of origin. Clarity is vital. An interviewee who has constantly to ask for a question to be repeated is more likely to become irritated than cooperative. You may be tempted to say, 'I have a right to use what accent I like. My part of the world and its accents are as good as anybody's!' So they may be, and if you want to use them at home that is your business. But we not talking about your habits at home or your rights, we are talking about your effectiveness in a specific job. Here you have no 'right' to an obscure method of speech that may be taken as a sign of bad manners by your interviewee.

The problem exists not merely with regional accents. Clear articulation rather than a slurring of words is necessary. In recent years it has become fashionable in some quarters to drawl words out like a string of sausages rather than a string of finely cut diamonds. One may agree or disagree with the social and political sub-text to this; the fact is that in utilitarian terms this drawling mode of speech is a handicap to an interviewer. Questions should not be uttered in a long trail of vowels with the consonants unstressed. This form of speech is difficult to decode, and perhaps impossible if the interviewee is nervous or partly deaf.

A hearing test I had at the Design Centre in London while covering a demonstration of new hearing testing equipment showed that I was slightly treble deaf in the left ear. This is not an uncommon affliction. After that, if I had to interview a non-consonant-sounding interviewee I tried my best to arrange that my right ear was nearest to him. As the interviewer, I had to do the adjusting. Had I been the interviewee, and found myself with a mumbler talking into my least effective ear, I would not have been keen to prolong the interview.

I repeat: if the interviewee's hearing is not 101 per cent, such as it may not be in an elderly or even middle-aged person, bad articulation on your part will put him at such a disadvantage that he may well become irritated with you and the whole idea of the interview. If there is poor communication with the interviewee, it is *your* fault, full stop. It is no use denouncing him back at the office for being deaf; even if he was deaf, it was up to you to pitch your voice in such a way that he could hear all the questions clearly. There is no need to shout, which just makes a difficult voice even more difficult to understand. Carefully modulated speech in all circumstances can be vital. Tolerance of slovenly speech does no good to anyone, certainly not a potential interviewer.

If those are the only two choices, it is better to be thought patronizing than to be indistinct. Once, after I had dictated from a battery of press telephones at some conference an interview I had just conducted, a French journalist waiting to use a telephone told me: 'Remarkable! Your diction was so clear that I understood every word you said, though it was in a foreign language. Your copytakers must love you.' I did not risk denting my halo by admitting that occasionally, on the contrary, the copytakers had accused me of mouthing my words to them as if they were idiots. I was always unrepentant: being thought patronizing is a passing cloud, being indistinct is potentially disastrous. Similarly, when actually interviewing, I would rather be confident that the interviewee was cunningly ignoring my question than battle with the suspicion that he may simply have misheard it because I wasn't talking clearly enough.

Clearer consonants are often an instant way of improving one's diction. Try saying, 'Was the game of football fast and furious?' Then say it again, cutting out some of the consonants: 'Wa er ama ooball assan urios?' Which question would you rather answer?

I would add only one qualification. In America less stress is put on consonants. Sounding them as you would in Britain may lead to incomprehension. In a bar on my first visit to New York, I asked for a Manhattan cocktail. Conversation around me came to a dead stop. Even I could detect that in these surroundings my voice must have come across as effete rather than educated, inflaming those prejudices the Americans sometimes have about the British. More importantly, the bartender had simply not understood my request. Only when I repeated my order, this time more slowly and in a more expansive tone, lengthening the vowels and not bearing down so hard on the consonants, did I get what I had asked for.

This was a lesson well learnt *before* I attempted to interview anyone in the USA. Only with its aid did I survive the fact that though Britain and the USA may have a common language, they do not speak it in the same way. But with this proviso I stand by the central point that from the first remark you address to an interviewee, you should make sure that your voice is properly audible. You should certainly make sure it is audible after the preliminaries have been completed.

At this stage keep pleasantries to a minimum; the time for commenting on the weather and your journey was during the few seconds after the handshake; it has now gone. It is best to open with a direct question on the substance of the interview, though not the most deep and difficult one you could ask. Throwing the interviewee a googly at the start of an interview was popular in the 1950s and 1960s before public relations men got to work on potential interviewees, and the element of surprise might shake a truth out of the interviewee. Not any more. The interviewee, faced with a first question like, 'Your new novel is just a collection of contemporary stereotypes, isn't it?' is more than likely to give a polite, quite unrevealing answer. At the same time, he will be thinking, 'This is going to be another one of *them*, is it?' The result is not likely to be profitable for the interviewer.

Chapter 3

Discipline and Spontaneity

Always go into an interview with a list of prepared questions. This applies even in the case of a speedily arranged pavement interview, for which you may have to think of the questions very quickly, off the top of your head. But this is the vital point in all cases: make sure these prepared questions are your guide, not your master. Be ready instantly to rearrange the questions, to ask supplementary questions or to adopt a completely different line of questioning if you deem it necessary.

Your first question should be very flexible indeed. Perhaps you have decided that an actor who plays tough roles is like that in reality, and have so prepared a very direct first question. If, having shaken his hand and sat down with your notebook or recorder at the ready, you come to the conclusion that he is on the contrary rather a diffident, inarticulate person, relegate your first question for later use and start with something more tentative and easy to answer.

In particular, do not assume that because someone is far more well known than you are, either locally, nationally or internationally, he or she will be less nervous about this interview than you are. Do not assume, either, that his greater fame means that he must be more articulate than you are. If he is not naturally articulate, your first aim should be to make him feel as if he is articulate. Deceitful? Perhaps, but justified in the circumstances. If it makes you more comfortable, call it tact. Make sure that the first question is one that will, or at least could, make him talkative – one about himself, but about his latest work rather than his personal history. A personal question asked as the first one gives the flavour of an interrogation, whereas you want as far as possible to suggest a pleasant conversation, even if in fact a professional interview is nothing of the kind.

When, very early in my career, I took over a weekly show business column on a regional evening newspaper, I decided to revolutionize its content. Instead of the endless bald listings of future productions by local amateur theatre groups, I substituted an interview or interviews with professional actors or stars about to appear locally (there were at least a dozen theatres in or adjoining the paper's circulation area). These were interviewed in depth about their lives, motivations and so on, in a manner only just then becoming fashionable. It is arguable that local readers may well have been more interested in the banal list of local events than in my psychological confrontations, but let that pass.

I was less worldly than I thought. I assumed the interviewees would be as enamoured of the newly fashionable psychologically probing mode of interviewing as I was. In my interviews, I was certainly very direct from the start. They included the only two interviews that I have ever had aborted by the interviewees at almost the beginning of the interview.

The mistake lay in my first questions. My first interviewee was Joyce Grenfell, the much-loved comedienne and sketch writer of that time, whose favourite creation was a jolly-hockey-stick schoolmistress vainly trying to keep order in a difficult class. ('George, dear, do stop that. You're not to do that to poor Lucy.') My first question was: 'Do you think in this day and age that your style of humour has become socially patronizing?'

I had only just sat down when she stood up. That was the beginning and the end of the interview. Of course that fact gave me the intro for a piece on Joyce Grenfell in which I could spill out all my prejudices and produce a readable column; but with hindsight (or even at the time) it was obvious that an actual interview with her would have been better. I should have led up to that question, after first establishing myself as a friendly presence. At the time (but not now) I was astonished that she could not see that I was merely indulging in a debating game. The second non-interviewee was the well known dancer and singer of the time, Cicely Courtneidge. It was just before (it was a pity it was not just after, because I just might have been more cautious) the release of the film in which she played a benevolent lesbian – Bryan Forbes's scripted and directed version of Lynne Reid Banks's novel *The L-Shaped Room*, about a collection of people, principally a pregnant girl, struggling with their emotional problems in a 'Swinging Sixties' London rooming house.

I forget the exact words of the first question I put to her, but it was about her long marriage to the comic stage and film actor, the great favourite Jack Hulbert. I put it to her because they were a well-known and respected stage couple, a sort of Laurence Olivier and Vivien Leigh of the musical comedy stage. She evidently found something underhand and insinuating about it (it must have been about the time *The L-Shaped Room* was being made) and ended the interview there and then. We were standing at the theatre bar at the time – with Jack

Hulbert, who first looked disconcerted, then looked apologetic and then beat a diplomatic retreat. Had I been as worldly as I thought I was, I would have taken a more perceptive measure of the horsey singer and dancer, a great favourite with women audiences, and kept the questioning to purely professional matters until confidence had been established.

In any case, by intuition, that was what I rightly decided to do thenceforth. It is a good maxim: the personal questions only after the interviewee has acquired confidence and is even perhaps prepared to offer personal material without being asked.

This formula saved me from a possible disaster with Agatha Christie, the crime writer who was known to be resolutely averse to giving media interviews. A series of three one-act plays built around her stories were to be previewed, prior to London, at the theatre which was at the heart of my paper's circulation area. The theatre management on this occasion took me to one side and asked if, because the arranged interview with me was so rare for her, I could be fairly impersonal in my questioning.

I gave no undertaking (rightly – too many 'deals' of this sort can be limiting) but said I took note nonetheless. This was just as well, because Agatha Christie's emotional life had at one time been intensely painful, a fact not well known before the Vanessa Redgrave–Dustin Hoffman film *Agatha* appeared in the 1970s. She had effectively been left by her husband for a younger, possibly more pliant woman who was her friend. Agatha Christie 'disappeared'. She in fact ran away to a hotel in Scarborough, where she signed in under the name of the younger woman. The multi-layered emotional suffering implied in all this can be well imagined – now. None of it was public property at the time of my interview but in the light of my experience with Joyce Grenfell and Cicely Courtneidge I decided to get her talking about her stories and the resultant plays before passing on to more personal matters. Time, perhaps mercifully, ran out before I could get on to personal questions and another forceful woman's blacklist.

Though in the intervening years the style of interviews has become less inhibited, especially when dealing with artists of one sort and another, the point still has, and will always have, a general application.

Do not, then, ask as your first question something like, 'Is the part you are playing in your new film anything like the real you?' (Preferably do not ask it at all, since it must by now be one of the worst reach-me-down clichés of all time; if you do, at least ask it in less hackneyed language.) Do not ask the local mayor, 'Does your divorced wife agree with your attitude to the new ice skating rink?' Do not ask a government minister campaigning against income tax evasion whether his own accountant ever suggests ways in which he could pay less income tax. All these personal questions are askable, but better near the end of the interview than at the beginning.

Instead ask questions which are broad and catch-all enough to make it easy for the interviewee to answer in any way he or she likes. You could ask, 'Did you find this book difficult to write?' Or, 'Did you find this part difficult to play'. Or, 'Did you find this selection of poems difficult to choose?' Or, 'Did you find this portrait easy to paint?'

You merely need to throw the interviewee the sort of question that he must have thought about and can therefore answer easily – and at sufficient length to give you the basis for several of your subsequent questions. The interviewee must feel good about the first question – or, rather, he must feel good about his answer to it. He must feel, after answering it, that he could go on in this fashion for hours, or at least for the length of the interview. He must not feel that he is dealing with an ignoramus, but he must not feel either that he is dealing with a smart alec who thinks he knows more about the subject than he does. Ideally he should be saying to himself at this point, 'Here is an intelligent fellow who doesn't know as much about the subject as I do, so I'd better put him into the picture.'

Once the opening question has been answered, you should have found out quite a lot about the interviewee and his attitude to the interview. You may have provisionally decided, once you have put the first exploratory question, to proceed with a list of questions on a certain aspect of his life and work. But if you judge that he is a reticent type and that the ideal moment for asking such questions has not yet arrived, shelve that whole tranche of questions and move on to an easier range of queries. If, on the other hand, the interviewee seems to be fighting fit and spoiling for a battle of wills ask him the difficult questions immediately after the first question before he has had a chance to tire of the whole process and, perhaps, discover that you are not such a pussy-cat as an interviewer as he first assumed you to be.

The danger of seeming too humble at any point is that the interviewee will seek to manipulate you for his own purposes. This, at very least, will waste a lot of time as you struggle to ask your own questions rather than the ones the interviewee would like to answer. Combined with an inability or unwillingness to alter the batting order of questions or completely replace them with others, this sort of humility can lead to worse professional failures than failing to deal briskly with waste of time.

The balance in any interviewer must be between discipline and spontaneity. Too much barrack-square-type discipline in the form of a mechanical list of questions will stifle what might have been a live and revealing conversation, and prevent you asking supplementary questions that should have been asked. Too much spontaneity, too much contempt for the prepared list, and questions that should have been asked will simply be forgotten in the vivacity of the moment. Nothing is worse than leaving what you have regarded as a thoroughly satisfactory interview only to find that a quite central question that you had in mind has not been put because you were bemused by the excellence of other answers.

I have found over the years that a useful technique has been writing out in clear handwriting in a notebook a list of questions you want to ask, dividing these up into sections by drawing a red line at the beginning and end of a section of questions which seem to be closely related to one another. As each question is answered as satisfactorily as you want, cross it out. But if an answer suggests that there is a very good reason for moving on at once to a different section altogether, then by all means move on to it and complete that section, again crossing out the questions after they are answered, before moving back to the previous section of questions.

A further advantage of this compartmental approach is that it helps you to have a very clear idea of the significance of the questions you are asking, rather than seeing them all as a sort of endless chain. But while you jump about between sections as required, the interviewee should not be conscious of how intensely you are thinking on your feet, because you should make your verbal contributions as clear and polished as possible. Here a broadcaster's technique of providing streamlined questions can be helpful, too, to the print media interviewer.

The type of notebook you use, even if you are doing the interview for radio, is relevant here.

There are several disadvantages in using so-called Reporter's Notebooks, about eight by five inches and bound by a wire spiral horizontally at the top. In my personal view – others may think differently – their chief advantage is to the sort of beginners who want to impress themselves and others with their status as journalists. Yet your best chance of being effective as a journalist may often lie in your seeming not too much like a stereotype of one. These sort of notebooks are too large to be slipped into the average pocket and must therefore be carried conspicuously even when the circumstances suggest that they might be off-putting. Because they are bound at the top, pages have to be swirled upwards in a conspicuous manner before falling at the back of the notebook, out of sight. There is thus nowhere to write notes and further questions except on the page you are using to take down notes of replies, which can make for confusion.

For whatever purpose, I have always used a smaller notebook, about three by five inches, stapled together vertically. As you work with such a book, you can see not one but two pages open before you. You can take down your notes of the answers on to the page on the right, while scribbling notes or further questions to be asked later on to the left-hand page. It doesn't intrude like a professional flag between you and the interviewee. In my experience, a small notebook of this type is better than something more conspicuous like a Reporter's Notebook or a clipboard (excusable, I think, only in the more exhibitionistic medium of television) or their reverse, the back of the proverbial envelope. Such an envelope suggests that if you have not prepared better for the interview in this respect, you have not prepared for it in any other respect, and that you are a self-satisfied sort of cove who takes life far too casually and will probably get all the quotes wrong.

A small type of notebook such as I have used also makes it easy to transcribe your shorthand or brief longhand notes afterwards on to the left-hand page.

Especially in a long interview, all these factors can be a distinct advantage.

Used properly, the prepared list of questions can be an aid rather than a hindrance to spontaneity. The very act of writing out the questions in progressive order will focus them in your mind and give you far more confidence during the interview – so much confidence that you may hardly have to glance at your questions more than occasionally, because their content and their order will be firmly fixed in your mind.

The less you have to study your questions in your notebook while the interview is going on, the better. It depersonalizes the contact between you and the interviewee more than is necessary. It reminds him that however pleasant he may find you, and however intelligent and congenial your questions, this is really a formal interview for some sort of publication and that he should therefore be cautious. It may also suggest to him that what he is being subjected to is no more than a routine, mechanical process. You have probably asked these questions dozens of times before, and now you are asking him! He is probably number 103 in some sort of queue! Not very flattering!

But the written-out questions will help you to keep the thread, and that is what you must do in all circumstances. When Senator Edward Kennedy, brother of the assassinated John F. Kennedy, was health spokesman for the Democrats, he flew to Britain in well-publicized circumstances to look at a wide variety of British medical establishments. I was then already on *The Guardian*, arguably the newspaper with most interest in the National Health field, and read by many nurses and doctors.

There was a press conference at the end of his visit, but I judged that would be full of rhetoric and polite clichés. The only way I could see of making some sort of sense of his in-and-out-of-limousine visit was to be with him in the limousine and to ask him after each stop, or at least as many stops as he could endure my interrogation, what he made of what he had seen.

This I did. Between stops I had the chance to prepare further questions and keep the thread. I do not think that if I had waited until the end of the tour and asked him questions the answers would have been as fresh – certainly not if I were competing with Fleet Street and the broadcasting media.

I did a similar string-of-pearls interview, chaotic in potential if not in the result because well-planned, when the Republican President Richard Nixon's ex-aide Chuck Colson came to Britain. This was to boost his memoirs and take part in a fundamentalist religious service in Surrey (after exposure he had Seen the Light). It was after Nixon had been ousted following the Watergate scandal involving the bugging of Democrat offices in Washington. I negotiated to travel in the car taking Colson from the centre of London to the service in Surrey. I prepared a series of questions (mild) for the journey out, and a series of questions (more pointed) for the journey back.

Strictly speaking I did not need either list. We had scarcely taken our seats in the back of the limousine when he launched into an explanation of how he had become involved in illegal activities for Nixon: he and his colleagues had thought they were so much in the right that whatever means they used to achieve their end must be right, too. He was rarely at a loss for words and only when he was lost did my prepared questions come in handy. Otherwise I was getting what I wanted just by shutting my mouth and letting him talk.

But a list of questions will come to your aid if an interviewee himself suddenly loses the thread and gets bogged down. It helps you keep your own thread, so that you know in general and specific terms whether you are getting what you want or not. Without that list of questions as some sort of yardstick, you might not be so sure about whether you were getting bogged down or not.

Chapter 4

Divided Aim

It is nearly always risky to try to interview more than one person at a time, especially if you are working for the print media.

In a radio or television interview with two or more people, they will perhaps not want to show themselves in a bad light by interrupting one another, talking over each other so that no one can hear anything and generally indulging in behaviour likely to cause the interviewer and the public confusion. In a print interview, this restraint does not apply and two or more interviewees taking part in the same interview will quite possibly, if not certainly, cause you trouble.

You may have to interview more than one person at once, but you should rarely deliberately choose to. Perhaps an exception would be a comedy duo who will give you a comedy routine straight into your notebook/microphone. Another might be a husband and wife explorer team just back from some distant land. Or a husband and wife sailing team who have just sailed in some unusual way round the world. All these could not logically be separated.

But, in the light of my own experience, the exceptions remain a minority.

It is dangerous to talk to two people at once even if one of them may be there nominally as a 'minder'. Minders are vain like anyone else and may insist in putting their conversational oar in.

Not only will an interview with more than one person at a time be physically harder work. The chances of confusion, misattribution, mishearing and later complaints will be increased by several hundred per cent.

Use a small cassette recorder for long interviews whenever possible. These are some check on what has been said, though I would be cautious about believing that they solve all problems. Contentious quotes may well occur at times when more than one person is speaking at once. Your ear may be able to follow one voice through this clash, just as your ear may be able to continue listening to a person at

41

a cocktail party or in a bar though surrounding voices are louder or at least as loud. But the recording machine has no such discrimination. If more than one person is talking at once, it will record an unintelligible mish-mash of sound. Unlike you, it has no mental selectivity. It is best to take shorthand notes even when using a recorder, and doubly so when there are two or more interviewees.

If you are landed willy-nilly with more than one interviewee, much stronger stage-management is needed than when you are dealing with one person only. At the start of the interview you might well simply tell the truth by saying, 'To prevent any confusion in my notes, could we have only one person talking at a time? Could I deal with you first, Mr Blank, and then come to Mrs Blank?' This arrangment may well break down as Mr Blank gets under way and Mrs Blank decides she must get into the picture, too; but it may hold long enough for you to establish some basic facts.

If it doesn't work, blame technology. Say something like, 'I'm sorry, but if you all talk at once the machine can't hear any of you and I shall be in a mess when I come to playing the tape back.' Say this even if you are pretty sure you will not need to refer to the tape at all, because you are taking shorthand notes. Or blame your shorthand: 'Sorry, but it makes it difficult for me to take a note of either of you if you both talk across one another.' You can say this even if they haven't in fact been talking across one another, only in too rapid succession for you to be totally sure you are attributing each remark to the right source; they may well both see the danger of too rapid changes of speaker and the advantages of each allowing the other to pursue their individual point.

You may feel that such techniques will suggest to the interviewee that you are incompetent. In my experience, the one thing that even the most difficult interviewees will accept and act on is any suggestion that their 'line' will not get across properly. If you make your requests in aid of clarity and against confusion in a confident as well as diffident manner, the interviewees will assume they are incompetent interviewees rather than that you are an incompetent interviewer.

Never, however, say anything that could directly imply they are incompetent interviewees. Let them feel it, but don't yourself hint at it.

I would not suggest any manoeuvres such as I have mentioned in the case of one-to-one interviews, only in the case of dual or treble or more interviewees: if you get muddled by a single interviewee, facing you on a one-to-one basis, he or she is liable to draw the most dire conclusions about you.

Trying to stage interviews among a whole group of people, as in a classroom or boardroom, can be a trial.

I happened to be in Jamaica when Michael Manley returned to power as Prime Minister after an interval of several years. I was there about something else entirely. But since there was a great deal of speculation at the time that Manley would align Jamaica to Fidel Castro's Cuba and thus to the Russian-leaning parts of what was then known as the Third World, I immediately applied to Government House for an interview with the new Prime Minister. I had only a basic knowledge of Jamaican affairs, but enough to put to him a few questions about how he saw Jamaica's alignment *vis-à-vis* East and West now that he had returned to power. Then I would put a few questions about trade with Britain – Jamaica was fearful that its exports of luscious sugar-cane would be depleted by Britain's reliance on less luscious but more economic home-grown sugar-beet. All I would need then would be a telephone to get my story back to London.

When I walked into Manley's office he was not alone. He had his entire Cabinet with him. A dozen or more people sat on one side of a desk and I sat on the other. Furthermore it soon became clear that each member regarded it as a matter of honour or perhaps ambition to make a contribution. This, taken with my lack of detailed knowledge of the issues on the minds of the various government department heads, threatened confusion.

It was a situation which any interviewer, in essence, may have to face at any time, in some shape or form: confronting a bigger opposing team than one has bargained for. It is difficult when you are on firm ground, such as a specialist interviewer might be when interviewing other specialists; it is extremely difficult if you are a non-specialist who just happens to be on the spot.

In such unexpected circumstances it is not enough to float along hoping that things will somehow get better. They won't. It is necessary to evolve a central strategy that will work in view of all the circumstances. Such a strategy should have the result of keeping a coherent single thread. I evolved this strategy: since I wanted the final result to be an interview with the Prime Minister and since I wanted to avoid confusion in areas in which I was not an expert, I would take every intervention by a Cabinet member and put it to the Prime Minister, seeing whether he would accept it or dispute it.

I applied this strategy and it worked. It had the additional advantage that, while I was putting various statements made by Cabinet members to the Prime Minister, under the umbrella of courtesy, it gave me more time to think of the issues involved and of more possible questions.

The principle is a general one. Confronted by multiple interviewees, it is always necessary to evolve, and quickly, a method of operation suited to the exact circumstances. Otherwise confusion will almost certainly reign. What should and could have been a revealing and informative interview will end in a muddle or a final published interview more dogged by caution than it should and could have been.

The Jamaican solution would have worked only in those precise circumstances. But the sensitivities of those in high office are not the central ingredient of the difficulties in interviewing more than one person at a time. The potentially most disastrous example for me had no 'celebrity' connotations. It was when I was in Cyprus writing about the life of the RAF in the major communications centre covering the Middle East and beyond. I was in fact conducting interviews for my book on the people of the modern RAF, *Guarding the Skies*, but it would have been substantially the same (but for the more imminent deadline) had I been working for a newspaper, magazine or broadcasting organization.

In order not to neglect the female side, I had asked to meet some women of all ranks. It would not have been easy to talk to them while they were in the course of their work, especially if it were to do with communications. I had expected to be able to talk to them individually on a sort of dentist's waiting room arrangement I had used on other occasions.

Instead I was led into a large meeting room full of female members of the RAF. Obviously I was expected virtually to hold a public meeting. Panic and despair almost took over, but by the time I had reached my seat facing them, some ten seconds later, I had somehow managed to cobble together in my mind not only a series of questions but also a method for handling the situation.

It has been said that journalists have to have a quick rather than profound intelligence. True. Here that precept was tested to the full.

The first necessary technique in such a situation, since you will not be able to keep track of actual names, is to take a detailed mental photograph of every person as they speak and to preface their comments in your notebook with an abbreviation of their most obvious characteristic. If the speaker has a large nose, you write Nose; if fair hair, Blond; if spectacles, Specs and so on. If she is obese, write Fat; if she is thin, write Thin; if she is physically unprepossessing, write Ugly. This will enable you to keep track of what everyone says even if they are interrupting one another, since you will not need to look back in your notes for a name: the physical appearance of the speaker, constantly before you, will immediately suggest it.

If you follow this system, you must naturally take very good care indeed not to let the people you have been talking to see your notes. 'Belly' or 'Sheep' could take some explaining away.

Always be aware, however, that there are (albeit a limited number of) cases where it can be distinctly profitable to interview two or more people at the same time.

Don't be too much in love with your own preconceptions. If interviewing two comics – or anyone else – produces an entertaining or enlightening bedlam, that is better than trying to stage manage the joint interviewees into your own pre-set pattern.

But, to reiterate, in most other cases very firm stage management is needed if you interview more than one person. If you can avoid it altogether, then do so. If you can't, be prepared for considerably more work and hassle. Be sure to have plenty of tricks not only in your repertoire, but at the very forefront of your mind.

Chapter 5

Vox Pop

There is one interviewing technique that is almost in direct contrast to asking different questions of a number of people at once. It is what is termed 'Vox Pop', where you ask the same question of a lot of people individually in the hope of finding out what the public is thinking on a particular issue of the day. The results can be either revealing or idiotic, according to the skills of the interviewer.

The whole business is inherently somewhat unreliable, as professional polling organizations have discovered to their cost. Suddenly faced with an interviewer at a street corner or on the telephone, asking questions on sensitive or controversial subjects, interviewees may well lie in order to give an answer they believe is more generally acceptable than their own view.

I have done very many vox pop operations, mostly in general and by-election campaigns. The method I devised over the years was simple. You stop ten people in the street and ask them who they are voting for. You then go to another part of the district and ask another ten people. And perhaps another ten if you feel like it. There is only one proviso: you absolutely must *never* be selective in who you approach. You must point your eyes arbitrarily in a certain direction, focus on the very first person you see and ask him or her the question, having first established that he is a voter in the constituency. It does not matter if the man is wearing a bowler hat and therefore looks quite untypical. It does not matter if he is wearing a pull-on woolly and so looks equally untypical. It does not matter if the person looks the sort of person no sane person would want to talk to. It does not matter if the person next to him looks far more amenable. You must interview the person on whom your eye first alights.

And the question you put to each must be precisely the same, even in the intonation with which you ask it. However fed up you may have become with the same question, this downbeat mood must not be conveyed in the manner in which you ask the question. If you smile in one case, you must smile in every case. The best stance is a neutral expression and impression, as far as any human being can contrive this, and a rather mechanical if not exactly Dalek-like tone of voice.

In using this method, three things quickly became obvious to me. First, the results in the two (or more) tests of ten people produced almost exactly the same result. Second, this result was virtually the same as the professional opinion polls with a catchment of a thousand or more people compared with your humble ten. Third, when the results of the actual election are known, both your vox pop and the professional pollsters will be inaccurate to almost precisely the same degree.

In short, people as individuals or in the mass do not always reply truthfully when asked about their views and intentions. Indeed, why should they? Is it any business of the interviewer which way they are going to vote? There may be incontestable reasons for asking a politician his intentions, but do they apply to a random selection of people approached in the street or by telephone?

Nevertheless, the vox pop can have its uses as entertainment and as some guide to the emotional temperature around any given issue. For instance, it may establish that there is *no* emotional temperature around an issue, however much Parliamentary figures are getting steamed up about it.

On the first anniversary of the government's sell-off of what had previously been unified and nationalized railways, the London *Evening Standard* did a vox pop among travellers at Waterloo station, one of the busiest used by commuters. It was sensibly conducted and presented by Sally Pook, whose conclusion was that most passengers found their train service had altered very little and that those who detected minor improvements, such as better rolling stock, were not certain that these were anything to do with privatization.

The main interest lay in the way the individuals questioned were reluctant to jump onto any political bandwaggon on the issue of rail privatization. One said she hadn't noticed any difference, though the service certainly hadn't got worse; what mainly annoyed her in the past were the engineering works on the Weymouth and Southampton routes; there were fewer now, but this might not have anything to do with privatization. Another said that the trains seemed to be more on time and the coaches seemed a lot cleaner, but that might be a sheer fluke; and that the staff were just as miserable as they always had been. A bank manager from Fleet in Hampshire said he would have expected some services to be cut, but they hadn't been. A broker from Cobham, Kent, said that the 'amazing' service hadn't changed in the past year.

It might have been expected that the older people interviewed would have been united in their nostalgia about the past, but this was not so. One 62-year-old said the service to Windsor from Mortlake now consisted of four trains an hour instead of two, while a 65-year-old man said the Bracknell service was about the same – 'except that a lot of people are making money out of it.'

The impression I drew from the published material was that this was a case where people were distinctly unopinionated. Only persistent and skilful interviewing by the reporter had produced useful views on a subject about which people cared not very much. I do not know the interviewer's own views, but they did not emerge by inference in the treatment of the vox pop. This was as it should be. The comment about people 'making money out of it' came at the very end of the resultant piece and was thus the pay-off line; but that may have been accidental or owing to the way the story was handled by the sub-editors.

This was a useful example of the way a vox pop can be used to test the temperature of the water: it came up with the fact that people did not think as they were expected to think by the more politically conscious or partisan. It is often the case that the results of a vox pop will illuminate more than the direct question, and for this reason alone it is a form that any interviewer or would-be interviewer on a larger and deeper scale should take seriously.

Chapter 6

Barging In

Do not believe that interview techniques and refinements are applicable only to big, half-page or half-hour interviews. Any contact with a human being when on a news or feature story is in fact an interview and should be given some degree of thought as such. It is never enough to open your notebook and hope that the right sort of material will fall into it. 'It's a job,' may be a sensible attitude; 'It's only a job,' never.

Any question-and-answer session, however brief, should be regarded as an interview and given the hard preliminary thought necessary in any interview, even if the time for such thought is brief. Because work of this sort often does entail a very brief period for thought indeed, and is often regarded as the rough end of the business, it often requires more 'nerve' to make an approach than for a full-scale interview which has been set up in advance and for which both sides are therefore receptive and prepared.

It is having this sort of nerve in making approaches, in juxtaposition with the sort of sensitivity that makes it possible to frame a seductive question, that makes a good interviewer. I have often joked that in Fleet Street and the media as a whole, foot-in-the-door merchants who ask mechanical questions are ten a penny, and sensitive spirits who can frame sensitive questions but can't push their way in to ask them are ten a penny; it is foot-in-the-door merchants who can ask sensitive questions, if necessary in a hurly-burly, and then present them intelligently, who are like gold-dust.

Don't be frightened to jump the counter that divides you from an interviewee you want to interview, but make sure that your manners and visible intelligence are not those of a counter-jumper. Certainly for brief, unpremeditated interviews foot-in-the-door techniques can be useful, especially if they are applied with an element of finesse. The more you are in fact barging in for an interview, the less your manner and manners should suggest that you are doing so.

When she had just been made Leader of the Conservative Party, Mrs

Margaret Thatcher was the prominent guest invited to the Ideal Home Exhibition to open and inspect that year's show house, usually a source of controversial ideas on patterns of living. I thought her ideas on that, during or after she had inspected the show house, would make one of the two weekly columns I was then writing for *The Guardian*.

The snag was that I did not know until the last minute that she was due to make the appearance: for security reasons, the movements of politicians were not publicized far in advance. For the same reason I did not think it would be easy to get close enough to bend Mrs Thatcher's ear with any questions. In such conditions my maxim that a journalist should look as little like a journalist as possible tends to be worth remembering. I can see no advantage to a journalist in looking like a journalist, except perhaps when covering a war zone.

Sure enough, the reporters and photographers who were beginning to gather at the exhibition were kept well back behind silken ropes. Fortunately there was no one in the press pack I knew or who knew me. I wore my usual grey suit, formal shirt and plain dark necktie: inconspicuous and respectable, perhaps depressing but useful.

Mrs Thatcher arrived with her entourage to the clicking of kept-at-bay cameras. She cut the tape in front of the show-house door and disappeared inside. No media person got near her – although they were eventually allowed to follow the visiting party at a respectful distance (i.e. out of earshot).

Looking, I imagine, rather like a conformist borough surveyor, I walked unimpeded into the house by the back door. As Mrs Thatcher came to the last rooms of the house and was nearly at the back door, I stepped forward in front of her with my notebook plainly in front of me, told her who I was, and asked her for her opinion of the house.

It is important in such cases that the first question not only be one that it would interest the interviewee to answer but also one that it would seem merely silly to *refuse* to answer. Her protectors looked a little uneasy, but she didn't miss a beat, giving her opinions with that incisiveness that even her opponents had to acknowledge. I then moved on to more complex questions about what she looked for in a home and the dangers of having people living in inadequate homes. She considered all questions, which were put in as non-pushy tones as I could contrive, with birdlike attention, then gave well-phrased and useful answers. I asked four or five questions in this way, as the minders understandably grew more twitchy, and then, before I wore out my welcome or had my collar felt, thanked her as if I were a guest who was leaving after being invited to tea, heard her say, 'No, thank *you*,' and backed off. As far as I know no one else talked to her.

I had the basis for a piece on homes as domestic, social and political entities, led with her own views. The whole interview could not have taken much longer than two minutes, though it seemed an hour at the time as I made escape impossible simply by standing there. I would not have been able to do this had I gone 'through the proper channels' because as soon as she exited from the house the Leader of the Opposition was simply – and predictably – hustled away. For such mini-interviews, you must choose the psychological moment.

Above all, you must make it seem easier and more pleasant to answer your questions than to have a confrontation about it. Don't behave pushily like a stereotypical journalist. I have no doubt that had I not been neatly dressed, clean shaven, bespectacled and using BBC standard English; if I had been in dirty jeans which were fashionable at the time, bearded and talking in cockney or Birmingham accents, I would have been brushed aside. I have no doubt that if my articulate questions had not been in vivid counterpoint to the hard foot-in-the-door technique which made it possible for me to ask them, I would have been brushed aside, if not by her then by someone in her entourage. It emphasizes my point that even a brief encounter like this deserves both pre-planning and a display of interviewer's skills at the time.

It also involves a capacity for taking what you are offered and doing something with it rather than having in your mind the quote you want and ignoring everything but the nearest approximation to that – a style of interviewing technique which has never seemed to me the most creative or accurate: distortion rather than insight.

At the other end of the political spectrum to Mrs Thatcher, Tony Benn could be equally courteous to members of the wicked capitalist press who approached him in a way that suggested the ability to listen rather than prejudge.

For the hundredth anniversary of the birth of Ernest Bevin, the leader of the Transport and General Workers Union who became Minister of Labour in Churchill's wartime coalition Cabinet and then, after the war, Foreign Secretary, there was a party for Labour's elite and foot-soldiers, held in Bloomsbury. It was a time when the Labour Party was polarizing into left and right factions in internecine strife which would help keep the party out of office for almost a generation. In his lifetime Bevin had been regarded as being on the political right of the Labour Party, an upholder of the 'traditional' line which had been followed in practice by Labour in office: welfare at home plus reliance on America as financial helper and guardian against the Russians. For my column I decided to ask as many guests as possible what the great Bevin would think of the struggles then going on in the party over Clause Four (the one in the party's constitution pledging adherence to the nationalization of the means of production and distribution) and other matters.

It was apparent at the party that no formal arrangement for interviews would be laid on, and I didn't really expect it. So I just had to barge in on as many conversations as possible to get the answers I wanted. Barging in on a conversation is something that I find difficult as a private citizen; I would go out of my way to avoid it. A journalist cannot afford such squeamishness. There is only one way to do it. Approach the group containing the person you want to interview, wait for whoever is talking to complete their sentence, then cut in by introducing yourself directly to the person you want to interview, hoping that the medium you are representing is one that will curry favour, explain what you are doing and then put the first question straightaway without having stopped speaking.

The interviewee may turn away from the group to talk to you (the best solution from your point of view) or he may continue with the group, but answer your questions as if it were conversation at large. For this you will possibly have to suppress more personal embarrassment but there is this advantage: if you want to talk to another person or persons in that group, it saves you the trouble of explaining yourself all over again.

I asked Tony Benn: 'What do you think Ernest Bevin would think of the Clause Four debate?'

Tony Benn regarded me with utmost courtesy from his considerable height. 'I do not need,' he said, fiddling in his hip pocket, 'to speculate on what Ernest Bevin would think about the Clause Four debate. I *know* what Ernest Bevin would think about the Clause Four debate.'

I wondered what made him so certain. I also wondered what it had got to do with his hip pocket. I was soon to find out. He produced a pristine copy of the little red rule book of the Labour Party, and pronounced it to be forty or more years old.

This was, he said, the copy of the Labour Party rule book he had acquired as a young lad, when he had gone round helping his father to do doorstep canvassing.

'It's all there!' he said. He read out the pledge to nationalize the means of production and distribution as if it had been the Sermon on the Mount or a Shakespeare sonnet.

'That's what Ernest Bevin would have thought,' he said.

How could he be so sure?

'Because it says so here.'

But could he be sure that Ernest Bevin's thoughts would not have moved on in the intervening years? Especially bearing in mind that he had been thought of as a right-wing member of the party?

'He would have stuck to what it says here.'

This and other questions and their answers provided me with some amusing and enlightening material.

There is no way to produce such mini-interviews at such occasions other than the crude one of barging in. It is best done almost mechanically, as if you yourself had no personal diffidence. However embarrassed you may be, it must not show or you may well embarrass other people, even politicians who are thought to be almost unembarrassable. If the thought of it defeats (as distinct from merely agitating) you, you are in the wrong job. Get a behind-the-scenes job like sub-editing other people's material.

One of the most extreme cases of barging in I have ever perpetrated, based on a hunch that nothing else would produce results, was over President Richard Nixon and his supporter John Wayne, the rugged film star. Nixon was in deep trouble over allegations that he or his minions were responsible for tapping Democratic Party telephones at the Watergate apartment complex in Washington and over tapes made of Presidential Oval Office conversations, which turned out to have a high proportion of paranoid or foul language and, though apparently recorded as a precaution against enemies turned out to be a shot into Nixon's own foot.

Few famous people in America at that stage were keen to come forward as enthusiastic supporters of the President; everyone was fearful of their own reputations. An exception, and one in line with the sort of Wild West law enforcer or Green Beret characters he played in Hollywood films, including many distinguished John Ford Westerns, was the late, great John Wayne.

Wayne was known to be a supporter of President Nixon, and had remained so. In America, he had stirred up some in the liberal media because of his attitude. Would he take the same line in London? London was keen to hear. He came to London to promote his latest film, *McQ*, and to make a spectacular for a British ITV company. A 'press reception' (not press conference) was called at the well-known hotel, Grosvenor House, in Park Lane. A press conference is where someone usually mounts a platform to talk to the press *en masse*, a press reception is where someone may or may not mingle with reporters, and may or may not answer questions. The reception was more full than a tube station in the rush hour. I asked one of the organizers whether Mr Wayne would be taking questions and he managed to say, before being dragged backwards into the crowd, that we would have to see what he felt like after his flight.

I did not regard this as a good omen. When Wayne appeared in the doorway, hesitating and surrounded by heavies, I regarded it as even less of a good omen. I estimated anyone's chance of having anything resembling a civilized conversation with John Wayne as absolutely nil. In this sort of situation you have to consider how you can contrive anything positive out of what appears to be a wholly negative situation. I came to the conclusion that I had nothing to lose and everything to gain by direct action. It is a conclusion not to be risked lightly or often. I might not have come to it had I been a Hollywood feature writer in a continuous professional relationship with the actor; it might have cost me a useful contact. But sometimes, as in this case, I thought it necessary.

Accordingly I forced my way towards the doorway in which the six-foot-four Wayne and his entourage were hesitating and when I was within three feet of him, asked, carefully projecting my voice over the surrounding row and making the question deliberately challenging since I reckoned I had nothing to lose, 'Did you come over here to defend President Nixon?'

'No, but if you give me a few minutes, I sure will.'

I did not believe he would be able to make good his promise, even if he wanted to. I immediately put another question. 'Isn't Nixon bad for American life?'

'The sad thing,' he shouted over other people's heads, 'is not President Nixon. The sad thing about life is politics. Politics of any kind.'

The fact that other reporters, noting our conversation, were now pressing towards us, prevented other questions, as I knew it would. He was just able to shout over the heads, 'President Nixon has brought the boys home from Vietnam and achieved détente with China. He should be in his crowning glory. Give me time and I'll answer anything you want,' before his minders pulled him away. He was tugged far more violently than his minders or anyone else would have dared had he really been one of the tough guys he played with such conviction. I took a bet with myself on whether this promise would be honoured. I stayed on until he left under fifteen minutes later, shadowing him and the surrounding press. There was no press conference and he gave no answer to questions about President Nixon.

I won my bet.

Yes, but was what I got worth much? The answer is that it was better than nothing, which is what the opposition media got. Had his minder grabbed at him a second later than he did, I might have got seven or eight useful sentences instead of six. The point is that there are situations in which a mini interview is going to be very mini indeed; but even one or two brief questions answered are better than nothing. It may chime in with what you know already and enable you to create a useful piece with the one or two new sentences as the intro.

Most in-passing interviewees will tend to answer a single question if it is one which is easily answered with a sentence or two. Such questions may require more concentrated thought beforehand than a question in a longer interview. They do not always receive it. Sometimes I am tempted to think that capital punishment should be brought back for any media interviewer who asks the question, 'How do you feel?' It is asked of sprinters who have just won an Olympic race, widows five minutes after their husbands have been found dead in a mountain avalanche, Members of Parliament after they have lost their parliamentary seats, bricklayers after they have just won £20,000,000 on the National Lottery, scientists who have made a breakthrough in curing cancer. What sort of answer do they really expect? Do they expect the sprinter to say, 'I'm disappointed – I wanted to lose'? Do they expect the widow to say, 'I'm delighted he's dead'? Do they expect the MP to say, 'Oh, I'm very happy: since my constituents are such morons, I've wanted to hand over my seat to some poor mug for years'? Do they expect the bricklayer to say, 'I am suddenly and tragically confronted with the human problems associated with trying to handle effectively an entirely unaccustomed and disproportionate amount of money, which will probably destroy me'? Do they expect the scientist to say, 'Actually I'm very sad to have contributed to a possible cure, because I feel very affectionately towards cancer'?

There is no point in asking a question to which the answer is obvious, unless it produces an answer which is not obvious – which very rarely, if ever, happens. Any one of the five answers I have just suggested would be worth reporting, but in practice they never occur: the answer is always entirely predictable and therefore pointless. It is an attempt at wall-to-wall sensationalism: the sprinter is expected to whoop and jump in the air, the widow is expected to cry, the MP is expected to look gratifyingly gloomy, the bricklayer is expected to wave an open bottle of champagne in the air, flooding the entire landscape, the scientist is expected to look as if he knows more than God. It is pure wallpaper, not a shred of insight or information in it.

On the other hand, I do understand how any reporter, faced with a very mini interview opportunity, is tempted to shout out this vapid but at least catch-all question. It is a question which is probably easier to answer than rudely brush aside and there must always be the feeling, 'Well, it just might reveal something.' Small though this hope is, there is always something to be said for hope. But if this or any similar question produces nothing except the obvious and predictable, there is a good case for editing it out of the programme or the printed interview.

It is of course much easier and less heartbreaking to edit it out of a printed interview than a broadcast one, since pointlessness is easier to defend as 'good television' than good printed journalism. Showing a human being mouthing banalities or rubbish may or may not be visually arresting; trying to report it in print will soon reveal its lack of substance and interest.

Sometimes it is possible to get in first with your mini-interview, before the presence of a large press pack makes anything in the nature of a thoughtful question difficult or impossible.

Somehow you must get in before the competitive psycho-drama begins. In the case of a press conference or press reception this is often possible, especially if you keep your notebook out of sight (it will make your competing colleagues twitchy) and contrive to talk to the interviewee in as conversational, as opposed to as hard-pressing a tone as possible. Make up your mind who you want to interview and sidle up as early as possible, before the public proceedings have started. If everybody did it, it would be chaos, but everyone will not do it: many prefer to get going only when the competitive psycho-drama starts, and tradition supports them.

It was in this way that I approached Sir Laurence Olivier, Lord Olivier as he was to become, when he helped launch a series of television programmes which he had produced, using British and American actors, for Granada Television when its head was the literate David Plowright, brother of Olivier's wife Joan Plowright. There was a press reception and screening at the British Academy of Film and Television Arts. After refreshments the plan was that we would all adjourn to the Bafta theatre for a preview of one of the programmes and press conference conducted from the stage.

I have rarely found such loud-hailer press conferences very useful, so I decided to tackle Olivier when he was on his own in the bar before the show. I was then writing on alternate days with John Torode *The Guardian*'s London Letter column, and was less interested in the show being discussed than in the spectacle of Olivier holding a press conference, something very untypical of him.

Approaching him and introducing myself, I remarked on how untypical such razzmattaz was of him. Olivier gave me the appraising look of a man who is on duty and with all his antennae operating. In his best cathedral tones he enquired: 'I am supposed to be the producer and I therefore try to be the father of the occasion. Were you with us in 1956?'

1956? Presumably he was not asking was I born then, because my few grey hairs gave the obvious answer. Was he talking about the fiasco of the Suez Canal invasion and its portent that Britain's days as a world power were over? Was his mind on the invasion of Hungary by Warsaw Pact tanks and its message that the Cold War was still likely to go on for a long time?

I tried to find words that would indicate I didn't know what he meant without making myself look a complete ass – a prime skill for an interviewer. But he stepped in and saved me. '*That* press conference was with Marilyn. It started an hour late and I was the host. That took the hell of a lot to get out of.'

That explained the rarity of his press conferences; after which he was happily off with memories of that disastrous press conference with the late – in every sense – Marilyn Monroe, when he was at odds with her and her protective husband, Arthur Miller, was trying to keep the peace. I certainly got enough to support my thesis that press conferences were not normally considered Laurence Olivier's forte, and I got it only by barging in.

You might shrink from doing something similar because of the fear that you could be bursting in when the interviewee was trying to get his thoughts in order. That is a risk, but an experienced operator will usually have a general idea of what he is going to say by this point and will not finally extemporize until he is on his feet. A 'celebrity' will often stand alone at such functions because people are afraid to approach him, whereas he might well welcome the chance to start 'doing his duty' by starting to respond to an intelligent, non-confrontational question.

Sometimes at such events you may have to be very quick off the mark indeed to talk to the interviewee. Olivier was tied down to the proceedings, whereas that other member of the triumvirate of great British actors, Sir Ralph Richardson, was not so tied when he attended a press conference to launch a new scheme to take British actors and productions on American tours, thus prolonging the life and cash rewards of those productions. It was an interesting idea and there was the promise of many actors to discuss it.

But for lightness of foot, which I recommend, and a touch of blackmail, which neither I nor the great C.P. Scott of the *Manchester Guardian* would ever recommend, I would not have talked to the most distinguished actor expected to appear at the press conference, whom I was determined to target. When I saw Sir Ralph Richardson appear at the door of the reception room, wince at the sight of the crowd and turn tail and walk away, I asked one of the organizers where he was going. I was told the washroom but I didn't believe it. An investigation by me proved me correct: he had gone.

In the street, I saw his back disappear round the corner of the block. I chased him. This was not easy, as he stood six foot three, and his strides were considerably longer than mine. I broke into a trot. By the time he reached his enormous motor bike, parked about a quarter of a mile away, I was sweating.

He didn't respond to my first question. I looked at his motor bike, thinking I might have to content myself with a story about how a Garbo-esquely elusive Sir Ralph preferred motor biking about London to boosting British theatre productions. I took in every detail of the bike, including its elegant chromium road tax disc holder.

'Sir Ralph,' I said, as he was about to start the bike, 'do you realize that your road tax disc is several weeks out of date?'

'My dear fellow,' he said expansively. 'What do you want to know?'

Thus I got the only quotes from the great Sir Ralph that day. Call it opportunism rather than blackmail – and opportunism is definitely one of the interviewer's necessary skills. But of course the tone of my statement about the tax disc wasn't, 'I've got you now, so you'd better talk,' but 'You've been nicked, squire, give up and come quietly' – i.e. it was not serious coercion but a shared joke he could comfortably laugh at. Being light on one's feet does not mean only in the physical sense. Law and morality aside, serious threats of any kind are hardly ever likely to produce a useful interview.

Brief interviews created by barging in are often more useful in producing the nucleus of a story or the embellishment of a story rather than the story itself. I have found them especially handy for producing light touches. A great gala showing of a film in a Leicester Square cinema revealed the film to be of the sort that almost made me regret the exertion of donning my dinner jacket. I was on the wrong side of a red silken rope; the celebrities were on the other. I needed a witty remark on the film. Espying Sir Peter Ustinov among the famous faces assembled to give weight and diversity to the occasion, I ducked under the regal rope. I apologized profusely and indeed genuinely for the intrusion and then put my questions to him. He had wittily defended the film in terms that made it easy for me to seek other opinions before the organizers suggested my withdrawal to join the other *hoi polloi*.

I don't remember the film. I don't remember what Sir Peter Ustinov said. I do remember the nervousness I had to overcome to barge in, and the satisfaction I felt having done it. Barging in is a very useful interviewer's art. But always mind your manners – except for the act of barging in itself. Your behaviour should not be that of a barging-in yob but of a sensitive man forced in the course of duty to do things his diffidence would not normally permit.

Which, ideally, may even be true.

Chapter 7

Working Inwards

Sometimes public relations and publicity people promise more than they can personally deliver in the way of interviews.

This may apply most frequently, though not exclusively, in show business. You may have asked for an interview with a film star who is currently filming. The PR person, especially if you are a regular interviewer for a reputable medium, will not wish to offend you as a valuable contact. He does not want to say, 'Sorry, it's simply not on: So-and-so's wife has just been ill and he's sorting out some tax problems, so he's not very keen on talking to anybody just now.' Not only does he not want to offend you, he doesn't want to discuss his client's private difficulties with the media. So he doesn't say it. He may promise or half-promise an interview, but ask you to be on set or location and 'approach So-and-so only if it seems the right moment – feel your way'.

This sounds reasonable. You may well feel it is the best offer you are likely to get; that it is better than no interview at all. But once you arrive you may find in practice that the star, for reasons you don't know and can't guess, is apparently determined that there should be no right moment. You have only to move in his direction for him to move off in another. At lunch break, he heads for the bar, only to change his mind in favour of apparent teetotalism when you head for the bar too.

By this time you may well be getting irritated. You had intended to play by the unwritten rules of procedure by starting inconspicuously at the outer rim of the target's consciousness and working inwards towards him in the hope that ultimately you would be able to exchange words without frightening him to death. But the rules – or what you took to be the rules – don't seem to be working. You are beginning to curse not only the star but also the PR person who let you in for all this.

You may ultimately have to decide: do you write off your chances

of an interview or do you, at some point, stand directly in front of the
star so that he can't pass, introduce yourself and ask if you can have
ten minutes if not more with him, either here and now or at some time
more convenient to him?

I would instinctively favour the latter course, especially if you reach
the point where you feel you have nothing to lose. But it should not
be embarked on without some speculation as to the possible cause of
the star's reticence. If you can, before you set foot upon the set or
location, press the PR intermediaries about the possible causes of non-
cooperation. They may at least be able to give you a hint, without
divulging too much of their client's business.

I was warned when I set out to do a feature on the making of the
James Bond film *Live and Let Die* in Jamaica that Roger Moore might
be difficult to approach. It was his first film as Bond. A rather different type of personality, he was taking over from Sean Connery, who
many people thought had made James Bond so much his own that no
other actor could successfully play him. Moore had an international
reputation as one of the few British stars who could compete with the
Hollywood matinee idol mould. He would have been a fool, which he
certainly wasn't, not to realize that his international reputation was on
the line as he took over from Connery in a series of films which were
among the most lucrative British films ever made. If box office takings
went down, the accusatory finger would be pointing straight at him,
however unjustly.

Naturally, therefore, he wanted to concentrate on creating his own
Bond, not on talking to journalists. This was made clear to me by the
publicity people. It was entirely understandable. Fortunately I was
working for *The Guardian*, a newspaper whose readers did not swoon
at the very thought of stars; they did not simple-mindedly believe that
stars, however important, made up the dialogue unsupervised as they
went along. In other words I could, if it came to the point, write a
valid piece on the making of the film without exchanging a word with
Moore.

In these circumstances I took a flight to Montego Bay, near the location shooting. Dan Slater, the experienced and helpful publicity man
on the spot, advised caution about approaching Moore, but helped me
organize interviews with other members of the cast and with the
producer Harry Saltzman, who told me (and *The Guardian* audience)
that he had always regretted leaving Unesco after the war: he ought to
have given his life to it. An unlikely (but diverting) story.

I also arranged for myself a number of interviews not directly
concerned with the film, including tracking down a witch-doctor who
was anxious to advise the cast and film crew and what they should and

shouldn't do with their lives, and who insisted he was not a voodoo doctor (this was bad magic and only applied in Haiti, he said) but a doctor of benevolent obeah. I did not avail myself of his services, except as an interviewee; I gather some of the cast were more adventurous or credulous.

This was all most interesting, but it was not apparently getting me any closer to Roger Moore. I watched him by the poolside of the hotel complex overlooking the brilliant blue bay. I watched him from a few seats behind at a live variety show at the local cinema, with many of the local population trying to see both the show and the James Bond cast through doors open in the swelteringly humid heat; in the second half they had the variety show to themselves, because the film cast had called it a day. This was all good back-up material but no more than that.

I watched, and he must have been advised that I was watching, but I got no signal, direct or indirect, that an approach might be in order. Someone on the publicity side told me about the woman journalist in London who had once been offered an alternative cast member to the one she had wanted to interview and had refused the offer, insisting on the interviewee she wanted. Could I understand such an attitude?

Yes, I said briefly, I could.

Oh!

In such discouraging circumstances it is necessary to send out two signals: (1) Resolute determination to get the interview you want and (2) Absolute human consideration about the time, place and method of the interview. One is no good without the other.

The determination can be conveyed in two ways, through the publicity minders and directly. I was careful to make my continued interest in talking to Moore personally about his concept of 007 clear to the publicity machine and to shadow Roger Moore like a gumshoe from a bad B movie, so that not only he but also his beautiful Italian wife could not fail to realize I was there. The aim was to persuade them that giving me an interview would be less distracting than having me hanging around in the middle distance like a heat-seeking missile.

But in such a case, it is vital to make it clear that you will accept any arrangement within reason for the interview. Your personal convenience must be put completely to one side. If the interviewee insists on having the interview over breakfast at 5 am, that is the time you will have it. If the interviewee wants the interview held in bits and pieces between takes, that is how you will do it. If he wants it held over lunch at your expense that (if your employer or freelance market finds this acceptable) is the way you will do it. If he insists on having a cassette recorder running and you haven't got one, buy or borrow one. If he doesn't want a recorder running, don't use one however used you are to using one. If he insists that you don't take notes of any sort, agree but with the proviso that if he is not quoted absolutely correctly, the responsibility will be his rather than yours: you will be surprised at the speed with which the objection to the notebook will fade.

Just before I was due to fly back to London, I got my interview with Roger Moore. His wife was also present in one of the chalets of the hotel complex, and the interview proceeded smoothly if understandably guardedly – the actor must have known that any rash remarks about playing James Bond could live to haunt him if things didn't work out. They did work out; his Bond, though different from Sean Connery's, took on an English upper-crust life of its own; he needn't have worried – though there was no way he or I could know that at the time. Therefore the interview was sometimes halting. At one point, so determined was I not to disturb the flow in any way that I neglected to point out that there was, as only I could see, a bright green lizard on the wall directly behind him that seemed about to jump down his neck. Fortunately the lizard did not have a journalist's gift of intrusiveness and eventually made off.

The interview was unimpeded. It slotted in with, and supported, the material I had got so far. But I might not have got it but for the two-pronged approach of visible determination to get the interview with willingness to be flexible in the actual arrangements for it.

The working inwards interview is certainly not for the thin-skinned. The paradox is that though a thick skin may be necessary to snare the interviewee, a degree of sensitivity, its opposite, helps in the conduct of the interview itself.

At the height of his youthful fame, Cliff Richard was due to appear live in the Midlands town in which I then worked as theatre columnist and critic. His venue for the previous week was a town in East Anglia. I rang the manager of the cinema in East Anglia and asked if I could interview the pop star for use just before he was due in the Midlands. He referred me to the Richard management, but said he would keep an eye open for me and smooth my path if I had any difficulties. When I telephoned the management, I was told there was no objection to an interview, but I would have to take my chance at the time of his concert. I could go behind the scenes, but they couldn't guarantee that Cliff would want to talk to me.

Especially as pop music has never been something about which I have claimed expertise, research was necessary. Fortunately I had already done much of it, in reviewing his autobiography which he had written at the age of twenty, *It's Great To Be Young*. I knew from this that the former Harry Webb, son of a worker in an electrical equipment factory, thought English girls the warmest in the world, though he hadn't a steady date. He designed his own shirts. His latest record had sold 123,000 at a time when 40,000 was the average. He liked the approval of his fans, however inconvenient it could be at times. He did not even resent a girl who snatched a necklet crucifix off him after the police had ordered the fire hoses to be brought in. After all, she had given him her rosary in return: 'I want her to know that I have still got that rosary, and I hope she has still got my crucifix.'

Just as the intimations of religious belief were there, so were the intimations of worldly shrewdness, the shrewdness of a survivor. He had, he said, made his stage name Richard instead of the more usual Richards specifically so that people would get his name wrong, thus enabling him to draw attention to himself by pointing out the mistake.

All this material, I thought, could be useful, especially if my working inwards didn't succeed and he decided absolutely that he didn't want to talk to me. But I have always regarded previous material as an insurance in an interview, not a way of curtailing the effort of doing one's own questioning.

I doubted whether the pop icon or his management would have read my review of his book, the summation of which was: 'Mr Richard's life story, in fact, is equable to the point of anaemia.' If they had, it would certainly not have helped me get through the mêlée of his backing group, entourage and fans backstage. A rugby scrum would have been relatively relaxing, but I managed to shoulder my way through, waving a notebook to show I was on business, until I was at least in sight of him. It was a very hot day. He and his friends were sitting round drinking from bottles – lemonade, I supposed – and chatting. The cinema manager had understandably retreated after seeing that I was safely backstage, and no one from the Richard entourage made any attempt to greet me.

In such a situation you cannot know or even guess with any reliability whether the interviewee is discussing urgent business that he will resent being interrupted, or merely commenting on the weather or the flavour of the lemonade. I allowed a decent interval to elapse – about a couple of minutes – and then, when there seemed no change in the prospects, I pushed myself through the hordes with a great and graceless heave, introduced myself to the boyish singer and let him have my first question straight between the eyes. Like him, I was rather young at the time.

'Mr Richard,' I said, 'you are now twenty. Since the age of eighteen you have lived in the padded world of applause. What has this done for your ego?'

In the light of experience, I might have rephrased that question. I might have toned down the interrogatory aura and asked, 'Mr Richard, for the past two years you've had more applause than most artists can hope for in their lifetime. What does an experience like that do for the ego?' The essence of the question would still have been there but the almost accusatory finger would not have been.

However, bearing in mind that I was very junior myself, having no grey hairs to give me authority in an era when grey hairs still had advantages, and that the interview was of the working-inwards variety, in which it is all too easy to be simply brushed aside, an arresting and provocative first question was quite legitimate. It was better than a bland one which could easily be ignored. In interviewing, as in life, it is sometimes better to take a sledgehammer to crack a nut than to leave the nut uncracked. As you get more experienced, you can scale down the size of the hammer and still get the results you want.

Only with reluctance would I today, given similar circumstances, ask that first question I did ask: 'Mr Richard, you are now twenty. Since the age of eighteen you have lived in the padded world of applause. What has this done for your ego?'

At least it got an answer. 'Well,' he replied straight-faced, 'I suppose if you have *really* got a big head, you don't know it.'

I still can't make up my mind whether that was a deliberate or accidental hit. In view of his Christianity perhaps it was an accidental one, but I wasn't sure. I didn't retreat: 'Do you regard perfectionism as the antidote to conceit?'

Cliff Richard: 'Huh?'

I tried again: 'Do you think striving for perfection is a way of stopping yourself getting conceited?'

'I think if I am big-headed, then it is because I am trying to get better and better.'

Pardon?

There is a moral here. Any interviewer should tailor not only the content but also the tone of his questions to his interviewee. Mine in this case had all the delicacy of a charging elephant, coupled with the charm of a guided missile. If not exactly rude, they were as a whole too intense to put to a twenty-year-old pop singer who had never pretended to be an intellectual. Certainly they were the sort of questions one is sometimes tempted to put in 'working inwards' interviews which may peter out at any moment and where an abrasive question may yield some sort of revealing answer, whereas a bland question may well receive a bland and useless answer or none at all before the interviewee decides it is time he was doing something else. But this process has its risks: it can gum up an interview even before it starts.

Fortunately for me, Cliff Richard was considerably more durable than he then looked, and I was not so obdurate as I sounded. I tried a little flattery: 'You have already had a long life for a pop singer, and your influence seems just as strong, especially among the younger listeners.'

At which the singer relaxed enough to show his sharply analytical side: 'Among the fourteens, yes, audiences are gradually getting calmer and we are tailoring our act to the audience. About 75 per cent rock 'n' roll and 25 per cent ballads now . . . I don't blush at the reaction of the audience. You want a woman to like you. Even if she is a girl of fourteen, I can't understand anyone who says it just passes over him.'

I shook this point like a dog: 'Your critics might say that to work on a teenage audience, as you do, you must be a cynic.'

The use of the omnibus term 'your critics' is useful in an interview. It enables you to express a hostile point of view without suggesting that you yourself are necessarily hostile. In fact, I doubt whether any critic had actually suggested that Cliff Richard must be a cynic: I was drawing the hostile point of view out of the empty air or my own cynicism – a quite valid manoeuvre for an interviewer to make unless overdone.

Cliff Richard replied: 'I'm only cynical against the press. We do the act for old people's clubs and blind people's clubs. It is for everybody.'

The only thing he didn't like about fans, he added, was when elderly people came up to him and asked him for his autograph, pretending it was for their nephew or niece.

'Perhaps,' I zoomed in, 'it *is* for their nephew or niece?'

'I don't like it when they do that, not at all! It is as if they said to you, "Someone else likes you, but I don't!" – you know? It makes me feel funny inside.'

'You said in your recent autobiography,' I pointed out, 'that you started singing because you liked it. Do you keep on because of the profit?'

Provocative questions usually fail against timid people and succeed against survivors. I should have made more of Cliff Richard's unruffled answer: 'As soon as that happens, you are dead. You have to like, all the time, what you are doing. I love the fans. Whatever they do in the theatre is fine. The only time I get embarrassed with them is when I am walking down the street. Money? Personally, I don't spend much. On clothes, mainly. I have bought my mother and father a house and a car. I have a car myself. I have an accountant who deals with all the money matters. I care what happens to money. But I don't think I have got a business head.'

This was quite a shrewd self-assessment for a person of twenty. I didn't expressly say so in the printed interview, but I allowed the quote to stand verbatim to illustrate the point. Time has proved that if he does not have a business head, he certainly has the hard head of a born survivor, which is not necessarily to be taken for granted in the world of pop music, where hard hearts and soft heads are, as in the case of the Bourbons, arguably more usual.

My piece pleased my employers, who rather liked the hard-edged tone: 'their man' was up to grilling the youthful idols then beginning to dominate entertainment. It read well. But I can see now that I did not take sufficient perceptive note of his character as distinct from his flamboyant popular reputation: he might have talked even more revealingly if I had not flung sharp questions at an icon but tried to establish the atmosphere of a conversation between two intelligent people.

At any rate, I gave him a more respectful and I hope good-humoured time when, years later and now on *The Guardian*, I interviewed him again. This was when, after leaving pop for Christian works and then returning to pop without abandoning Christian works, he helped promote the launch of the *The Good News Bible* in Britain in the late 1970s. I increased my stock of signed first editions by getting him to sign my copy (the authors not being available), acknowledging frankly that it was for me rather than for any nephews and nieces. Flattery, especially if sincere, can be a better loosening up interviewing tool than what sounds like hectoring. But this time the interview, though more brief, was set up and I did not have to struggle through crowds. If I had had to carve my way through a fracas for a working inwards type of interview, my technique might have had to be closer to the one I had used twenty years previously.

By and large, interviews are now more professionally arranged and regulated than they were. An interviewer, especially for a reputable medium, is more seldom faced with being at the periphery and having to ingratiate or force himself to the centre of the charmed circle and then charm or provoke a response from the interviewee.

But it remains an interviewer's skill that is best acquired, even if it is relatively rarely used.

Chapter 8

The Hitchcock Syndrome

I call it the Hitchcock Syndrome because it was my interview with that great suspense director of the cinema, Alfred Hitchcock, that first made me vividly aware of it.

The syndrome is when you are treading on the interviewee's toes in some way you don't understand, but neither push ahead to capitalize on it nor retreat gracefully until, perhaps nearer the end of the interview, you offer the same line of questioning, safe in the knowledge that even if you are thrown out, you have enough material 'in the can'. Instead, you just stand there, as it were, like a rabbit paralysed by the headlights of an approaching lorry. That is the Hitchcock Syndrome, and it is to be avoided if possible.

I interviewed the maker of *Psycho*, *North By Northwest*, *Strangers on a Train* and *Shadow of a Doubt* at Pinewood Studios near London at the beginning of the 1970s. Already elderly, he was making *Frenzy*, his first film in Britain for thirty years, about a serial killer in the old Covent Garden fruit and vegetable market who strangles women with neckties. Hitchcock's reputation was on the wane.

The interview was one of the most difficult to set up in my entire career, which should have given me a warning of troubles ahead, but didn't. I spoke with his press spokesman several times on the telephone before it was agreed that I should appear at Pinewood at 9.30 the following morning, so that I could be a fly on the wall when he was shooting and talk to him when he was not. Hitchcock had vetoed my suggestion of 8.30 am: as what is now known as a control freak, he would not have wanted me there half an hour before he himself was due to arrive.

Once there, I did several things that were right. Seeing that Hitchcock was busy, I spoke to his devoted wife and ex-collaborator, the scriptwriter Alma Reville. I knew that she always held the keys to Fort Hitchcock. What I first said to her was not, however, politic. My explanation for my desire to interview him at length during a day's

67

shooting – my personal admiration for his films stretching back to my boyhood – may have caused suspicion. It was quite true. But it was *not* the sort of thing that is usually said by an honest journalist. It is usually said by some huckster intent on setting someone up.

But it was the Hitchcock Syndrome proper which for a while clammed up the interview.

At this stage of his career, we now know via the American academic author Donald Spoto and others (but as I did not then know) the situation of Hitchcock was parlous. His health was poor; he found it difficult to get his proposed films financed; his infatuation with Ingrid Bergman still hurt his pride; he had never got over his undignified and fruitless attempts mentally and physically to take over one of his string of screen blondes, Tippi Hedren of *Marnie* and *The Birds*, by threats to ruin her career. He was drinking vodka by the tumblerful and had become a psychological if not actual groper.

Furthermore, something else I did not know, in the 1930s his films had been consistently trashed in *The Spectator* by the British novelist Graham Greene. There was at the time no reason why I should have known this. The damning reviews had first appeared when I was a toddler and were not republished in book form, edited by John Russell Taylor under the title *The Pleasure Dome*, until long *after* my interview with Hitchcock.

Greene had written of *The Thirty-Nine Steps* that the film consisted of a series of small 'amusing' melodramatic situations: the murderer's button dropped on the baccarat board; the strangled organist's hands prolonging the note in the empty church. Hitchcock, in the view of Greene, built up these 'trick situations' very perfunctorily, paying no attention to inconsistencies, loose ends or psychological absurdities. Then he dropped them: they meant nothing, they led to nothing.

All seemed well in the great director's caravan (literally a caravan like you might see on the M5 in summer). The only snag seemed to be that though I was about the same height as Hitchcock, I was only half his weight. As we sat facing one another on either side of the caravan, his twenty stone so tilted it that I and my cassette recorder were in constant danger of sliding into his Buddha-like lap.

That might not have mattered. My line of questioning did. Knowing that he and Bergman had once had some sort of spat on a set I asked him why. He looked panic-stricken. I should have asked myself why. Whenever an innocent question (as mine was) produces a disproportionate effect an interviewer should ask himself why and proceed with care.

At last, after a very long pause, he said, 'I don't like quarrelling. It is a waste of energy. Hating people is ... ridiculous ... it is ...

unprofitable. Any quarrelsomeness offends me. I don't clash with other people's temperaments. I am a man without temperament – for clashing purposes, anyway. I would rather have fun and enjoy what I am doing. Ingrid Bergman said what she said, about me being a man you couldn't quarrel with over some ... technicality. Something I wanted her to do and she didn't want to do. I walked out and she was calling the walls names, not me. I walked away.'

I changed the subject. This was in itself the right thing to do, especially as I had decided to revert to it later. Unfortunately I changed the subject to another hero of mine, Graham Greene. As his world seemed in some ways similar to what was called Greeneland, had he, I asked, ever wanted to do a film of a Graham Greene novel?

The length of the pause should have persuaded me either to get off the subject or to pursue it with great vigour and damn the consequences. I did neither. I just waited for him to go on.

Eventually he said carefully, with many painful pauses: 'It has never worked out. . . . It has never come my way. Would I like to? Yes . . . I think they have a . . . dry humour. But I have never been offered the rights of a Graham Greene story. Never.'

Had he ever tried to acquire such rights? This must have seemed to him like asking Winston Churchill whether, in the middle of World War Two, he had ever been asked by Adolf Hitler to come over to dinner.

It produced a longer pause. 'No . . . most of them were already done . . . it just didn't happen . . . that they . . . came my way.'

I can now see, being fully aware of the existence and nature of the Hitchcock Syndrome, why his minders were afterwards constantly on the phone, trying to find out what I was going to write.

'But you spent *all day* with him! You asked all sorts of questions!'

'Well, I rather thought that was the whole idea.'

And so on.

Always have in mind the possibility that, without knowing it, you may be walking on eggshells. The interviewee may have some aspects of his personal life that he would not want revealed. In the light of the libel laws, you might not be able to reveal them in any case; but if you stroll near them by accident you may gum up the interview. Learn to recognize the signs and take evasive action.

It pays to *know* as many facts as possible about the interviewee that the interviewee himself might prefer to forget – but sometimes only so that you can steer well clear of them or anything reminiscent of them. In short, if the interviewee has a wife on two bottles of gin a day, you may well freeze him into mistrustful silence if you innocently ask his opinion of the licensing laws.

Either pursue touchy subjects rigorously, accepting the risks, or back off. Use your imagination to divine what may be the trouble: I should have guessed that Hitchcock might notice Bergman personally as well as professionally and I should have sensed that Greene and Hitchcock, both dwellers on the dark side of the street, would find one another embarrassing rather than sympathetic. If not a bad interview, it could have been better. Pursue or retreat, albeit temporarily. Don't just stand there. Avoid the Hitchcock Syndrome.

The reverse of the Hitchcock Syndrome is what I think of as the Jackie Collins Syndrome. In this the interviewee is oppressed by the interviewer's obvious suspicion of dark secrets which don't in fact exist. When the first of her Hollywood bonkbusters, *Lovehead*, came out, I interviewed Miss Collins for *The Guardian*, at her elegant flat in Belgravia. When a few months later my own second novel, *The Scandalisers*, appeared, the arts page editor Michael McNay mischievously asked Jackie Collins to interview me. I suggested that this be at her flat rather than my own.

She obviously brooded over this. Would my domestic arrangements not bear scrutiny? Was I perchance sharing my flat with six girl groupies, eight gay plumbers or thirty parakeets? In fact, no. It was merely my vanity. I didn't want to put on show my small book-lined Hampstead flat after seeing her large Belgravia residence.

Always remember that interviewees will probably have more self-perceived inadequacies than dark vices.

Chapter 9

Don't Be a Sheep

By all means be sensitive to the public's current opinion of any inter-viewee, but do not be imprisoned by it.

Recognize that the heights and depths of reputation can be transi-tory. Yesterday's idol can be today's fallen idol and today's fallen idol can be tomorrow's idol. Don't assume that some quite pretty girl who makes her living by wearing clothes and walking up and down will still be an icon and role model in five years' time. Do not assume that a distinguished actor who has had one flop is to be written off. Form your own assessment of the interviewee. Use those skills of human understanding that every interviewer must have and develop.

Where is the interviewee now in terms of public reputation? Where is he likely to be in five years' time? From past happenings in his life, what can you infer about his possible future? Is he in some way under attack, and is he likely to succumb to that attack or survive it? Is he the sort of person who can take a cool view of events or the sort of emotion-led person who will always tend to find himself in difficulties which are, to him, inexplicable? You will produce a more interesting interview if you bear in mind all these things rather than simply, in effect, cheering or jeering with the crowd.

He wasn't aware of it, but it was David Frost who taught me this.

Frost first became famous in the early 1960s as the cropped-haired anchor man of the BBC Saturday night satire show, *That Was The Week That Was*. It ridiculed politicians and other icons in a way unheard of previously. The nation watched compulsively. It was a scandalous success. Its stars – Frost himself, Millicent Martin, Roy Kinnear and Lance Percival – though all very young, were more familiar figures than many government ministers. Then suddenly the position of the show's protector, the BBC's Director General, Hugh Carleton Greene, brother of the novelist Graham Greene, was weakened by political infighting and the show was terminated.

The stars – except for Bernard Levin, who still had a newspaper platform – were suddenly adrift without exposure. Those in the media who had always hated the programme crowed at their discomfiture. David Frost took to touring the provincial musical halls, much as the doomed comic Tony Hancock had done, with a revue called *Doing A Grand Job*.

When the show reached Birmingham, a city within the remit of the regional newspaper for which I then worked, the *Express and Star* of Wolverhampton, I set up an interview with Frost at the Birmingham Hippodrome.

I arranged to meet him at 5.15 pm in the theatre foyer. At 5.45 pm he burst through the door from the auditorium, breathless, wearing a creased blue blazer, baggy grey flannels and scuffed slip-on shoes. He told me he had come into the theatre by the wrong door, and that his car had broken down on the way back from lunch at Cambridge. He piloted me to his dressing room door, which he failed to open with the key, the pile of magazines under his arm sliding to the floor as he repeatedly tried.

I took the key from him and opened the door at the first try. Was this the man who had so confidently ridiculed the Prime Minister Harold Macmillan for mismanaging the country? The tone of the interview was rather lack-lustre. His complexion was sallow and his manner far from sparkling. It would have been easy for me to have written a crowing interview taking him down several pegs. I might have done just that if, outside on the pavement with him as he courteously bade me farewell, I hadn't mentioned that I had once submitted a sketch to *That Was The Week That Was* and told him the gist of it.

He laughed. His rather hooded eyes suddenly came alive. His back straightened. He became a different person. If I had any more ideas for sketches, I was to send them direct to him: yes, he meant it.

I revised my opinion of him as a possibly busted flush. This was not self-interestedly because I intended taking advantage of his offer; I never did. It was because I had seen this extraordinary transformation, this sudden coming alive, when faced with an idea. This was not the attitude of a human failure, it was the attitude of some sort of future impresario, someone who could recognize and deploy other people's ideas as well as his own.

David Frost's current reputation confirms my 1960s impression; but at the time of our meeting it would have been all too easy to write a snidely knocking interview. I like to think that I didn't do so because I am not a sheep.

On the other hand, one failure of mine makes the central point equally well. When interviewing one of many high-ranking officers for my book on the people of the modern British Army, *Soldiering On*, he told me: 'There are some of us who think the Soviet Empire will crumble – so that in that area there will be everything to play for.'

This was in 1979. I had never heard such an opinion expressed before. There was, as far as I could see, absolutely no reason for believing anything of the kind. To me it seemed merely the spirit of gung-ho gone mad.

I ignored the remark and guided the conversation to other matters. Oh dear! At least I vowed later not to make the same mistake twice. If any intelligent interviewee ever says to me, 'Though it is apparently at the height of its world supremacy, some of us think that management capitalism is suffering from the ills of hubris and, if it is not careful, is in fact doomed,' I promise not to dismiss the remark out of hand but to question the interviewee further.

Chapter 10

Political Pressures

Pressures from politicians and others to slant an interview in accordance with their own priorities rather than those of the interviewer are not easy to resist. However, a vigilant attempt at resistance must always be made.

Such pressures among politicians in particular began to accelerate in the 1960s under Harold Wilson as Prime Minister and the process continued progressively under James Callaghan and Mrs Margaret Thatcher. With the media growing more powerful, it was perhaps understandable that politicians should in self-defence try to manipulate the media rather than be manipulated by it; but however understandable the pressures may be, it is up to interviewers to play their own hand watchfully and strongly, knowing that the politicians will certainly be playing theirs with far more skill than they would have done thirty years ago.

A few examples from the turning point of the 1960s/1970s readily spring to mind as signs of what was coming.

Just before the 1970 general election, *The Guardian* wanted to create a public forum on the issue of Law and Order, which was being talked up by the Conservatives as one way of unsettling the Labour government. I was asked to interview the Home Secretary James Callaghan and the Opposition shadow spokesman on home affairs, Quintin Hogg (Lord Hailsham), putting broadly the same questions to both. I prepared a list of questions.

It seemed to be a simple task. It wasn't.

Quintin Hogg, receiving me in his barrister's chambers, was a textbook example of one technique interviewers must watch out for: talking-out.

I began the interview by saying: 'The issue—'

I got the chance to say no more. 'I will tell you what the issue is!' he burst forth. He then told me, at well over 200 words a minute. This ensured that I was so busy with my shorthand, keeping up with him, that it was difficult to think up ways I might interrupt him and seize control of the interview.

After what seemed to be about ten minutes of this, with me still thinking about how I might interrupt him, he said, 'So much for the evidence-in-chief. Now for your cross-examination.'

Ah! But my sigh of relief was a mistake, for it enabled him to start telling me at great length what my cross-examination was.

This technique was the forerunner of the technique now commonly used by politicians on programmes such as BBC Radio 4's *Today*: answering not the question asked but one which the politician wished *had* been asked. It amounts to killing with kindness. It appears to be obliging but in fact is intended to prevent the interviewer asking the questions *he* wants to ask.

The remedy, which I adopted in this case, is twofold. First, keep your temper and, in your mind, a note of exactly what you want to ask, and when finally the interviewee runs out of steam, ask away. Secondly, decline all attempts to end the interview before you have obtained answers to the questions you have come to ask, however uncomfortable you may feel at seeming impolite, and insensitive to the fact that you have overstayed your welcome. Have no scruples whatever about taking up more time than has been budgeted for, pointing out if necessary the reason.

The Home Secretary James Callaghan's technique was an equally clear example of another technique emerging more strongly by the year: seeking to vary the terms of the interview at the outset, by replacing the interviewer's questions with more amenable ones.

First, when I arrived in the Home Office building, his officials asked to see my list of questions, unmoved by my assurance that they were the same ones I had put to Quintin Hogg. Then they told me that the Home Secretary saw no point in answering my questions, as he was not to be equated with a mere Opposition spokesman. I asked the officials to point out to him that unless Labour's arguments were put, and put effectively, he might no longer be Home Secretary.

Another wait. Then the officials returned and said the Home Secretary said he wanted to get across what he was trying to do in Northern Ireland, of which he was very proud, and not waste time arguing with the Tories about Law and Order.

In such circumstances never take dismissals as dismissals. Fine, I said, Northern Ireland was certainly part of the Law and Order issue, so if they would give me ten minutes I would draft some additional questions on Northern Ireland.

When I finally got into the Home Secretary's room with my augmented list of questions he threw them across the polished table at me so that they skidded off and landed at my feet. I had to get down on my knees to pick them up.

Such events should be a powerful incentive to any interviewer to continue at all costs, and in this case they certainly were. Though it felt as if steam were coming out of my head by the end of it, I got my questions answered; and at the general election a few days later the Home Secretary James Callaghan became James Callaghan the ex-Home Secretary, a displacement I took with considerable fortitude.

My resistance was a painful textbook example of how to circumvent question-bargaining. But I made one mistake. In such a case, the interviewer should ask himself what sort of politician he is facing: pragmatist or ideologue? In the case of an ideologue who is congenitally sure of what he wants to do, the broadest question (or no question at all) may be all that is required to get him talking about anything under the sun. In the case of a pragmatist, it is safer to build questions around specific propositions which he can either embrace or reject.

James Callaghan was a pragmatic politician. Yet the new questions I drafted for him were broad, catch-all questions of the, 'What do you see as your next step in Northern Ireland?' variety. They should have been of the, 'Would you support power sharing based on proportional representation?' variety. He would have talked more readily on that basis.

Another technique also had increasing currency in that period: asking to see a copy of the interview before it appeared. The request may be valid in the case of an interview involving a complicated technical subject like brain surgery, but should be resisted in the case of a politician or other non-specialist. If it is not resisted, your interview will in effect be composed by a committee.

When she was removed from her last office and, it was wrongly thought, public life itself, the veteran Labour minister Mrs Barbara Castle submitted to an interview with me for *The Guardian*. I wanted a human, affectionate piece on her past life and what she would do now. Instead she asked to see the interview before it appeared and when I declined, she called in her secretary and insisted she sit in on the interview, taking notes. This I had to accept.

I was doubly wrong. Firstly, I should have referred her request for a sight of the interview to the office hierarchy and let them either overturn my principles or take the odium, in her eyes, of refusing her request. That would at least have made her realize that I was not personally antagonistic.

Secondly, I should have resisted the presence of the secretary at all costs. Nothing is more calculated to gum up an interview, especially one intended to be about human considerations, than to have one of the interviewee's subordinates present. It is a recipe for the striking of public attitudes rather than the revelation of private truths. Getting Barbara Castle to 'come over' as a human being involved more hard labour than should have been necessary. I should have pointed out, in as innocuous-sounding words as possible, that the presence of the note-taking secretary would make the proceedings too formal.

In any sphere, however, facing extremely testing and demanding difficulties may have positive possibilities that can be exploited by an alert interviewer.

Chapter 11
Victory in Defeat

A difficult interview can sometimes be transformed into a final result which is better than an easier interview could have provided. The difficulties may in fact make some or most of the 'copy' if treated in the right way by the interviewer. A smoothly slick interview may induce professional admiration; but an uphill struggle, if acknowledged and chronicled openly, may be more endearing and amusing to the average reader, listener or viewer.

The earlier in the proceedings you realize what you are up against, and that the finished result is likely to be the story of your uphill struggle, the more successful the final interview is likely to be. When I was asked by *The Guardian* to interview the great but reticent English orchestral conductor Sir Adrian Boult about the publication of his autobiography, it finally made the better part of a broadsheet page. But at the outset I had mixed feelings, which were well justified by the preliminaries to the interview.

Tall, bald and, in the 1970s, still with the flowing moustache of the archetypal English gentleman circa 1900, Sir Adrian could interpret Elgar, Vaughan Williams, Gustav Holst and other British composers with an unrivalled blend of virility, dignity and fire. But I knew that the title of his autobiography, *Blowing My Own Trumpet*, was likely to be the biggest literary misnomer of the century. He *hated* anything in the nature of self-display, taking the public school position that it was a game only cads played. This was why most interviewers had long since given up on him. At least I was a non-specialist: I had dozens of his records in my collection, but I was not a music writer against whom he might be prejudiced.

After checking first with Sir Adrian that he had no objections, the publishers gave me his telephone number. I rang it and was immediately through to an austere and waspish headmaster who, when I asked for an interview, briskly demanded of me, as if I were a schoolboy putting up his hand to go to the lavatory, whether it was really necessary. I assured him it was.

'Oh dear, *must* we? Could you do it over the telephone and have done with it?'

Fortunately, it was at this early point that I sensed that any inter-view was going to be a 'victory in defeat' interview, the story of the chase of a singularly elusive man. I took down the brief telephone conversation in my notebook, sensing (rightly) that it would end up as the intro of the interview as it appeared.

'I'm afraid not, Sir Adrian.'

'Oh well, let's keep it short. Eleven thirty on Monday.'

Especially with a difficult interviewee in such a situation, it is essential to have read the whole book, not just the blurb; and I had. I did not want him to abort the interview on the grounds of my lack of homework.

I saw him in his office near the Wigmore Hall in the West End of London. His desk was ancient, wide and intimidating. There was an old-fashioned free-standing oak coat-and-hat-hanger in one corner of the room. On it hung a tin hat and gas mask. The war had then been over for twenty-eight years.

I asked him an 'easy' first question, one that he couldn't possibly object to. 'How did it come about that you wrote this autobiography?'

He banged the top of his desk with the flat of his hand. '*Oh dear!*' he roared. 'That is a rather scurrilous story.'

It wasn't, of course; but his explosive emphases in the telling of it made it appear so.

Practically every question I asked produced the thwacking of the desk top with the flat of the hand. My theory about 'Greek' and 'Roman' composers and conductors was especially rewarding, given the approach I was now determined to adopt. I put it to him that the 'Greeks' like Mozart and Bruno Walter valued beauty above power and the 'Romans', Beethoven and Arturo Toscanini, valued power above beauty. I guessed that he was a Roman, and might put Mozart well down his list of preferences?

The desk threatened to disintegrate under the thwacking. 'My dear *man*! *Must* we go on like this? *List*? I have no *list*. And if I had a *list*, Mozart would certainly not be at the bottom of any *list*.' He had just recorded some Mozart piano concertos with André Previn.

So it went on, each question like a red rag to a bull. Thwack, he couldn't remember the Musicians Organization for Peace, of which he had once been president. Thwack, when I praised his recent eightieth birthday concert. Thwack, when the photographer Frank Martin, as always a model of inconspicuous tact, arrived. Thwack, when I asked Sir Adrian about his famous stick technique, only the wrist moving, the rest of the body quite still.

The last question gave him his chance. He jumped up, grabbed a baton from his desk drawer, with which at first I thought he was going to attack me, and demonstrated first his own patrician technique and then that of a see-sawing exhibitionist. '*There*! Which was clearer?'

He remained standing. I took the hint and left.

In my cassette recorder was virtually the verbatim text of what became the long printed interview. Sir Adrian's answers themselves would not have justified ten lines. The blow-by-blow account of our joust, so revealing of the great and much loved conductor, was worth much more.

In such cases, the tone is most suitably one of wry amusement, not resentment or malice over the difficulties encountered. To show up the human comedy is permissible; to use your own last word for the purposes of acidic denigration almost certainly a graceless mistake.

One snag with the victory in defeat interview is that the interviewee, regretting the tough time he has given you, may relent and try to make amends.

This was so with the briefest of brief interviews I had with the celebrated American clarinetist and bandleader Benny Goodman. It was ten in the morning at his hotel in Park Lane at the start of his last British visit. In his room he fell fast asleep, with what I took to be an upturned whisky glass at his feet, during my first question: why did he think he and his style of jazz had lasted so long?

My saga of how I inconspicuously tried to wake him up for several minutes; how I finally in desperation fired that first question about the secret of his professional longevity at him again when he protested that he was due to see other media people waiting downstairs in the hotel lobby; and how he had finally explained, 'I make sure I get plenty of sleep!' was a delightful vignette. Unfortunately he rang the office later in the day with apologies and offers of restitution, pleading jet-lag.

I did not diplomatically make myself unavailable so that I could go ahead and use the saga of how he dealt with my question on the secret of his professional longevity. The integrity of the great and long-dead C.P. Scott still permeated *The Guardian*. But I can understand the temptation to be unavailable afterwards if one has such a victory in defeat interview in one's pocket and doesn't want it sabotaged by the interviewee's later compliance.

I indicated something of the difficulties in the way I wrote the interview up, but didn't write only about them. It was a compromise.

In some ways I was sorry that his obliging side had surfaced: a straight account of the difficulties might have been a more amusing victory in defeat saga. The essential point is that the most disastrous interview can be turned to account if your mind does not run on tramlines about what an interview should and shouldn't be.

Chapter 12

Special Cases

All interviewees are special cases and should be treated as such rather than as artefacts on the production line of your busy schedule. But some are greatly more special than others.

The disabled or otherwise physically disadvantaged are an obvious example. The physically or mentally ill, the blind, the crippled or the terminally sick cannot be dealt with as if they were in the full bloom of radiant health, though any suggestion of condescension, of talking down, must be avoided. And, in common humanity, you must realize that what you write may well have more of an impact on this sort of interviewee than it would have on a more average one.

It was a realization I had not fully come to when I interviewed the British actor and dwarf David Rappaport, who was about to appear at the National Theatre in Ben Jonson's *Volpone*, and who took his own life in California several years later.

The heading of the piece was 'Small Minority', which was justified by the line I took: because it was a rarity to be able to talk to an intelligent and apparently successful man about what it felt like to be a dwarf I concentrated on his dwarfishness rather than his acting.

This was my intro:

A dwarf talking: 'The weasel has nothing on me in getting to the bar. There is nothing but legs. To find a path, you have to predict which way these enormous legs are going to move. You are not dealing with people at all at this level, you are dealing with legs. You have none of the conventions of saying, "Excuse me", because you cannot say, "Excuse me" to a knee. A knee is an object. So you get to the bar first.'

My own breezy, almost flippant, style mirrored his own as he recounted his family background, his first experiences with girls, his efforts to become a teacher, his failed marriage, his turning to acting

81

and his previous appearance in *Illuminations* at the National Theatre. He was so upbeat about his life that I did not feel bound to ask myself, as perhaps I should have done, just how deep this upbeat attitude went. I dealt with his difficulties as a man rather than as an actor. Though this approach remains readable twenty years later, in a way that an account of his difficulties as an actor might not have done, I could without distorting my intentions have thrown in more references to his views on acting.

I gathered afterwards that he was wounded by the fact that I had not; that I had apparently not considered him, as an actor, worthy of more attention. If I had worked in a few more references to him as an actor, the piece would have been more encouraging to him and no less satisfying to the reader and to me.

If people are set apart from their fellows in any way, it is humane to think a little bit more about their vulnerability and their possible reactions to the way you handle them and anything you may write.

Children require special treatment, though the less obvious that is from your manner the better. The best method, I have found, is to regard them as adults who haven't quite got there yet. For all you know, you may be dealing with another Beethoven, Newton or Churchill who simply hasn't yet emerged in his distinctive final contours. If you attempt to patronize them, they will resent it as surely as you would in their position. Obvious wheedling, affected voices, silly laughter and forced familiarity should all be avoided.

If some sort of handicap is combined with extreme youth, any difficulties may be compounded. I once had to write about the winner of an art competition for the disabled held on the South Bank. The mentally handicapped winner had prepared a painting of remarkable power for a child, with both bold colour and arresting design. How had she produced these effects? Two or three questions showed me that I personally could not converse in any meaningful sense with the girl, yet I did not want to ignore her and talk instead to her special needs teacher. I was nonplussed, I hope, only momentarily. I took the teacher briefly aside and asked if she would cooperate in my idea. We returned and I addressed each question to the girl in the presence of the teacher, who conveyed her answer to me. I never looked at the teacher, only at the girl. It was not a perfect solution but it produced enough of an interview to stand as an informative piece about art for the mentally disabled, as seen through the eyes of a practitioner.

The elderly may also require well thought-out special approaches. There is one predominant question you must always ask yourself: however decrepit the body may be, how active is the brain? An emaciated form may be capable of incisive answers to interviewer's questions, a rubicund and apparently healthy body may house a sadly enfeebled brain.

Of course, usually no politician, actor, writer or any other public person will be exposed to the media unless they have their wits about them. It is still advisable to proceed with care and, even if the wits are still sharp, to have consideration for the ailing body.

The hundredth anniversary of the birth of the great war leader Winston S. Churchill was on 30 November 1974. All the surviving prime ministers – Anthony Eden, Harold Macmillan, Sir Alec Douglas Home, Harold Wilson and Edward Heath – and their relatives met in the River Room of the Savoy Hotel, overlooking the Thames, for a celebration. I was especially keen to find out what as many of these as I could interview thought the reputation in history of Winston S. Churchill would be, apart from the obvious one of being on the winning side in the Second World War.

The ex-prime ministers themselves were easy, but I approached the widow, Clementine Churchill, with considerable care. She was thin and obviously frail but since she was talking at length to her grandson Winston Churchill, it seemed she still had her wits about her. The grandson talked to her not by sitting beside her on the sofa, but by falling to his knees and talking directly into her ear.

When he finally moved away, I adopted the same technique. Lady Churchill spoke to me with graceful lucidity that was at some odds with her physical frailty. Had she faltered at any point, I would have had to apologize for disturbing her and withdraw. This did not become necessary.

The moral was that, especially with the elderly, an interviewer must physically adjust himself in all respects to the physical needs of the interviewee without regard to his own comfort and dignity. If you are not confident of being able to do this, do not contemplate the interview. The nature of television makes it difficult for practitioners in that medium physically to adjust themselves to the elderly, disabled or disadvantaged. Difficult, but not impossible.

All vulnerable interviewees should be dealt with in fact, if not in obvious appearance, as if their very large, fit and ultra-protective big brother or son were standing beside you with the beginnings of a scowl on his face. Try always to cause as little stress as possible, except to yourself, but never let the fact that you are taking care and making allowances show – or the interviewee may well feel patronized and therefore be uncooperative.

Chapter 13

Mood and Fairness

It is rather easier than you might expect to allow your mood, dictated by your own personal circumstances, to influence your reactions to an interviewee, just as the most elevated philosopher can be influenced by his own toothache.

You may be able to exclude your own political and social views from playing too strong a part in your attitude to the interviewee: the chances are that they will be too obvious, too visible, to produce any insidious results. Personal mood is a far more subtle bar to fairness: your headache may easily persuade you that an interviewee you would otherwise have regarded as merely irritating is a menace to the human race.

As an interviewer you should be able to put your own current preoccupations and moods firmly in the background, never allowing them to make you in any way unfair to the interviewee. Certainly you are entitled to take into account, and to describe if necessary, the context in which you are doing an interview. But if that context is one you find disagreeable for irrelevant and purely personal reasons of your own, it is wise to acknowledge this to yourself but otherwise ignore your own displeasure rather than to rationalize it into a dislike of, or irritation with, the interviewee.

Sir John Gielgud, who, alongside Robert Robinson, I interviewed on the BBC Radio 4 *Stop the Week* discussion programme, was a case in point. At any other time I would have approached the task of talking to that distinguished British actor with enthusiasm. The producer Michael Ember asked me, as the only member of that week's team to have met Sir John – albeit briefly at a demonstration a few weeks previously to save London theatres threatened by property developers – to be sure to arrive very early in the studio so that I could introduce him to other members of the team. Obviously I said I would be glad to.

The night before the recording, the IRA bombed a pub in Birmingham, their worst atrocity to date. And the night before the recording I happened to be *The Guardian*'s late duty reporter. Not without verbal fisticuffs, the night news editor Roy Harry, unimpressed by the fact that I had to meet Sir John Gielgud the next day, induced me to get up to Birmingham to back up staff already there. Trying to ask my way in pouring midnight rain towards a Birmingham Roman Catholic church which had been firebombed in retaliation, I was tripped into a surging river of a gutter by a gang of youths, and soaked to the skin.

I telephoned through my front page story. Roy Harry then asked me to do a vox pop the next day to discover whether Birmingham people approved the introduction of the death penalty for terrorist offences, which was to be debated in the House of Commons the following day. After that, would I cover a police press conference at midday?

By the time I arrived back in London, leaving my car on a yellow line outside Broadcasting House, I was crumpled and still unshaven, with the blood on the shattered pub walls still fresh in my mind.

Sir John Gielgud, as ever speaking beautifully, was wearing a beautifully cut camel cashmere jacket and a beautifully wafer-thin gold wristwatch. I was no longer in the mood to ask him questions about the reason for his appearance, his dear aunt, the Victorian thespian Ellen Terry, about whom a book had been published that week.

In such circumstances, where one word out of place can be one too many, it is necessary to hit on a plan to bring your own mood under control. It was not in the least Sir John Gielgud's fault that the IRA had the previous evening bombed a pub used by many of the press pack, including me, when I had been *The Guardian*'s Midlands correspondent.

Usually I was quite assertive when competing with questions on *Stop the Week*. This time I was very careful indeed before I spoke. It required a conscious adjusting of my voice and stubbled face every time I opened my mouth. I took other steps. I wrote down some questions, word for word, on the jotter in front of me so that I could expunge any words that might be out of key with the proceedings and was careful, as it were, to stick to the script.

It was good practice in the interviewer's art, if not of a sort I would wish to repeat often. It was a reminder that the personal feelings of the interviewer, unless they perhaps have an objective bearing on the matters being discussed, should be kept outside the door during any interview. Sir John Gielgud was an extreme case.

In *all* cases you must have careful control of your manner and your questions, whatever the circumstances in which they are deployed. One useful way of helping to achieve this is to concentrate wholly on your notebook and the intricacies of your note-taking until your feelings are under proper control. Concentrate on the reality that what is happening is *not* a conversation, however informal it may seem, but an interrogation concealed in the acted performance of a conversation.

One warning. Paradoxically, when firmly putting your own feelings into the background, it is possible to be too flat and detached, which can itself be off-putting to the interviewee. For my book *One Man's Estate*, about how the eighth Marquess of Hertford, of Ragley Hall in Warwickshire, had saved the family home after being told as a schoolboy at Eton that the family could no longer afford to live in it, I interviewed Lord Hertford many times.

Lord Hertford, with, as I put it, 'his 6,000 acres, his half a dozen tenanted farms, his hunting, his cigarette holder, his Berry Brothers Pale Dry Number 3 sherry and his meticulous accountancy and sales graphs, is more than an individual *in vacuo*. He could be regarded as symbolic of the British aristocracy as a whole, who, widely lampooned in these lean and nominally egalitarian times, have still somehow remained part of a country landscape that continues to provide comparatively sheltered, if not too-grandly-paid, employment'.

Many people, no doubt, would have had strong feelings one way or the other about Lord Hertford. Nevertheless, a few years previously he had been interviewed dispassionately by my colleague in *The Guardian*'s Midlands office, Roger Silver, and I intended to remain equally dispassionate during the much longer process of producing my book. I set out to ascertain what he had done to provide finances for the estate, and why. I tried to produce a piece of social history, not a polemic for or against the eighth Marquess. I allowed myself neither to like him nor to disapprove of him as an individual or a social phenomenon.

At the end of the process, I was rather pleased with my firmly dispassionate stand. At the last interview, having previously avoided anything in the nature of cosy chit-chat, I permitted myself to ask the eighth Marquess of Hertford how he had regarded my research.

'It was like being a bug under glass,' he said.

From which I gathered that my cool objectivity had sometimes come across as frostiness; and that if I had loosened my impartiality a little – even perhaps if the result had come across as humanly hostile – I might have got an even more colourful story with even more colourful quotes.

By all means discipline your personal feelings in pursuit of fairness, but always remember that you are not God. You should always come across as a human being: not an unrestrained human being, not a human being blinded by your own views and problems, but a human being nevertheless.

Chapter 14

The Telephone Interview

The telephone has obvious limitations as an interviewing tool and one or two not so obvious advantages. It is best in interviews where it is very much in your interests to get quickly to the point, pressing questions in a way that might seem rude if you were face to face.

A good example was the interview I did with the American stage impresario Joseph Papp, an expert in publicly funded theatre in otherwise highly commercial New York, when he came to London to try to persuade Glenda Jackson to play a female Hamlet. This was long before she took to politics as Labour MP for Hampstead and then Transport Minister in Tony Blair's government; she was still a highly individual and unusually powerful British film actress.

Joseph Papp's idea seemed idiosyncratic, certainly raising enough psychological questions to fill the regular column I then wrote for *Guardian* readers. Mr Papp's visit, however, would be a fleeting one; and a bad back problem which I faced confined my interviewing processes to a telephone box outside the doctor's surgery as I waited for my name to be called. After repeated telephone calls, Papp finally picked up the telephone in his hotel room.

The telephone demands and rewards getting down to business without too many preliminary courtesies. I bluntly asked Joseph Papp (which might not, face to face, have been my first question): 'Isn't it merely perverse to portray Hamlet as a woman?'

The interviewee was equally able to get right down to business without having to go through a ritual defensiveness: 'In Hamlet's character, there is a kind of non-sexuality, something of the female side in the man. When the role was first played here, it was the old Gielgudish effete sort of Hamlet. In recent years you have the Albert Finney, rougher type. Both extremes don't express the interesting composite of the man. Sexually he is right in the middle. There is nothing sexual in him, really. I want to explore the whole area of destroyed sexuality and the frustration of being in a kind of limbo, the frustration of being a woman trained to react as a man.'

Again, my next question was easier to ask over the telephone than it would have been face to face. 'Would all this have taken Shakespeare by surprise?'

No, there was historical/political justification for this interpretation, and the interviewee went on briskly to tell me what it was.

The interview continued in this brisk vein, giving me in very few minutes enough material for my column before I rushed back to the doctor's surgery to see if my name had been called.

If Glenda Jackson ever played a female Hamlet, Debrett's *People of Today* and *Who's Who* have both been unable to unearth the fact. But the column was a highly concentrated and entertaining speculative argument about the character of Hamlet – and one that might not have been improved had my scepticism been detected and Joseph Papp had been given all the time in the world to digress, in a face to face interview. Brevity is altogether more acceptable than in a face to face interview: it even comes across as a courtesy to the interviewee.

There is another advantage. The interviewee is secure on his own ground, be it home, office or hotel, and not directly faced by a personality he may or may not find congenial. He can take or leave you: it is far easier to put down a telephone receiver than show an interviewer the door.

But your attention *must* be concentrated. You cannot rely on a physical meeting to stimulate you and your questions. Your questions must be firmly established in your mind, preferably by writing them out in longhand in your notebook. You must command the interviewee's attention from the outset, because all he has to do, if he doesn't want to answer your questions, is to say someone is at the door and put down the telephone, ignoring it when you ring back.

The rule which applies is almost the exact reverse of that for the beginning of a face to face interview. Instead of asking a soft first question, you may do better to ask a very hard, pointed one, so that the interviewee feels he must address himself with equal concentration to what you are asking. There is a risk in postponing it: the interviewee may plead other business before you get round to it.

You might ask the leader of your local council, your MP or a government minister whether he is on the point of resigning. In each case, the interviewee will realize that if he puts the telephone down, that fact can be reported and will lend considerable weight to any rumours that are doing the rounds. Such a pointed first question in a face to face interview might well allow the interviewee to give a derisory laugh and say, 'You don't waste much time on pleasantries, do you?' before going on, 'Let's have some sensible questions now, shall we?' Such a response would not work on the telephone.

It is not, even, necessarily more difficult to detect lying on the telephone.

When I interviewed him by telephone in the late 1980s, the alleged American traitor Alger Hiss was still a cult figure among the left-wing intelligentsia of the West, though the scandal occurred in the 1940s. It had been the first Eastern 'spy' scandal since the war and it split Western opinion in what, for the East, must have been a gratifying way. For more than a generation afterwards what you believed about Hiss was less defined by judicial appraisal than by your political leanings. On the whole, if you were a conservative you believed Hiss to be guilty of passing secret documents from the US State Department to the Russians via an intermediary, Whittaker Chambers, who later denounced him. If you were a liberal you believed that Hiss was innocent and that Whittaker Chambers was an unsavoury perjurer. Hiss continued to deny his guilt throughout his two trials – the first one had a hung jury – and through a series of appeals, all unsuccessful.

His book, *Recollections of a Life*, again protesting his innocence, was published in Britain when he was 83. He was too old to travel to Britain to promote it, so I spoke to him on the telephone at his home in New Jersey. Realistically, all I hoped to do was paint a word-picture of the lifestyle of this old and still notorious man in his clapboard home, which I did. But in addition I thought a few questions about his culpability might enable me, even on the telephone, to make some sort of judgment about whether he was lying or not, especially as he might now be approaching senility.

In such circumstances, if you are denied sight of the person you are talking to, it may help if you also make yourself literally blind by closing your eyes as you listen to the answers. It is not easy to do unless the conversation is being recorded, because you cannot take shorthand notes, but it is surprising how much more you notice about the tone of voice if you can see nothing and have nothing to concentrate on except that voice.

I formed the impression, which I conveyed in the profile I wrote of him, of a man whose personality was so glacially sculpted, even at 83, that he had perfected a story, had stuck to it, and had a repertoire of answers for any question or any suggestion. I have rarely encountered such an impression of a man not really reacting to his fellow humans but uttering the words of a well-rehearsed, wittily brittle play. He did not vary his stance of innocence one iota.

I asked him whether, since so much had been written about it and he had given the same answers time and time again, he didn't have difficulty separating fact from imagination. 'Not at all. I know clearly what happened, and I know clearly the misrepresentations that have been made.'

I asked him, which I might or might not have been more inhibited about asking face to face, if he were not worried that he might one day, if senile, blurt out something that didn't square with his previously consistent version. The laugh was as sculpted as in a play. 'If there is nothing, I can't compromise my position! I don't see that I would be able to blurt out anything, because that would be contrary to the fact!'

I did not necessarily believe him.

Apart from drawing the word-picture of his life at 83, and describing the way he answered questions, I used his case as the basis for what amounted to an essay on one of mankind's less satisfactory characteristics: the willingness to believe as fact only things that squared with existing opinions.

I might have got rather more 'colour' had I sat opposite him instead of 3,000 miles away; but I suspect the telephone, used with more than a little experience of its limitations and advantages, enabled me to penetrate to the essence of the story that was available on that occasion.

But because the telephone is in a way a third party to any conversation, and one that may in effect discontinue your line of questioning in an instant, it is vital that you do not relax for a single moment, but firmly dominate it from start to finish. In a face to face interview, you may be able to let your mind idle along for a few seconds; in a telephone interview that can be quite fatal. Ideally, you must be fighting fit, mentally agile and well prepared.

The telephone, in short, is a good servant but a bad master.

It also officiously lacks all sense of humour and is quite likely to transform any attempt at humour on your part into something at which the interviewee at the other end of the line, misunderstanding, can take offence.

Do not try to be Oscar Wilde. Unless you already know the interviewee and his sense of humour, any attempts at humour which you make should be very tentative indeed and dropped immediately if they do not seem to take fire. Usually it is best to be rigorously, though not heavy-handedly, businesslike and polite throughout.

Chapter 15

Almost Interviews

Observation without conversation can sometimes be akin to an interview. Being in your sight if not in your hearing can sometimes make someone into an interviewee, body language and behaviour registering almost as loudly as words could do. That is what I mean by an almost interview.

I was keen to get a report of a Buckingham Palace garden party into *The Guardian* as a useful piece of sociological observation rather than as a pamphlet either for or against the monarchy. It was not going to be an easy task. The *hoi polloi*, including the press, were as usual to be kept well away from the smaller group of people who were to be lined up to meet and talk to the royal family. It would not be easy even to approach members of this select group afterwards with the standard, 'What did she/he say to you?' question.

Yet I thought I saw an angle that could legitimately be exploited even if I were to be kept out of earshot of what any members of the royal family might say. The then very young Prince Charles was going to make his first official appearance at a garden party that afternoon. This was certainly a news peg, but what could I hang on it?

In such cases it is wise to have a clear objective but to be willing to change that objective instantly if a better objective suggests itself. I would see, if not hear, how Prince Charles handled the situation and base what I wrote on that: a visual interview, as it were.

Buckingham Palace garden parties are held on the vast lawns behind Buckingham Palace itself. Exotic pink flamingos walked with long spindly legs in the royal lakes. There were marquees where the *hoi polloi* might have tea and cake and more exalted marquees where those destined to meet the royal family personally congregated. Civic dignitaries, high ranking churchmen, military chiefs, artists, writers and other worthies arrived in hired black limousines, whose drivers parked as best they could on the greensward of The Mall after delivering the guests. Car radios competed with police walkie-talkies.

In the middle of the afternoon, the Queen was due to walk along the line of those selected, shaking hands and making brief conversation, followed by Prince Philip, Prince Charles's mentor Lord Louis Mountbatten and lastly the newcomer Prince Charles.

I focussed on the young Prince as if I were a behavioural scientist.

Starting near the flamingo lakes the royal party worked its way up the line towards the back of the palace. The Queen did her usual measured and gracious routine of smiling and talking briefly to each person in turn. She then handed over to Prince Philip, who did more or less the same thing, perhaps rather more briskly. Directly behind Prince Philip and in front of Prince Charles, Lord Mountbatten managed his greetings with discipline and panache – a broad smile, showing plenty of teeth, a few well-chosen words (none of which, of course, I could hear from my vantage point some thirty feet away) and then a switch-off of the smile, a brisk turning away to the next guest, a resumption of the smile and the conversation for that guest, and so on. Each guest took about ten seconds.

Prince Charles, however, fell well behind the advancing royal line. His smile was not mechanical, but came and went as any other human being's might have done during a conversation. And the conversations he was having were taking longer. Lord Louis kept staring pointedly back over his shoulder, but Prince Charles maintained his slow pace, talking to people as if he were genuinely interested in the answers as well as doing his duty.

On the negative side, he might have been accused of greater lugubriousness than such an occasion warranted. On the positive side, he could be seen as a man who was signalling that he was going to take his own approach to his future job, and was already prepared to take his future subjects seriously enough to make more than routine conversation with them.

I mentally photographed all this in my mind and took supporting notes. It is essential in such circumstances not to rely on memory alone. The human memory is fallible. Memories are quickly overlaid by later events and lost. Few of us are cursed with total recall, which would eventually choke our minds with stale rubbish even if it would be distinctly useful in an almost interview.

Lord Louis Mountbatten still kept pointedly looking over his shoulder, keeping any reproach concealed behind smiling teeth but obviously signalling to Prince Charles to get a move on. The heir to the throne continued to give provincial mayors and charity workers his full attention, even after Lord Mountbatten had walked back and whispered in his ear.

Good for him, I thought and felt. There seemed to be a lot of encouraging tidings in Prince Charles's appearance, behaviour and body language that day. He seemed as if he were genuinely trying to care, even if there were also signs of youthful self-absorption and perhaps a consequent slowness to tune in to what a particular situation required.

That was the gist of the piece I wrote, without talking to him myself, or hearing a word he said to anybody else or conducting anything approximating to what is normally understood as an interview. It was what I call an almost interview, requiring a technique of its own. I may have been among the first to notice, in that almost interview with the heir to the throne, some of the attributes that were perhaps to be so significant decades later.

For almost interviews of this type, which may consist of watching an almost interviewee at a palace, a playing field, a concert hall, a theatre rehearsal or a film set, you need precise observation, some understanding of how human beings can react under pressure and what it may signify, and imagination; not the sort of imagination you need to make things up, but the sort that enables you to get inside other people's minds and hearts.

A lot will depend on your powers of description: it is not enough to interpret, you must first describe what you are interpreting. You are a humble fly on the wall, but with an efficient mental camera.

It requires a diametrically opposite temperament and skill to those of the columnist and polemicist whose own opinions, thoughts and feelings are always, sometimes tediously but necessarily, centre-stage.

Arguably one of the most baleful effects of the emergence of the celebrity interviewer on television or in the glossy 'fan' magazine press has been that celebrities, concerned with their own egos rather than the thoughts and feelings of the people they are interviewing, are so bad at it. They are quite unable to bring out what their interviewees are really like. In an almost interview they would be totally out of their shallow depth, because estimates of an almost interviewee have to be based on slimmer evidence backed up by an empathetic imagination they haven't got.

The competent almost interviewer must be almost their exact antithesis. With no words to rely on, his meticulously accurate observation and his human understanding are absolutely vital. With their help, he can make a ceremony, rehearsal or other apparently impenetrable event – and the human beings at the centre of it – take on enough life to inform and entertain the reader, listener or viewer.

Chapter 16

Personal and Functional

Establishing the right balance between the interviewee as a human being and as a functionary is an important part of the interviewer's skill. You should have that balance clear in your mind, in relation to the circumstances of the moment, well before you arrive for the interview – though, as with much else in the interviewer's craft, you should be prepared instantly to alter your approach if what happens in the interviewing process itself suggests it.

Politicians normally entail the greatest emphasis on the functional, the least on personal factors. You need to know how the Prime Minister is going to treat the country, not his pet cat. There are exceptions, as when a politician is being selected for some new reason for human examination, when changing parties, facing serious illness or contemplating possible resignation, for instance. In such cases personal philosophies and personal details may suddenly seem more relevant. But normally if you talk to a politician you will be talking chiefly about his policies, his ideas, the controversies that surround him; not his childhood, his marriage, his children and his religious beliefs.

At the other end of the scale are the sort of professionals who regard their personal circumstances as part of their self-promotion campaign: actors, models, television personalities, pop artists, popular musicians and so on. Some of these regard discussing their alcoholism, abortions, speeding offences, crack habits and sexual deviations as a personal advertising campaign. Also at this end of the personal/functional scale are people who have no 'name' but who suddenly become interesting because their personal lives are either, on the one hand, unusual or, on the other hand, suddenly thought to be representative of the lives of a significant number of other 'ordinary' people. They may be people who have survived misfortunes or diseases or have undergone traumas, such as having been made homeless or made to retire early because of employment policies or health reasons.

How much personal detail and how much functional detail should you seek to explore in such cases? One thing is certain. You cannot afford to leave it to others (the sub-editor in the case of a printed interview, the editor in the case of a radio or television interview) to arrange the balance for you by making cuts. That way, the final balance will not be as you want it: it never is, when other people take such a decisive hand in presenting your work. Of course you may have to yield to editing; but you should have a fairly clear idea of the balance you are aiming at and impose it on yourself, not have it imposed on you.

Ideally, whether you are a staff journalist, a contract freelance or a speculative freelance, you should discuss with whoever commissions the interview the sort of balance you are aiming at. Is this one where lots of personal history will have to be explored, or one where the views of the interviewee on some sort of new situation are paramount, while the interviewee's personal history can be condensed into a few lines to establish his status in relation to the issue being discussed? The commissioning editor may tell you to use your own judgment in relation to what emerges once you are face to face with the interviewee, in which case he will have no legitimate complaint later if his ideas turn out after all to be different from yours.

Possibly the easiest (but not the most productive) interview to conduct is one in which few personal details are sought. People will talk about functional matters freely while being reticent about personal ones.

For this reason, interviews in which primarily personal information is sought are often best commenced in a more impersonal way by putting questions about the interviewee's function. Later, questions can be introduced which will bring the interviewee into sharper focus as a human being. Even if, in the result, you are going to have a content of 50 per cent or more relating to personal matters, it may be wisest to proceed at first as if the focus were almost entirely functional, especially if the individual is unused to talking for public consumption.

One such case was an interview I did in New York at a time when kidnappings, muggings and acts of violence in the street were spectacularly on the increase. I sought out the famous detective agency Pinkertons, located in downtown New York and in many famous crime novels, and asked them if I could talk to one of their agents who specialized in personal protection.

My intention was to produce a personal portrait of his life. Why did he enter the business? How did he live with the inherent and apparently multiplying risks? What did his wife think of his job? How did it affect his children? How had it changed his view of the world and the people in it? Did he see the boom in the personal security guard business as a sign that America, and perhaps the Western world as a whole, was in deepening trouble?

Stanley, as I called him, was a massive man of few words, with a bulging gun under his left armpit. He had a policeman's affinity with officialese. He was more keen to talk about security in general than about himself. Though that was not what I wanted, I let him talk in general terms for some little time before gently quizzing him about the pattern of his own working week. Only having been given a demonstration of the fact that I was interested in the whole subject did he open up about himself. I was able to piece together the personal story I wanted, which would through a narrow, personal focus, illuminate an ominous social trend. If I had first asked 'Stanley' for personal details about himself, as distinct from his general function, I think he would have clammed up and the interview would not have been nearly as satisfactory.

Stanley involved an actual, if not, I hope, visible tussle. It is important to keep your patience and good humour during such a tussle. It is equally important that you quickly realize when you and the interviewee are in fact in broad agreement about the personal/functional content of what you want to talk about, and that you go along with what he wants to say rather than perversely, out of mistaken professional pride, trying to impose your own precise pattern of questions.

When I went to interview the distinguished British film-maker Richard Attenborough (first Sir Richard Attenborough, then Lord Attenborough) he had just been appointed chairman of Channel 4 television. For years a stalwart of the British film industry, especially with his director and screenwriter partner Bryan Forbes, Richard Attenborough had latterly had unique successes in getting films set up with American money while not slavishly mimicking American mores.

At the outset in such a case, you must ask yourself which of three categories this interview will fall into:

1) An interview about the interviewee's intentions at Channel 4.
2) An interview about the interviewee, including his intentions at Channel 4.
3) An interview about the interviewee, pegged to his assumption of the chairmanship of Channel 4.

You will see at once the differences between the three possibilities. (1) is the most impersonal: you could present the interview without any personal detail at all. (2) will be about him functionally but will possibly have personal details, while (3) will hardly mention his intentions at Channel 4 – this assumption of a new job will be just a pretext or peg for presenting a personal profile that could have appeared at almost any time.

You will also see that the choice between the three will vary very largely according to the market you are writing or broadcasting for; the public importance or not of policy at Channel 4; and the intrinsic interest of the personality involved. In the case of Richard Attenborough option (1) would have been rather sterile, a sort of policy statement *in vacuo*. Option (3) would have been largely redundant, since Sir Richard, as he then was, was already a well-known figure and there was no point in what would amount to a premature obituary. Only option (2) would cover both the human interest of the person and the functional story of him in relation to Channel 4.

On this occasion, the market I was writing for was Peter Fiddick's media page in *The Guardian*. This fact suggested that the interviewee's views and intentions concerning Channel 4 rather than anything else should have priority (though not exclusive priority), especially as the status of Channel 4 as a provider of television for otherwise neglected minorities was clearly in the area of important public policy. But the intrinsic interest of the personality involved was high, especially as, after years of devotion to British films, Richard Attenborough was at that time almost uniquely successful in attracting American money for films such as *Gandhi*.

As usual I had a prepared list of questions from which I was prepared at once to deviate if the situation required. I proposed first to ask him what he would now seek to do at Channel 4 and in what future directions he saw the station moving; and then to move on to his present and future cinema film commitments.

He entered like a whirlwind and was soon busy telling me, almost without my opening my mouth, how he saw his connection with Channel 4 and what future directions it was likely to take.

Professional vanity suggested that I try to assert control of the interview by arbitrarily introducing quite different questions. Fortunately commonsense prevailed. Once I had seen that the interviewee's concept of the personal/functional balance of the interview was almost precisely my own, I settled down for a comfortable as well as productive ride.

In many cases, if there is any doubt in your mind that your wishes and those of the interviewee will coincide, it may pay you to discuss the matter at the start of the interview. In other cases, such as Stanley, it may be best to do nothing of the kind but to adopt subterfuge.

But be prepared for the fact that in many cases, the circumstances of the interview and the intelligence of the interviewee as well as your own will exert their own logic in a way recognized by both parties. In such cases, be prepared to let the interviewee do your work for you, moulding his performance (the one you have already decided you essentially want) in the gentlest possible way if he is not as forthcoming in maintaining the personal/functional balance as you would wish.

Never, however, relax *too* much. Richard Attenborough talked to me about his hopes for Channel 4; his fears about satellite broadcasting, then in its infancy; his film on the death of the black freedom fighter Steve Biko; his proposed film on Tom Paine, which he even then had been trying to set up for years; and he talked about them roughly in the same order as I had prepared my questions, so that I was on the whole quite content to let him orchestrate the performance.

Towards the end of my references to Channel 4 I quoted Sir Richard as saying that artists, including makers of sociological and documentary programmes, had to express themselves in their own way; they had to have a degree of freedom 'at the appropriate time'. Then I wrote: 'He used the phrase twice, and one took it as meaning that he sees Channel 4's freedom as being used for serious purposes rather than being abused by immature attention-seekers desiring to utter four letter words when the kiddies are still up. In other words, if Channel 4 runs into trouble, it had better be on ground of its own deliberate choosing.'

That was indeed a very fair inference on my part, but somewhat of a brief abdication of the interviewer's craft, which should never rely too much on inferences. At whatever cost I should have cut into Sir Richard's flow and *asked* him precisely what he *did* mean. That might have produced something more revealing both personally and functionally.

In establishing the personal/functional balance, be as little visibly assertive as possible. But be prepared to come up decisively with the right question if something you think should be spelled out has not been spelled out. Otherwise when you come to look at your notes you may find you have not enough material to orchestrate the balance you had in mind.

Chapter 17

In Action

Following an interviewee in some sort of action may produce a more gripping interview than facing him from an armchair. It is certainly more demanding.

More often than not, the environment in which you conduct an interview will be irrelevant. You could as easily have talked to the interviewee in his office, your office, his home, your home, or the nearest restaurant suitable both to your expenses ceiling and his self-regard.

At other times, the venue may be significant or even crucial, especially when it is one which is on the move. Catching an interviewee in the course of his unusually interesting work is very much a case in point. Here the work may be of equal interest to the man or at least may greatly enhance his own interest. You may need dexterity and fleetness of foot to follow it, taking sufficient notes while on the move, but your dedication could be rewarded with a more than averagely interesting interview.

I could not catch the last public hangman in Britain, Syd Dernley, actually at serious work. By the time I conducted my interview with him on the publication of his autobiography *The Hangman's Tale*, hanging had been abolished in Britain for over thirty years, much to his disappointment. He was aged sixty-eight at the time of the interview, a tiny wizened elf of a man and the only British survivor of a calling which had been made most famous by his hero and mentor, the public hangman Albert Pierrepoint, who prided himself that he was able to execute a prisoner within eight seconds of touching him on the shoulder in the death cell.

I saw Dernley on the eve of the publication of his book, which set out how a serious-minded lower middle class boy with ambition had been drawn into what he and his family regarded as an important social service. As usual for such an interview, I had read the book from cover to cover, not just those passages which I could infer from the press release would be the most obviously useful to an interviewer. An interviewer should always stick to his *own* ideas on what is relevant and what is not. He can do that only by reading everything that is available to be read.

Before such an interview, apart from doing your reading, you need to have cleared your mind of prejudice, focusing only on what is likely to be the most *productive* attitude to adopt towards the interviewee. Plainly letting a mistrust of judicial killing in general, and hanging in particular, come abrasively between you and your interviewee would be counter-productive. Since you cannot visit a gallows in use, the minimum aim must be to draw a picture of the man, the facts of his trade, and his own attitude to them.

This is what I aimed to do: I would not write a polemic against hanging, which could have been written in any armchair during the past thirty years. I would take advantage of a unique reporting opportunity, and, being polite and encouraging but not faking any agreement or sympathy with him I did not feel, let the man reveal himself without any censorious finger-wagging from me. If he hanged himself verbally in the process, so be it.

At first the interview was conventional enough. We faced one another in two chairs in his publisher's office. A tiny man, Syd Dernley had skipped rather than walked into the room. He was breezy and chatty. At first I thought any piece I wrote would have to be based simply on the jarring counterpoint between the grisly nature of his former job and the cheerful banality of his personality and his treasurership of Mansfield Conservative Club. He told me he had been born in Mansfield where, after reading an Edgar Wallace crime novel at the age of eleven, he had decided to be a hangman. Later, when working in a colliery, 'I decided it would get me out of the rut for a day or two and perhaps let me meet people I wanted to, such as detectives and major criminals. My wife was astounded at first, but when my mother-in-law heard I was hanging people, she was delighted.'

There was a lot more of the same. It was certainly interesting, but it was all armchair discussion. The interview so far lacked the dimension of action. But I discovered that Dernley had brought with him some of the equipment he had used for hanging people. Could I see it? He brought it in from another room. When I saw the hood which was to be thrust over the head of the condemned man, the straps used to bind his hands behind his back and both his legs together, the noose of the rope which was placed round his neck, I saw a possible extra dimension. I could not see him at work, but I could do the nearest possible thing: I could *feel* him at work. On myself.

Dernley was especially anxious that I should understand that there was no 'long walk to the gallows', as suggested in so many feature films, and not much suffering on the part of the doomed prisoner, either. He emphasized that eight seconds from being tapped on the shoulder in the cell to the actual drop was the expected standard, and that Pierrepoint had regarded it as a blot on his standards when one took fifteen seconds.

'Some people think I am a brutal sod, but I am only stating facts,' he protested.

Actions can sometimes speak louder than words. It was at this point that I asked him to demonstrate the rapidity with which he would have hanged me, leaving out only the last drop. His little twitching fingers pinioning my arms and legs, pulling the hood over my head and adjusting the rope round my neck, finally pulling it tight though not, of course, tight enough (and rather outside the time limit) was, I reported, 'a memorable experience'.

This was, of course, an understatement: I hoped the average reader would take the point without the need for hyped language. In the published interview, I certainly did one thing right: I allowed the flavour of the man to appear without the help of any overt adverse comment from me. The piece was the more powerful for that decision, just as it was the more powerful for introducing an element of concrete action into a sea of contentious words.

Was I right simply to have described the action without explicit denunciations of the last public hangman? I am not sure. Should I have done what the satirical magazine *Private Eye* would have called a Glenda Slagg and emoted all over the page? The noose and its supplementary equipment was, after all, the grim star of the proceedings. Should I, as to some extent I think I did, have allowed my consideration for Dernley as a human being to stand in the way of expressing an instinctive and explicit, 'Yuk'?

On the whole I think I was right to sample the man in action, as it were, and to put the emphasis in the final printed interview on the actions and words of the last British hangman, not my own feelings.

The snag with action is that it can be hypnotic. It is not an interviewer's business to be hypnotized. A certain detachment must always be preserved. An in-action interview is often riveting, but the interviewer must never allow the excitement of the moment to wipe the 'Why?' as well as 'How?' questions from his mind. He must be able to maintain his own thread of narrative and thought however much the action may demand of him in terms of physical as well as mental effort.

When the left-wing controlled Greater London Council set up plans for some 'People's Art' on the South Bank to coincide with the

Queen's opening of the National Theatre, I went to see the flamboyant deputy leader of the council, Illtyd Harrington, a voluble
Welshman. An armchair discussion of what was planned would have
been as interesting as a railway timetable. Instead I asked if he would
take me with him on a tour of inspection of the various celebration
sites he was about to make, explaining as we went the significance of
what we were seeing.

It was hard work as we looked at the organ, the bandstand, the big
wheel of the funfair, the fireworks site and so on. My questions were
again aimed at the, 'Why?' as well as the, 'How?' designed to give the
left-winger a chance to come across as a wag as well as a civic impresario: 'Since the 1951 Festival of Britain, the South Bank has become
like pre-revolutionary Peking. Everyone in their own cantonment. One
doesn't want the Kulturkamp approach to life, so I said what was
wrong with people seeing it opened up?'

In such circumstances it is essential that your questions be noted
down as well as the answers; but preferably in abbreviated code rather
than word for word, or you will lose track of the answers and fail to
take them down. It was essential not to lose anything of what was often
witty word-display as well as information on what would be 'People's
Art' in the hinterland of the Queen's official opening ceremony.

'Careful,' a pin-striped official warned after Harrington had
referred to the London Firemen's demonstrations. 'The fire brigade do
not give displays. They are simply demonstrating the potential of their
equipment.'

'That's right,' said Harrington gravely. As I sweated over my notebook, tripping over my own feet, chalk-striped officials in the informal procession hid their grins at my ignominious progress. No matter.
For such a fast-moving occasion, a cassette recorder is not to be
trusted. If your interviewee is rushing hither and thither and throwing
comments at you over his shoulder, you as a human being can strain
your ears to catch what he is saying. A recorder can't do that: it will
record a mixture of noises as one impenetrable entity.

Far better the ignominious notebook and ballpoint. It is a classic
case of the maxim that the more sensitive a human being the interviewer is, the better he will deal with a situation. He will long since
have learned how to mask and utilize his own sensitivity, so that looking a bit of an idiot as he takes notes on the trot should not in the least
deter him.

Exact and detailed notes are especially necessary in interviews
amidst some form of action. One of the pin-striped officials who was
in the inspection party was worried about what clothes the left-wing
Harrington would wear to meet the Queen:

'My dog suit, of course.'

'Oh, how lovely!' said the official, his pin-striped radiance quite restored.

To be readable, an action interview must record every revealing act and phrase, however trivial they may have seemed at the time. Such an interview may not necessarily be on a par with reporting Bosnia, but it does illustrate the need for keeping a cool, note-taking head however arduous the action becomes. It is better to be looked at as if one were an idiot at the time of the interview than to get back to the office and find no notes about something you especially wanted to mention. It is the big difference between being thought an idiot and actually being one.

Chapter 18

Official Answers

Take a situation, any situation in which an interviewer could be faced with an official spokesman. How would the official be likely to handle questions and how should the interviewer handle the official?

As an exercise, Brian Hughes, head of corporate affairs of the West Sussex Health Authority, in whose National Health Service area a number of Community Trusts operate, agreed to play the part of a spokesman for the Authority in a particular situation. He was trying, more or less as he would do in a real interview, to explain that situation in the fullest way possible while hoping that certain difficult questions would not be asked.

It *was* an exercise. To protect confidentiality the name of a Community Trust and some of the facts as well as some of the positions taken by Brian Hughes were fictionalized. He would not necessarily have behaved in a precisely similar way had the interview been a real one: in some instances he acted 'difficult' with me specifically to help the exercise. His mandate was to adopt a 'glossing over' approach, which he would not necessarily have adopted in a 'real' interview. But the results may provide some useful lessons for interviewers trying to determine whether an official is being evasive or giving the best true explanation he can, which perhaps doesn't satisfy the interviewer purely because it isn't sensational enough.

Though in such a case the interviewer's aim will not be to paint a personal portrait of the official, the exchange will be an interview proper to the extent that what the interviewer gets and what the interviewer doesn't get will depend largely on his own interviewing skills and persistence.

This was the central situation:

West Sussex Health Authority had to reduce expenditure by £6 million. Part of 'finding' that amount of savings included asking local Health Trusts to make service reductions in areas that would have a minimal effect on patient care. One Community Trust was asked to make savings of £280,000. It identified a potential saving of £70,000 by withdrawing its night district nursing service, which had been used mainly by immobile, catheterized, terminally ill or incontinent patients.

The Trust assured the Health Authority as the body ultimately responsible for the provision of adequate care in the area that patients' needs could be met by the daytime and twilight shifts. Six patients regularly received some level of care throughout the night, of which three were thought not to be in care after midnight. The Trust met each of these patients and their carers to make sure that suitable arrangements were in place. In addition an average of five calls were made on the service each night on an *ad hoc* basis.

A joint statement had been made by the Health Authority and the Trust advising people needing urgent care during the night to call their GP on-call service. The Health Authority and the Trust waited until three days before their public statement before they wrote to the GPs potentially concerned and received the dusty answer that the care needed by these patients was nursing not medical and so was not their province. The GPs' letter said they would not attend these patients if it meant neglecting patients with medical needs, and that these patients would end up in nursing homes or even accident and emergency departments, thereby costing the National Health Service much more money in the long run.

The GPs' letter was sent to the local newspaper, and followed up by other media.

I had prepared a flexible list of thirteen questions for the official to answer, to which were eventually added eight supplementaries suggested by his answers.

My first question was simply: 'What is the current situation over the provision of night district nursing services in the Community Trust area?'

This was both a necessary and emollient first question, deliberately unchallenging. It merely requested information on what was happening. It enabled the interviewer to bring himself up to date on the facts and the interviewee to 'talk himself into' the subject without feeling he was necessarily facing high pressure tactics or hostility.

The reply was: 'This had been a very difficult problem for the Authority and the Trust. The Health Authority was faced with an impossible dilemma. On the one hand it wants to maintain the services for all patients currently receiving services and on the other hand it wants to preserve emergency admissions. There was no way we could afford to fund everything and therefore we decided that priority had to be given to emergency admissions. We think that most of the public would support our view that emergencies must come first.'

This was, no doubt, all very true; and interviewees have to feel their way forward in their first answers just as interviewers do. But it was not the answer to my question on what the situation was at present. It was the answer to another question which I had not in fact asked about the Authority's priorities.

Therefore, to get the spokesman to the front line of the crisis rather than allowing him to disappear into generalizations way behind the front line, I pointed out that the threatened services were there to deal with people, elderly and so on, who were the sort of people most likely to die or to need attention at night when, so to speak, there was no one else about. Had there been any specific failure to meet night care demands since the withdrawal of the night service?

OFFICIAL: The Trust have assured us that they will be working with the individual clinicians, that is the GPs and the district nurses, to make sure there is a package of support in place for each of the people who are currently making use of the night care service. We are confident that the Trust will be able to deliver that service to those patients and therefore as a Health Authority we have no immediate concerns.

This was an extremely reasonable answer, offered in a helpful tone of voice, but again it was not the answer to the question I had asked: had there been any specific failures to provide a service?

INTERVIEWER: What does that mean, other than generalities – the package? It is rather difficult to imagine what a satisfactory package could be to replace a specific service like this.

This was a sharp question, but not the one I should have asked. I had made a classic mistake in such circumstances: I had grabbed eagerly at a new subject before I had disposed of the one in my original question. I had let the interviewee off the hook of saying specifically whether there had or had not been any specific failures to provide treatment. It enabled the interviewee to move even further away from the front line by pointing out his lack of medical specialist knowledge, which he proceeded to do.

OFFICIAL: You understand that I am not a doctor and am therefore not able to give you details of the package, but the sort of package we would be expecting the Trust to have in place would have been discussed with the carer and the GP and the people who run the existing service.

INTERVIEWER: What could that be? Are we talking about doctors? Are we talking about – I don't know – emergency services at hospitals? What specifically is available by way of support in that package?

Though I had failed to stay with the original question designed to find out whether there had been failures of services, I at least pressed the interviewee about the detail of the alternative arrangements. This was quite legitimate on my part: the Health Authority was ultimately responsible for health care in its area and its spokesman was therefore open to be asked specific questions. That is another reason why I should have pressed my question on whether there had been any failures of service.

OFFICIAL: One of the things we have agreed with the Trust is to fund a special fast response team which, whilst it is primarily based on daylight hours will be available to provide some support out of hours, and that is mainly district nurses going on an *ad hoc* basis to help carers at home.

INTERVIEWER: So there will be or could be available at home people on call, but not officially available as it were? Is that the only difference?

OFFICIAL: As I understand it, the difference for the patient and carer is that instead of being a service that has been allocated only for these eight people – and I must emphasize that the service is being used regularly only by eight people – they will access a service that is available on a wider pool.

I should at this juncture have cleared up the point of whether there were on average six regular users or eight regular users. My omission was doubly expensive for me because the answer, whatever it had been, might almost accidentally have alerted me, as we shall see later, to a more important question I should have asked but did not.

INTERVIEWER: If six patients were originally identified as regularly needing some level of care throughout the night, how is it that three of these were suddenly not felt to need care after midnight?

OFFICIAL: I think that is a very technical question relating to the position of an individual patient which I can't answer. I would ask you to talk to the director of community services at the Trust.

That may be a legitimate response for a spokesman to make, but an interviewer is entitled to point out where the ultimate responsibility rests and to ask questions relating to that. I did so, and then moved on to an even touchier matter.

INTERVIEWER: When were you, as an Authority, first aware of the Trust's decision?

OFFICIAL: Let me describe to you the process we have gone through on this. We would have alerted the Trust roughly in December, along with all the other trusts, to the financial problem facing the Authority and this was refined during January. That came after we knew the public accounts committee allocation for the Authority. What we then had to do was work out what was the shortfall for each of the individual trusts and we found the shortfall for the Community Care Trust was approximately £250,000. We had been in detailed negotiations with the Trust over that period of time as to how exactly that quarter of a million gap could best be met.

As a Health Authority we do rely on the advice from the experts which the Trust employs. They put up a number of proposals, each of which was very difficult to contemplate and said to us, as a Health Authority, 'These are the things that would have the least impact on patient care.' What we have been discussing over the past few months is exactly which of those we should implement.

This was a skilful answer to a question which had not been asked and in effect an evasion of the one which had been asked, a favourite technique of any official spokesman seeing or sensing a tight corner. In such circumstances, the interviewer is entitled to put the question again in the same terms as he put it previously. This can be a pointed way of signalling that this is an issue from which the interviewer does not intend to be deflected.

INTERVIEWER: Yes, but my question was, when were you first aware of the Trust's decision to take this particular stance?
OFFICIAL: The decision was made public by the Trust last Monday, as a result of a meeting with its own staff at which this issue was raised and it was thought it was time to bring it out into the open . . .
INTERVIEWER: So, in other words, the Trust told its staff before it told you?

Note that in this question I was not asking the spokesman to attribute blame, I was merely asking for confirmation of what appeared to be a self-evident fact. If I had asked, 'Wasn't it wrong for the Trust to tell its staff before it told you?' the interviewee might have shied away from the question altogether. As it was, I asked only for confirmation of a *fact* of timing, not at this stage about its implications.

OFFICIAL: I think it is fair to say that the Trust announced it as a firm decision at the same time as we were in the process of finalizing it. It had been agreed but we hadn't actually signed the paper. There was no difference of opinion between us as a Health Authority and the Trust as to whether this was the least harmful action to take.

This was a virtual admission that the Trust had indeed notified its own staff before the Health Authority. The fact being established, the interviewer in such circumstances may move on to examining the reactions to the bare facts.

INTERVIEWER: Was it a surprise to you, the action? [*By the Trust.*]
OFFICIAL: I think it is very important for the Trust to be talking to its staff. These are the people delivering the service and closest to the patients. It is important that they are kept very aware of what is going on.

Here, if not precisely answering the interviewer's question, the interviewee was pointing to the positive side of the Trust's action in talking to its staff before the Authority. I was by now used to remembering to put the same question twice.

INTERVIEWER: But were you surprised yourself as an Authority when you heard the decision via the fact they were talking to their own people about it?
OFFICIAL: We weren't aware they were making the announcement at that time, that is correct.
INTERVIEWER: You *were* surprised about it. Why did the Health Authority and the Trust in their joint statement of April 14 advise people needing urgent care during the night to call their GPs' on-call service, when they had unilaterally advised the GPs of this only three days previously, and there had been no consultation?
OFFICIAL: You are referring to a document issued by whom?
INTERVIEWER: I gather there was a joint statement issued between the Authority and the Trust on April 14 and in that statement you had advised people needing urgent care during the night to call their GPs' on-call service. My question is, why did the Authority participate in that joint statement when they had – the Trust – unilaterally advised the GPs of their decision only three days previously without consultation with the GPs?
OFFICIAL: Consultation with GPs is a very difficult issue. The way this had been handled, the Trust and the Health Authority had produced a list of potential service reductions which had been discussed both by the Trust and GPs. I think it is fair to say that whilst the GPs were aware of the potential reductions, service cuts, they weren't aware that this specific reduction was going to be announced. So though there had been consultations with the GPs, they were aware of the options, but it is true to say they weren't aware of that particular option being announced at that time.

Not without difficulty, I had now established that the doctors had been left in the dark until the last moment. What did the Health Authority think about that?

INTERVIEWER: Do you think the Trust should have enabled the GPs to consult, consider and put their point of view?

OFFICIAL: We didn't of course cut the service immediately at that point. The Trust and the contracts staff from the Health Authority met with the GP locality group, it was three days later, and discussed this in some detail. What we actually put to the GPs was the difficult choices the Health Authority and the Trust were faced with and what alternatives you could take. I think it was fair to say that the GPs were very unhappy that this reduction in services was being made, but did very reluctantly accept that the Health Authority didn't have any better option in terms of service reduction.

INTERVIEWER: Were you – the Health Authority – surprised when the GPs responded that the care required was nursing care not medical care and therefore not their responsibility?

OFFICIAL: I think this was a misunderstanding on the part of GPs of the kind of work that was likely to be involved. It is true that some of the procedures out of hours may require nursing support and we are hoping that the fast response team that has been newly set up, only the first of April this year, will be able to help with the majority of those urgent requests. Clearly if the patient's condition deteriorates in such a way that it actually requires medical intervention or possibly admission into hospital, that is legitimately the job of the GP.

Sensing that this was as far I would get on this line, I switched the subject. On balance, I should probably have put my original question again.

INTERVIEWER: Is it true or likely, as the GPs asserted, that patients who ended up in accident and emergency departments would cost the National Health Service much more money in the long run?

OFFICIAL: That response or comment is firstly largely hypothetical.

The official went on to suggest why. But when any official spokesman calls something in a question 'hypothetical', the interviewer should be on his guard. If the Ministry of Defence had been asked during the Cold War what it would do if the Warsaw Pact armies attempted to invade Western Europe, it would have been no answer to say, 'That is a hypothetical question.' Everything that may possibly happen is hypothetical until it happens, by which time it may be too late to do anything about it. Any authority is constituted precisely to deal with hypothetical possibilities.

In this case, the interviewee had shrewdly gone on talking for so long after his use of the word 'hypothetical' that it would have been easy to lose sight of it. Almost always, interviewers should feel entitled to tackle the interviewee from a slightly different angle if told that something or other is 'hypothetical'. However, in this case the interviewee had gone on to answer the substance of the question, so I let it go and moved on.

INTERVIEWER: Had the Health Authority attempted to justify the abolition of the night district nursing service publicly before the letter from the GPs was leaked to the local press to be picked up by the other media?

OFFICIAL: No, we hadn't gone out into the public arena to explain this in detail. I think – this all happened very quickly between the announcement by the Trust, the reaction from staff and GPs and then us talking to the GPs – we felt that our top priority was to talk to GPs who are after all the agents of the patients and to the carers, and to, in a sense, come to an understanding with them about how this was going to be handled.

INTERVIEWER: Do you think the Trust concerned deliberately proposed some unworkable cuts in order to put pressure on the Health Authority to moderate its cuts – £280,000 – required of the Trust?

Such a sudden change of subject into a highly sensitive area can sometimes yield results, though the adroit official spokesman will usually gain time to think by expressing surprise at any such question being asked.

OFFICIAL: That is a rather surprising question to ask me perhaps as a representative of a statutory body but—

INTERVIEWER: You are taking the flak—

OFFICIAL: I think both the Trust and us are accepting our responsibility for this. We are not ducking it, we are accepting that we are responsible, we are accountable for what we are doing. We are trying to do our best in an extremely difficult situation.

While appearing to be utterly frank, the interviewee had deftly mislaid the specific question he had been asked. By this stage in an interview, however, the interviewer should be well on his guard.

INTERVIEWER: My question was, do you think the Trust deliberately proposed some unworkable cuts in order to get you to moderate your demand for cuts?

OFFICIAL: I don't think there has been any evidence of that.

INTERVIEWER: Presumably there isn't any 'evidence' unless you are inside their heads. But is that a reasonable conjecture in view of the rather unlikely cut (it strikes me as unlikely) – that it was a deliberate measure to get you to moderate your demands for cuts?

OFFICIAL: We work very closely with the Community Trust. Our chairman

and their chairman, our chief executive and their chief executive have regular meetings . . . I can't conceive of a situation in which one health service
body would place another in that position.

I was reluctant to let the point – the possibility that the Trust was to
some extent politicking with the Health Authority – go.

INTERVIEWER: They may have the patients' interest at heart, but they can
conceive of that in different ways. Would it be deplorable in your view if a
Trust, in trying to protect its services, had put pressure on you in this kind
of way? Is it a legitimate, as it were, office-political move?

OFFICIAL: I don't think it would be seen as helpful or constructive in any
way, by any player within the National Health Service system, to treat this
as a game. I think it is hard to conceive of a situation in which the people
I know personally in this locality would behave in that way.

Sensing that this was as far as I would get, and that it was possibly
further than the interviewee had intended to go, I moved on. After
some factual discussion about the procedures that would now be
adopted, I opted again for the tactic of surprise.

INTERVIEWER: Are there going to be any other instances of cuts without
consultation?

OFFICIAL: I can assure you that our intention has been and always will be to
ensure that there is appropriate consultation whenever there are significant
service changes. And there are times when for practical reasons it doesn't
go as well as we would like. We have had considerable discussion with the
Community Health Councils over this particular instance and it is quite
clear that there are one or two lessons to be learned.

What I was really seeking was an assurance that someone had put out
feelers throughout the system to make sure there were not going to be
other instances. I should have put the question that baldly. But I
thought it might be more profitable to ask about the lessons that had
been learned. Should I have pressed my original point, or would that
have produced only more fencing? I am undecided.

INTERVIEWER: What are they?

OFFICIAL: Probably the main lesson to be learnt is to try and plan the
communication to each of the groups so that it happens at the same time.
It is unrealistic to expect that you ask one particular group – it might have
been the GPs we had gone to first – to maintain a silence before you tell the
next group. And, whether we had told the GPs first or the staff first, clearly

the potential for the information being misunderstood is quite considerable.

The lesson is to try to tell all groups at the same time. As I said, that isn't always easy to achieve. One of the good things about being in PR in the National Health Service is that actually you are not always out there talking and telling, you are actually out there listening and hearing. A much bigger part of my job is actually going out to meet all the voluntary groups, the community groups, the community health councils and actually showing what they see as their concerns.

I have seen that that role actually helps my colleagues in looking at priorities and I would hope that is more the contribution that PR people in the National Health Service make.

INTERVIEWER: Good, I think I will probably leave it there. I am glad you seem a little tired. I am, and I expect that I let many of your googlies go by.

That was the end of the interview with the official Brian Hughes more or less as I would have conducted it for real. I was impressed by his oblique stonewalling and emollient handling of awkward facts and not excessively pleased with my own performance. I asked him, in his opinion as a man who knew the actual facts of the issue, what sort of questions I should have asked and didn't and what points I had failed to follow up when I should have done.

Brian Hughes's verdict was that what had made him most uncomfortable was the way I had followed up on the specifics. He saw his job as avoiding the specifics. He was often running out of alternative ways of phrasing the same thing. Secondly, some people who interviewed him allowed him either not to answer the question that had been put or to answer the question that had not been put. I didn't, for most of the time. He found it tougher going than the average.

It was perfectly legitimate of me to have asked for details but it was equally legitimate for a Health Authority to say that beyond a certain point it could not go into detail. (Nevertheless I stick to my view that any interviewer must pursue detail in view of the fact that the devil can often be in the detail of grand plans.)

He said he had desperately not wanted to be asked about what else the Health Authority could have cut. I had asked, but I did not pursue it very far. The Health Authority would have found it difficult to defend logically how it had made its decisions. Sometimes a decision was made because it was easier to take decision A than decision B, not because logic supported decision A over decision B. That was a reality. I had touched on it, but we had then moved on.

Costs of hospitalization were something he did not want pursued. I had pursued it some way but not as far as he had feared. The Health

Authority was vulnerable on that, because it would cost much more if patients were hospitalized.

But my biggest failure, he said, was not to press further on the issue of the eight people who were regular users. The point here was that although there were an average of eight calling on the system at any one time, there was in fact a much larger pool – some twenty-five to thirty – of people who used the service, though not all on the same night. If they had all needed hospital attention, the cost would have been great. He had been keen always to focus attention on the eight, and to rely on the media not pressing the question of how many individuals did in fact use the service at one time or other. That had been 'helpful' to the Authority. But in terms of upset people, there were more than these eight people and their carers.

The area in which I had made things difficult for him had been the nature of the care package. But he thought that no reporter except a specialist health reporter would have been able to pursue him beyond his own level of knowledge. He sometimes had to rely on that. But the specialist reporter was also the one who would most understand the Health Authority's own difficulties. What he had done in this particular case was to repeat generalizations and avoid specifics as much as possible.

I had to concede that his technique had worked in this instance because I did not have enough specialist knowledge to pursue the point: the more an interviewer knows, even if it means mugging up for a specific interview, the better.

His own technique when discussing the £70,000 cuts required of the Community Trust would be, he said, to start talking about the large financial sums that needed to be cut in the Health Authority's area as a whole so that the figure of £70,000, by the time he got round to it, was in 'context' – i.e. sounded even smaller than it was.

I asked him how he rated most journalistic interviewers generally at the present time. He said that he and his colleagues knew a certain number of things in advance: the interviewers had a limited amount of time, they had pressures on them to be going off somewhere else, so they couldn't hang around for ever. The ones who were irate were usually those ones who did not know a great deal about it, and the ones who really did know and could make life difficult tended also to be the ones who understood.

'The minute they think, "Hello, there isn't a headline in this," they lose interest. They will be polite, they will continue asking a few questions, but you almost see them consciously lowering their level of interest.'

Let me make my own comment on this. In one sense, this practice is quite valid: if there is no newsworthy scandal, there may simply not be a story. In another sense, it is something that any interviewer needs to watch: it does not follow that, because there is no bloodstained corpse on the carpet, there has been no malpractice and no story. The fact of a crisis or deficiency in the National Health Service is a story in itself, whether or not there has been scandalous behaviour on the part of any party concerned.

For his part, Brian Hughes said that his job was sometimes to take a line whose content and tone almost suggested there was no headline.

One question I could have asked and didn't, in Brian Hughes's view, was whether the cuts were in fact all the fault of underfunding by the government. I did not ask this because I already knew that he would not answer it; but with hindsight I think I should have asked it nevertheless.

I might, for instance, have asked whether the Health Authority would consider lobbying government against the cuts the government's underfunding had made necessary: the very fact the question had been asked and evaded, and the tone of the evasion, might have been worth including in any print or electronic media report.

As a wrap-up, I asked this official to suggest one or two points that any interviewer of an official spokesman should bear in mind. He produced these:

1. Recognize as a fact, whether you like it or not, that the authority you are questioning may not always be its own master.
2. The government and any other official body could not except in extraordinary circumstances be critized by another, even if it was at fault.
3. If the interviewer can enable the spokesman to put a positive message alongside the negative message, the official will feel better about it and be readier to be interviewed on future occasions on difficult topics.
4. What may seem important to the interviewer may be in terms of the organization, which is concerned with other big issues, no more than 'a little blip'.

I would *de facto*, if unwillingly, go along with these maxims except the last: any bad happening affecting only one person is not in the least made better by the surrounding context, any more than a postman can defend himself on the grounds that though he has put one vital letter through the wrong letterbox he has put thousands through the right letter boxes, or an accountant can maintain that an error of £10,000 in the accounts doesn't matter because the organization's turnover is £100 million.

A 'sense of proportion' should be watched when it is invoked by officialdom. As with other elements of official presentation, though understandable from the point of view of officialdom itself, it should be penetrated if possible by the interviewer. A highly skilled official spokesman, whose manner is quietly reassuring, can sometimes lull any interviewer into lapses of concentration and failures of persistence. I have reproduced the question and answer session almost verbatim in order to show how the sheer weight and flow of an accomplished official spokesman can so easily edge an interviewer off course.

The maxim of this particular official spokesman which I agree with quite cheerfully, as distinct from merely accepting as a political fact, is number three. Certainly you should always be fair to any interviewee by allowing him to put his own side and his own strong points, and you should include these in the finished interview.

The function of all journalism, it could be argued, is to reveal vice. It is certainly not to stifle virtue, to obliterate the positive side of the interviewee, his cause and his case.

Chapter 19

Transcribing Notes

One of the most unnerving moments in the whole interviewing process, especially in the case of a long interview, may come immediately after you have said goodbye to the interviewee, and you suddenly realize that you can remember hardly a single word of what has been said.

It sounds unlikely if the person you have just interviewed is interesting and humanly vivid; but it is quite likely even in such a case, perhaps more likely in such a case, if my own experience is at all typical. The memory comes back slowly, and often requires prompting.

It may be a form of stage fright, such as affects the the after-dinner speaker who cannot remember a word of what he has said once he has sat down. The bigger and better the interview, the greater excitement experienced by the interviewer during the course of it, the worse this form of retrospective stage fright can be. The act of concentration necessary to improvise questions, to allow the interviewee to blossom, but nevertheless to keep control of the interview, promotes a sort of tunnel vision. When you emerge from the tunnel you are apt to be quite lost in the sudden light of day.

The panicky failure of memory may be especially overwhelming if the interview has been tape recorded. You will in a sense have unconsciously 'left it to the machine' to do the memorizing. Your mind will therefore have legitimately switched itself off as a recording machine, concentrating entirely on the present moment and the future questions throughout the interview.

But you have the tape cassette to help you remember, so what's the worry? The worry is that a recorded audio tape can seem, in such highly-strung circumstances, more impenetrable than Fort Knox. All the information you need is in that little four inch by two and a half inch box, but you can't see any of it. Unlike the situation if you have depended entirely on a notebook and shorthand, you cannot riffle through the pages and see, with the aid of key words written conspicuously in longhand, what you have got. What you have got in the case of a cassette is a lump of plastic that yields nothing whatever to casual inspection. Any panic in the interviewer is apt to increase.

The precaution you should have adopted is to note down briefly in a notebook, even if a recorder is running, the sequence of the subjects and some key words from especially interesting answers, written large and in longhand. Consulting your notebook briefly afterwards, you will be able to do two things: refresh your memory of the whole interview and discover broadly where on the tape you will find the best quotes.

If you are pressed to produce the completed interview to a tight deadline, it is tempting not to transcribe the whole tape, but merely to dip into it at strategic points, or even to use the best quotes from memory.

Using quotes from memory is inadvisable. I have been amazed at how rarely one gets the wording of a remembered quote – even a most vivid and easily remembered quote – exactly right. One will remember the sense accurately, but the structure of the sentence or sentences is often inaccurate. Direct quotes in an interview should be exact, otherwise the flavour of what is being said, if not the sense, will be distorted. Your memory tends either to iron out individualities of speech or to accentuate them unduly, so that the finished result will either be more bland or more sensationalized than the original, but not accurate.

Whenever possible after a long recorded interview I have transcribed the tape word for word and then looked at the transcript as a whole. This is time-consuming but highly beneficial to the final result. You can see at once the shape of the interview and where the emphasis should be placed in what you write. Only if you are cursed with a photographic memory can you hope to do this without transcribing the whole tape.

Get on the word processor keyboard and put the cassette recorder beside you. Play the first sentence and type that out. Play the second and type that out, and so on. You can manage quite well if you have to by simply switching the recorder off and on by hand, rewinding if you have missed something. But there are devices operated by the foot that can switch the tape forwards and backwards without your having to take your hands off the keyboard. These will speed things up considerably.

Generally speaking the more time you spend on transcription the less time you will have to spend on writing up the result. To some extent the material will have written itself up. Most written-up interviews will flow more naturally if they follow the sequence of question and answer. If this is not so, then your sequence of questions was probably misconceived.

Certainly you may use for an intro anything from anywhere in the tape or notebook; but after that it usually pays to revert in due course to the face-to-face sequence, because that will have its own logic and progression.

If you have to chop and change the order of sections of the interview, it may be because you did not question the interviewee in some sort of logical order in the first place. In conducting an interview, the *easiest* way is to follow up every 'lead' fed you by the interviewee immediately as it happens, entirely forgetting the next question you had in mind. This, however, will be the most *difficult* interview to write up, because, unless you are aiming at some sort of scatty character study, you will have to rearrange the order of the sections of the interview so that they appear to make a sensible progression to the reader (or listener or viewer, though here you may well find the producer or editor will do for you what you could and should have done for yourself during the interview.)

By all means follow up immediately avenues of thought suggested by the interviewee's answers if your hunch tells you that is the best thing to do in this particular interview, though usually it is better to file the follow-up in your mind for use later in the interview. But if you do follow up at once, departing from your prepared next question, don't lose sight of your intended question. And don't follow up on any subject at once without making a *written* note of it in your notebook, with at least one word in longhand that does not have to be transcribed and is immediately recognizable. This will enable you quickly to locate on the tape or in your notes the various topics discussed, and lead you to the most interesting quotes.

The quality of the interview as experienced by you and the interviewee will depend on the way you conduct the question and answer process. But the quality of the interview as experienced by the most important person in the whole exercise – the reader, listener or viewer – will depend on the way you (preferably) or somebody else writes it up and presents it.

It is a lonely task. Whereas a born extrovert may have found the conversation itself less harrowing, the thinking introvert may find the writing-up process less like trying to find his way through a maze. As most of us are a bit of both basic types of personality, this should not cause too much alarm.

Chapter 20

Writing it up

Your intro is vital. Until you have the intro, you haven't found the essential nature of the interview – what it says, why it is there, why it was worth doing. Once you have got the intro, the rest should flow naturally or at least give the appearance of flowing naturally.

Cut straight into the interviewee. Do not preface it with 200 clever-clever words of your own which are no more than self-indulgent, armchair drooling in front of the word processor screen: they are to journalism what humming out of tune in the bath is to symphonic composition. The reader, listener or viewer wants to meet the interviewee, not to be told by you how clever you are.

These redundant 'limbering up' words are irritating in any form of journalism and even more irritating than average in interviews. Take a newspaper and go through all its features, including interviews, and simply strike out the first paragraph. You will be surprised how often nothing whatever is lost and a greater sense of urgency gained. In such cases the real intro is the second paragraph, not the first.

The habit of almost automatically sticking a wodge of flowery word-spinning at the head of pieces of journalism is a comparatively recent one and would certainly not survive a national emergency and paper shortage. It patronizes the reader by assuming that he cannot take the subject 'straight' but must be lured by a form of performance art which may have only a tenuous bearing on the subject, at best gets in the way of the real point, and at worst so irritates and frustrates the potentially interested reader that he turns away and reads something else.

Let me give a fictitious example of what I mean:

> I have often thought that offices are dangerous places, but this is ridiculous. You can't be polite to female colleagues without getting yourself into trouble? My Uncle Jocelyn might have agreed, because he claimed that if you were polite to a secretary she would take it as a proposition

and if you laughed at her jokes she would take it as a proposal of marriage. Now it's rather different. If you remain studiously polite to your female colleagues, they may accuse you of shutting them out from the circle of comfortable male bonding. If you make a joke, they may accuse you of insulting them. If you find your secretary crying and put a hand on her shoulder she may accuse you of sexual assault.

Burt Zurek, the American anti-feminist writer who believes that men should refuse to work in the same offices as women because it is getting increasingly dangerous for them to do so in a feminist age, arrived in this country yesterday to debate the issue with feminists at a London seminar and launch his new book, *Leave Them To It: An Office Guide For Persecuted Men.*

The first paragraph is self-indulgent stream-of-consciousness waffle apparently arising out of nothing and nowhere. Why is it being said? Why is it being said *now*? Where is it being said? By whom? These are among the questions the intro doesn't answer. The second paragraph gets to the point and should have been the intro. It introduces the interviewee immediately to the reader. All the detail of his claims can then be dealt with in direct quotes from him, not flung at the reader from cloud nine.

The art is not to blather picturesquely in the first paragraph, it is to make the first paragraph dive into the point in a way which is both factual and intriguing. You do this by the words you use to elaborate or qualify the simple factual thrust.

Perhaps you think that a bald, direct, factual intro will lack punch. If it does, it will be because of the weakness of your human understanding or vocabulary. The intro should take the reader straight to the interviewee and the point of interviewing him, but in language that enriches and illuminates the bare facts. I have often smiled at journalists whose best intro is in effect to take the first paragraph of the news agency report and stick two or three adjectives into it in the hope that the result will be Art.

An example? Here is the news agency report:

Eighty year-old pilot Sam Gutz flew himself into London from New York today to urge the British government to support liberalization of the laws on those entitled to pilot private aircraft.

Here is the adjectivized version:

A gallantly assertive 80-year-old aviation pioneer flew himself into London from New York today to urge an apparently indifferent British

government to liberalize the draconian laws restricting those valiant but
elderly spirits who still wish to fly.

Far better to close your dictionary, forget adjectives and let Sam Gutz
speak for himself:

> 'I can fly better and more safely now than I could when I was twenty,'
> 80-year-old Sam Gutz claimed today as he left the cockpit of his private
> jet after flying it into London from New York – 'a flight I first did in my
> twenties and will still be doing in my nineties.' In London to urge the
> British government to support . . .

The aim is to get your effects by giving examples of what Gutz said
and did rather than by using 'mood' adjectives like posters clapped on
to the interview with wallpaper paste. Adjectives tend to sanitize and
reduce everything to a formula. Many years ago, every front page lead
in the *Daily Mirror* had to have the word 'dramatic' in its second paragraph – always the second, never the first or third. This gave at least
one reader the beginnings of a nervous tic as he reached every second
paragraph and left him with an objection (a dramatic objection?) to
run-of-the-mill adjectives, even to exotic adjectives unless required by
or strictly suited to the context.

In the intro, do not gild the lily: describe what you are dealing with
as specifically and as interestingly as you can, and move on.

When it comes to the body of the interview, there are two main
dangers to be avoided. The first is putting together the gist of the interview from memory, dipping into the notebook or tape only occasionally to aid your recollection. The danger here is that your final piece
will be skimped, with insufficient direct quotes and concrete facts:
opinions are easier and safer to precis than direct quotes and facts.
Usually you fall into this error when you are pushed for time and when
you decide the face-to-face encounter was not as interesting as you
thought it would be. Whatever the motive, the result will tend to be
that instead of giving the reader the facts and quotes you will spin out
your own thoughts on the interviewee as a make-weight to thin material. You will provide a lot of interpretation, perhaps even words dancing on the head of a pin, when you should be simply reporting what
the interviewee said and did. At worst, it is lazy evasion.

The remedy is to type out a copy of the questions and answers in
full before you begin to work, as previously recommended. You will
then have at your fingertips all the facts and direct quotes you need.
You will not need to pontificate in order simply to fill the space.

The second danger is the direct reverse: that you will put so much effort into preparing a complete transcript that you will be reluctant to let any of the material go to waste. You will therefore be tempted merely to open your notebook or recorder and pour, as it were, the entire contents straight onto the keyboard, with insufficient distinction between what is important and what is not. We have all made this mistake in a long interview, and the result can be slack and uncompulsive. Tighten up the result by cutting out the duller material and the interview will have more tension, thrust and point. It will become much more memorable.

The danger especially affects direct quotes. Every journalist is legitimately proud of a direct quote. But especially in long interviews not every direct quote can earn its space. If the interviewee expresses something dully, try at the time to get him to say it again in clearer terms or report it in third person speech or merely say that such-and-such is his opinion or position. If he expresses something vividly, then make sure to use the direct quote: the reader will not thank you for getting between him and the interviewee in order to give your own interpretation.

One of the most uncomfortable hazards of the writing-up process is premature staleness. You will by this time have 'lived with' the interviewee in some way or other for some considerable time – thinking of whom to interview, arranging the interview with the interviewee or his representative, planning the questions you will ask the interviewee, getting to the venue suggested by the interviewee, conducting the interview with the interviewee, returning from the interviewee, transcribing your notes and tape of the interviewee's replies.

The danger is that by this stage ennui will have set in. You may already be thinking about your next assignment. The interview with this interviewee took longer than you had anticipated, and you are by no means certain that the material gained justified the expenditure of time. Some of the interviewee's answers that you can remember seemed very substantial or great fun at the time but do they really amount to what you thought they did?

If the interviewee had a weak personality, will readers really care what he says? If the interviewee had a strong personality, are you slightly resentful of him for monopolizing and manipulating you for so long?

All this can be a way of unconsciously trying to defer writing it all up. If you are a sociable person, you may have enjoyed the conversation itself, however much the interviewee may have displayed his cleverness by jumping from one subject to another, but are you really without resentment at the thought of the long struggle to produce a coherent and interesting final result? If you are more introspective by temperament, did the conversation bring you out in such a sweat that the thought of sitting down and sorting it all out fills you with edgy despair?

All these difficulties must be resisted. The best way to do so is to expunge from your mind all matters except writing up the interview. Don't think about your next interview. Remove yourself if you can from all irritating sights and sounds. If you are part of an organization and work best while solitary, try to arrange to write up the interview at home. Play your latest Beethoven CD by all means if you work well to music, but escape from the sound of the children's pop music if you don't like it. Don't ask your wife, husband or partner to bring you cups of tea unless you actively enjoy being interrupted. If you are in the house alone, consider switching off the front door bell and leaving the telephone off the hook.

You have to 'live with' the person you have interviewed for a bit longer and any distractions will almost certainly heighten any sense of irritation with him or her, as well as with yourself for not carrying off the interview better. (You really are in trouble if you come out of an interview thinking you have handled it as well as it could have been handled. You may think this years later with the benefit of long hindsight, but if you think it at the time you are almost certainly too easily pleased with yourself.)

You may well find that, if you have a transcript of your notes to hand, it is easier to work in the office. Here there will certainly be noise and conversation, but none that need involve or concern you. Any journalist must get used to working at top concentration in Waterloo station during the rush hour. Though writing up a long interview requires more sustained concentration than drafting a short news story before phoning it in, you should be able to exclude extraneous noises from your mind in any situation.

Domestic demands are less easy mentally to cut out: you are emotionally involved. If your wife or partner wants to be reminded of a friend's telephone number or your young daughter wants to show you the messy pudding she has just made with mummy's help, you will feel such a monster if you try to ignore it that your concentration will be more disturbed than if you had simply taken time out to admire the pudding and then resumed work.

But broadly, as long as you can maintain your interest in the interviewee and not suffer from premature staleness, all distractions will be manageable. Tell yourself firmly that the concentration is only temporary, a sustained burst, before freedom from the interviewee and all his ways. Your life has not really been taken over by someone you may never meet again and perhaps hope you will never meet again.

The other danger is that you will become so accomplished at deal-ing with all interviewees and writing them up at commendable speed that you will become blasé and regard interviews as a string of sausages. On the whole, as with many other things in life, it is better to be uncomfortable than smug. It is better to find an interview diffi-cult to write up than to devise an easier-for-you-way of doing it mechanically. It is better to struggle maladroitly than to work in a limited and limiting way.

Some ways of writing up an interview amount, of course, to more than maladroitness or cutting corners because of premature staleness. They amount to malpractice and should be consciously resisted.

One malpractice certainly to be avoided is putting quotes into the interviewee's mouth. Sometimes it is legitimate to put a sentiment to the interviewee and, if he agrees, to give that as his opinion, in the third person, when you come to write the interview up. If you say to a minister, 'Are the other European countries being uncooperative over this issue?' and he says, 'Yes,' it is legitimate to write that the minister said that other European countries were being uncooperative over this issue. It is less defensible if you put much more emotive language to the interviewee, like, 'Are the other European countries behaving like little Hitlers about this?', he says, 'I suppose so,' and you then report in direct quotes the minister saying, 'The other European countries are behaving like little Hitlers about this.'

The sin lies in the fact that you are attributing to the interviewee degrees of intense feeling that he may not in fact have, and language he would not normally use. If you say to a woman Rural Dean, 'Do you think some of the male priests have been complete shits in resist-ing women in the priesthood?' she may say yes, not disputing your language because she politely does not wish to appear a censorious fuddy-duddy. It would be quite unfair if you were to reward this politeness by ascribing to her the direct quote: 'I think some of the male priests have been complete shits in resisting women in the priest-hood.' It would imply that a dignitary of the church had herself used questionable language.

It is true that more sophisticated interviewees will proof themselves against this danger. The minister might reply, 'No, I would not say the other European countries are being like little Hitlers, but . . .' Even this course would leave him open to being quoted in those terms, as if dragging a suggestion up on the pretence of denying it. 'I did not say that,' (without saying what the 'that' is) is probably the most difficult manoeuvre for the unprincipled interviewer to get past. But such manoeuvres should not really be necessary.

The world of the media, like most professional worlds, is a small one. Word gets around. An interviewer whose failings lapse into malpractice is soon identified and his own position is infinitely weakened. To attack the interviewee in the written-up or broadcast interview may be legitimate, though honest revelation is a much more potent weapon than partisan attack. To misrepresent the interviewee in any way, either by misquoting him or by putting words into his mouth that he would not normally use, is professionally and morally indefensible. It is not just a private dispute between interviewers and interviewees. It befouls and corrupts the mainstream of public debate and discourse.

Foot-in-the-door methods of getting material may be justified if the results are morally in the clear. Ordering the interviewee a rather too generous glass of brandy after lunch may be defensible if it leads to revelation of the truth. The television and radio interviewer may occasionally be blunt to the point of rudeness if the result is to break down a persistent evasion on an issue about which the public have a right to be informed. Minor corner-cutting may be excused if the resultant interview is a true one as well as being factually accurate.

But malpractice operates on the principle of diminishing returns. The offender and his techniques become familiar and interviewees (if they will agree to be interviewed at all) will be on their guard. Malpractice is unlikely to usher in an enduring career as any sort of media interviewer.

A felicitous treatment of interviewees and a sensible accuracy in writing them up – such as that employed in their vintage years by Terry Coleman, Lynda Lee-Potter, Pauline Peters and many others who have lasted well – is the more promising course for the shrewdly ambitious.

The first interviewers likely to spring to mind today may be those of the electronic media. But the principle of fair dealing and accuracy, and the ability when required to discipline one's own ego in the pursuit of the interviewee, which originated in the print media at its best should still apply to all interviewers.

Part Two:
How Others Interview

Chapter 21
The Big Political Set Piece

Important politicians, especially prime ministers or presidents, submit themselves to long and wide-ranging interviews in print or in the electronic media only when two sets of circumstances respectively dictate it and allow it. These are when their positions are markedly and publicly dire or at least critical; and when they are sure they will be able to put over their own points without undue obstruction or harassment.

There may be some who would dispute the words 'set piece' in this chapter heading, on the grounds that such interviews are not actually scripted in advance. Of course they are not, in the literal sense. But no leading politician would submit himself to one of these long interviews unless he were sure he could get over, at some length, the points he wanted to make. That is the unwritten pact behind the whole operation.

Understandably, senior politicians do it rarely. When, in December 1996, in the middle of a big public and Parliamentary row about Britain entering or not entering the European Single Currency, the then Conservative Prime Minister John Major did a fifty-minute interview with one of the BBC's most formidable interviewers, John Humphrys, on the Sunday midday television political programme *On the Record*, it was one of those rarities.

With such interviews, the terms will be settled in advance at the most sophisticated level. They may be hammered out in overt negotiations or they may 'emerge' as understood.

The Major interview took place in the Prime Minister's own private home, thus putting any interviewer in the role of guest. Guests are expected to be on their best behaviour. If the Prime Minister had chosen a television studio the result might have been less secure from his point of view as well as less 'real' – and the impression of absolute veracity is what is sought by interviewees in these sort of circumstances. If he had chosen his official home, 10 Downing Street, it might have been thought self-important. The choice of venue can be crucial.

In this case, the precise venue was the conservatory of the Prime

Minister's house, overlooking potted plants and the garden – a fairly anonymous backdrop with which most viewers could identify themselves. Had the interview been in the living room, the Prime Minister would have had to display his personal taste, which might not have been that of many viewers. The precise location had the apparently contradictory virtues of being both homely and impersonal.

While it may be courtesy to concede the choice of venue to the interviewee, the experienced interviewer will make sure that it does not overawe or wrong-foot him in a way it must not do if the interview is to cover all the points that could and should be asked.

What are they? The answer must always be kept well in mind. They are the points that Joe Public would have asked had he been there, not necessarily the points the interviewee's best friends or worst enemies would have asked.

John Humphrys first set up his stall to be as arresting as possible. He mentioned as many as possible of the difficulties facing the Prime Minister, to get them out into the open at the outset. This technique has the effect of putting the issues to the public in such a way that the interviewee will feel forced to address them, even if he might want to evade some of them.

In fact, John Humphrys took two bites at this cherry, once with a short trailer a few minutes before the interview began, in which he said: 'Good afternoon, I'm in Huntingdon, at the home of the Prime Minister. The government is in crisis and I shall be talking to John Major, that's fifty minutes with the Prime Minister *On the Record* after the news is read by Chris Lowe.' The news led with warnings by senior Conservative party officials that the in-fighting among Tory politicians could cost the government the election.

Then John Humphrys was back again with what in print reads like a rather long or very long introductory question but did not seem so when he was saying it straight to camera (which illustrates the differences between the written word, which must have its own resonance and the spoken word, which can be gilded by the speaker's manner and delivery): 'The government has had what may be its worst week since John Major took over from Margaret Thatcher six years ago. The Prime Minister has lost his majority in the House of Commons.' (A few days previously the Conservative MP Sir John Gorst had said he would 'withdraw cooperation' from the government because of the failure to maintain an adequate accident and emergency service at a hospital in his London constituency, which effectively removed the government's majority of one.) 'And his backbenchers have been at each other's throats and his over Europe; some have been baying for Cabinet blood.

And all this with the general election at most only five months away. I'm with the Prime Minister now at his home in Huntingdon. Prime Minister, I would like to cover lots in this interview, including Northern Ireland, the economy, the state of the party. But let's start with Europe because clearly that's at the heart of your problems. What you are asking your party to accept is that Britain should perhaps at some stage go into a European Single Currency. Now that is plainly unacceptable to many of them. Haven't you got to change your mind?'

The Prime Minister replied that what he was asking everyone to accept was that decisions were being made over a single currency, but not only that, also that they were decisions which were important from the point of view of British interests. Whether we went into a single currency or stayed out of it, it was going to affect the United Kingdom in a whole series of ways. He intended to stay in the negotiations.

JOHN HUMPHRYS: But that is a question of keeping the opt-out. What I am really asking you about at the moment – which is, look, the European Single Currency is, as we speak, developing into a flawed system. Clearly a flawed system, because of fudged criteria and all the rest of it. Therefore it is not in Britain's interest to go in as it stands?

Again, in cold print, this question is less than immaculate. Nonetheless, on the screen it conveyed a feeling of spontaneity while raising a central point. An interviewer's 'question' need not have a question mark. In a minority of cases, it can be a statement which the interviewee is free to accept or dismiss. An interviewer should never make a statement flatly, as if there were no possible answer: the whole idea of any media question is precisely to *get* an answer. A statement of fact should be proffered, if at all, as if it were a tentative suggestion rather than an indictment.

PRIME MINISTER: Let us take your premise. A number of countries are moving towards a single currency. Some of them, for their own reasons, are very enthusiastic about it, for some of them it makes undeniable sense. There is a great head of steam, and all that is absolutely true. You say they are looking at a flawed way of going in and by that I assume you mean that they—
JH: Fudging the criteria?
PM: The criteria is a jargon. Fudging the economic circumstances that would make it prudent to go into a single currency. Well, let me take that proposition. Let us assume that is what they are doing. If they are fudging the criteria then there would be no question of Britain joining, none at all. [The PM then at length defended being in the negotiations so that Britain could vote

against fudging.] But giving ourselves a red card now and fleeing the field
when the game is still to be played seems to me dereliction of responsibility.
JH: But many of your critics would say that is a bad argument, say the game
is being played, yes, but the other side is cheating in such a way that clearly
it isn't going to be acceptable to us and that is already happening.

It was by now clear that the interviewer was going to keep a very loose
rein on his own syntax as well as on the interviewee, who was to be
allowed a lot of rope in expressing the same thing in a number of ways
– something which the same interviewer would have been unlikely to
have allowed him to do on the equally influential BBC radio early
morning *Today* programme. Here much shorter interviews and fairly
constant interruptions by interviewers are *de rigueur* at a time of day
when the public is hurrying to get to work on time.

In the long set-piece interview it is understood that many of the
questions will be merely triggers which will allow the interviewee to
deliver individual set pieces. Providing the interviewer is allowed to
come back at the end with supplementary questions, this is quite
acceptable in a long interview, where the interviewer will have plenty
of opportunities to raise again any points he thinks have not been
adequately answered. It is only in shorter interviews that the interviewer needs to thrash out every point as he goes along, knowing that
if he waits time may well conveniently run out.

In this fifty-minute interview, John Humphrys voiced sixty-two questions or interjections. In other words, he gave plenty of time for the
interviewee to expand his answers without interruption – almost a
minute between each of his own contributions, a good balance between
allowing the interviewee to meander on and ill-mannered hounding.

The interview continued with the Prime Minister repeatedly saying,
in different words, that Britain had to be part of the negotiations over
the European Single Currency, and could not logically withdraw if it
disliked what was going on now. After he had said he did not understand the logic of Britain's withdrawal from negotiations, John
Humphrys put this question:

Well, the logic is that if the economic criteria, these financial critera are
already being fudged: we have seen what the French have done,
Telecom pensions funds, the government has basically pinched the funds
and said, 'We have cut our bill for borrowing at a stroke' – now there's
a bit of fiddling going on there for a start. The Italians have done various things, the Spanish have done various things, some of those things
will affect the decision that has to be taken in some months' time, a
year's time, maybe, but it is already affecting the situation today to such

an extent that you really have little choice, they say; but you say, 'We cannot conceivably go in in the first wave; perhaps things will change later, perhaps, but we can't go in in the first wave because of what is already going on at the moment . . .'

This 'question' was a good example of the maxim that there is no such thing as a 'brilliant' media question, only a question (or statement) that elicits a useful answer. First, it was not a question at all, it was merely a bait to get the Prime Minister talking about the issues in hand. Second, the syntax was dreadful. This, though it could be sneered at by purists, can be a useful way of getting the interviewee to end the tortuous sentences by almost mercifully breaking in with an answer. In this case the Prime Minister immediately cut the 'question' short.

PM: But you absolutely make my point. You said a fudging the criteria, but we don't yet know—
JH (*cutting the beginnings of a possible evasion*): We know the French are fudging the criteria.
PM (*resisting the prod*): But we haven't yet reached a decision on whether the criteria can be met or not. [The PM again defended staying in negotiations so that he could argue against fudges.]
JH: But it is already happening. In that case . . . France for instance. Look, you can't be in it, the whole thing is—

Apart from interjections such as this, made in a teasing rather than hectoring tone, and invariably accompanied by smiles rather than frowns, the Prime Minister was obviously to continue to be allowed to put the points which he had equally obviously, from the start, been determined to make. Indeed, had he been prevented from doing so, it would have grated in this particular kind of fairly rare interview, when the viewer is far more inclined to listen to the interviewee at length than to the interviewer at length, however brilliant he or she is. The interesting thing about the sort of meandering sentences thus far uttered by both the interviewer and the interviewee is that in context, with the back-up of body language, all the sentences flowed smoothly and seemed to the viewer to make sense. Such sentences are an art form just as beautifully constructed syntax is an art form.

The Prime Minister went on to say that he had been saying for weeks, months, years, that the criteria were the most critical element of all. He again defended staying in the negotiations, in slightly different words.

JH: So your objective is not just to say Britain can't go on – clearly you have made that reasonably clear though we may come back to it – but if people are fiddling the figures, cooking the books, you say, on behalf of Britain, this system ought not to go ahead. You would take it as Britain's reponsibility to stop the system coming into being, full stop.

PM: Of course. Of course. And it is in the British national interest to do that if they are cooking the books and I again enter the word 'If' . . .

Had the interviewer on this occasion been more impatient, and had the interviewee been a more arresting and magnetic speaker rather than a soothingly reasonable one, it might have been more blazingly obvious to the viewer that enormous numbers of words were being used, virtually unchallenged, to say the same thing: that Britain should keep its vote in Europe and should use it against fudging criteria and other alleged malpractices. In the big set piece interview, it is, by custom, more acceptable to let the interviewee say things his way, more than once if necessary. The playwright and wit George Bernard Shaw, a brilliant debater, once said: 'Never argue; repeat your assertion.' This is fine from the interviewee's point of view, but something that has to be watched vigilantly by any interviewer.

True, there is a danger, if the interviewer says, 'But Prime Minister, you keep on saying the same thing,' that the interviewee could logically wrong-foot him by replying, 'Then ask me different questions – at the moment I am merely trying to answer the one you asked me.' But the interviewer must sometimes take this risk and gently point out, if necessary, that the point has already been well made. A statement made once is information, a statement made twice is emphasis, a statement made three or more times is propaganda. All interviewers should bear this in mind.

In this case, through no less than forty-four questions or interjections from John Humphrys, the Prime Minister continued to press, with some variations and embellishments, his central point: that the British government should keep its position open by staying in the European negotiating process. In any other sort of interview, especially in an era given (regrettably) to soundbites of a few seconds on even the most serious issues, he would have been moved on to other issues much more quickly.

There is a case for saying that, if an interviewer is going to be allowed to stay on one topic for long, then the style of interviewing should be very aggressive indeed, more aggressive than John Humphrys employed in this interview. This view would be unfair to an interviewer placed in an unusual interviewing slot. The principle would almost certainly have been applied in the case of anyone other than a prime minister or president, who would not have agreed to such a long interview in the first place unless he were sure that he could get his main points over in more or less his own way, hammering them home repeatedly if he so desired.

Perhaps a well-informed democracy demands such latitude, but it can put even the best and most independent of interviewers into an uncomfortable corset in which he has to fight hard to achieve normal movement. Such an interview, though it demands high skills of its own, certainly cannot be held up as a model for *all* interviews.

It would be unkind to all parties, including the reader, to give a detailed examination of the same expansive treatment given by the interviewee to the other subjects covered in the fifty-minute interview, such as the prospects for a lasting cease-fire with the IRA and the allowing of its political wing Sinn Fein into talks (it depended on intelligence of the IRA's real intentions rather than their words); the influence of rebellious Conservative MPs on government policy (they would not be allowed to hold the government to ransom); the recent Budget (just what industry and commerce wanted); the reliability of recent adverse opinion polls on the Conservative Party's chances of being elected (there had been adverse opinion polls just before the Conservatives had been re-elected in 1992); whether the 'wheels were coming off' the government (just the 'rumour mill' of Westminster); and whether the Prime Minister was becoming tired of all the hassle.

This last question must have indicated, to any remaining doubter, the inevitably ritualistic elements of this type of political marathon interview with a top politician in office. The interviewer is virtually obliged to ask, as his last question, a variant of, 'Aren't you tempted to chuck it all in tomorrow?' To which the interviewee replies with a variant of, 'No, I am going to stay for ever.'

JH: Aren't you also just a bit fed up with it all? You have been there for a fairly long time now. Don't you sometimes say, 'This is a lovely place to be, Huntingdon, nice garden out there, nice conservatory.' Do you think, 'Oh, for heaven's sake . . .'

PM: I love politics. That is the point you need to bear in mind. . . . Many of the things I would have liked to have done in this Parliament I have only begun to do . . . education changes . . . improved health reforms. . . . We have now got the economy in order. The government after the next election is going to be operating against the backcloth of the strongest economy we have seen in this country for generations. We can turn to the social agenda. . . . So if you think I am thinking of packing my bags and walking off, then you are wholly wrong.

JH: On and on?

PM: Hah. You are wholly wrong.

JH: Prime Minister, thank you very much indeed.
PM: Thank you.

A few months later, the 1997 general election gave Labour the biggest
landslide in its history and John Major was out of office. The defeat
was clearly foreshadowed in this interview by John Humphrys, without the interviewer adopting what could have been criticized as a
hostile, partisan tone.

Encouraged to expand by a polite and neutral tone, the interviewee
in effect listed all the problems facing the Conservative government,
thereby establishing how many there were and how serious they were.
An intensive grilling amounting to hounding would not have been
nearly as revealing; it would merely have seemed one-sided and
created sympathy for John Major, who was already more popular
personally than his party.

The big and almost ritualistic political set piece with leaders of
parties is not therefore necessarily the tame tool of government that
any government's enemies might like to think. There is no obvious
way a politician can give his answers to a problem without mentioning and confirming that problem in the public mind; and in discussing
it, he may well confirm in the minds of some of the electorate the
sheer daunting extent to which his party is facing a difficulty – in this
case principally, but by no means exclusively, Europe.

That fact is often overlooked by those journalists who despise the
big political set piece and believe that the interviewer is not doing his
job unless he trashes everything the politician says immediately after,
or even before, he opens his mouth. The big set-piece interview is an
example of how, without partisan dishonesty, an interviewer can get at
the truth and foreshadow the political future without mounting any
soap box of his own.

He needs, like John Humphrys with John Major, to be vigilant, to
make sure all the important chinks in the armour are discussed without himself showing signs of wanting to thrust a sword into those
chinks, only a bright light. His aim is to reveal truths as a spectator
rather than to secure victory as a combatant: the latter is a politician's,
not an interviewer's, job.

A very broad canvas like the big political set piece can be, in an
inconspicuous sort of way, quite effective in revealing truths. What of
other methods?

Chapter 22

In Writing

An interview which consists of a series of written questions which are answered in due course by a series of written answers may be thought to have mutual advantages, especially when the interview is one dealing with important and complex issues.

The interviewer has plenty of time to compose his questions, and can be fairly certain that all of them will be answered. A written question cannot be deflected or talked out as in a verbal exchange. The interviewee has time to consider his answers and – in theory, at any rate – can be more forthright because he is safe in the knowledge that such frankness cannot be used as a lever to extract further and even more revealing answers, as it can be in a verbal exchange.

The advantages can be summed up as the advantages of low adrenalin. The in-writing interview can be more calm, thoughtful and considered. But the low adrenalin will be manifest in other, less desirable, ways. At worst, the effect of such questions and answers, when they appear in print, will be of two people conversing under water or speaking like *Dr Who*'s Daleks rather than like human beings. An element of adrenalin is necessary to promote an aura of drama, which the most effective interview must have. This is difficult or impossible to achieve in a written exchange of questions and answers.

Another inevitable casualty will be a sense of spontaneity, of an exchange in which anything could conceivably happen. Answers to questions will not lead on naturally to a related question but to a previously thought-out question. This factor, important in print interviews, is even more important in those for the electronic media. Here it can be fatal to submit or mention in advance of the actual interview the exact questions to be asked; at best the interviewee may answer your question crisply and interestingly at that time, and then give a stale and drearily rehearsed answer in the interview itself.

Andrew Walker, former BBC World Service Commonwealth and defence correspondent, who as a member of the training committee of the Commonwealth Journalists Association, has helped instruct many budding journalists, is one of the experienced operators who has counselled against submitting questions in advance.

'This is not always possible with the powerful who sometimes make it a condition of granting an interview at all,' he has advised students. 'One solution is to tell them to go to hell; a better one is just to indicate the topics you want to ask about without going into detailed questions. An even more pernicious habit indulged in by some is giving written answers; don't agree.'

This argument also has force when applied to print journalism interviews conducted in writing. Incomplete or inadequate answers cannot easily be challenged. The reader may be dying to see the previous question pursued more rigorously, but will be pitchforked willynilly into a quite different question that may not interest or excite him nearly as much. At worst, this may give the impression that the interviewer has failed in his job by not trying to take an answer further.

The in-writing interview, therefore, has restricted applications and, even when done well, has inevitable limitations. One application that can be considered a journalistic and public service is the extraction of firm and specific policy intentions from politicians well before the frictions of an election campaign have started to produce more heat than light. One of the criticisms of Labour's campaign in the 1997 general election was that it wanted to be all things to all men, that it was more concerned with bland soundbites designed to offend no one than with firm policies.

About a month before polling day on 1 May, the London *Evening Standard* addressed fifty questions to the then Leader of the Opposition, Tony Blair. The questions were well chosen, beginning with the most controversial at that time – Labour's attitude to joining the European Single Currency – and working through tax and similar contentious issues to those of particular interest to London, such as the possibility of creating a mayor for the capital.

In such an exercise, it is vital that the questions should be a mixture of the basic and timeless (such as those dealing with underlying values) and the immediately newsworthy. Values without immediacies tend to lead to hot air, which would bore the reader. Immediacies without values would not enable the reader to identify where his heart and head truly belonged.

The answered questions were published a fortnight before polling day. They took up, with the neutral portrait of the interviewee which made him look thoughtful but not severe, two pages.

Question One was: *Will Labour take Britain into the European Single Currency?*

This was the answer:

> The final decision will be for the people of this country in a referendum, not the government. Any decision about Britain joining the single currency must be determined by a hard-headed assessment of Britain's economic interests. There are formidable obstacles in the way of Britain being in the first wave of membership, if European Monetary Union takes place on 1 January 1999. However, to exclude EMU for ever would be to destroy any influence we have over a process which will affect us whether we are in or out. We must therefore play a full part in the debate to influence it in Britain's interests. There are three preconditions which would have to be satisfied before Britain could join during the next Parliament. First the Cabinet would have to agree; then Parliament and finally the people would have to say Yes in a referendum.

Then came the next question, asking where Labour stood on whether or how a two-tier Europe should develop.

Certainly this question was directly related to the first one. But an interviewer in person would almost certainly not have chosen to put the second question at that point. Anyone face to face with Tony Blair would have realized that the answer, except for the referendum issue, could equally have (indeed, had) come from the Prime Minister John Major. The face-to-face interviewer would have pointed this out, and asked exactly where Labour's policy on the single currency differed from that of the Conservatives. That is a good illustration of the limitations of the in-writing interview, even when well conceived.

When such an interview is for a magazine rather than a newspaper, the deadline may be more generous. In such a case, it is technically possible for the interviewer, after perusing the answer, to get back to the interviewee and ask for elaboration or clarification. Many magazine interviewers, for example, would have been tempted to get back on the answer to the *Evening Standard*'s Question Seven, which was, *By what means will Labour enforce its compulsory homework policy?*

The answer was:

> We will introduce home-school contracts for all schools, which schools will be expected to develop with parents. We will issue guidelines for setting down recommended minimum periods for homework in primary and secondary schools.

The vital word in the question was obviously, 'enforce'. Anyone can lay it down that a child must do two hours homework. But how do you enforce it if there is no place in the home to study, if the rest of the family are noisy or deliberately obstructive, if the parents have no interest in or understanding of the child's educational needs? The question was plainly concerned not with the children whose parents would be likely to follow 'guidelines' but with those whose parents would not. In that sense, the question was not answered.

So should the interviewer, if the deadline permits, get back to the interviewee or his office, and say, 'Look, the point of the question has been ignored. Can we have a fuller answer to this question, please, specifically addressing the question of enforcement?'

This possibility raises issues of professional practice and integrity which are not as simple as might appear.

If the questions were being answered by, let us say, the president of the Women's Institute or the local chairman of the marriage guidance agency Relate, there would be no objection to the interviewer asking the interviewee to make his answer more complete and convincing. It would be a service to the reader and to the blameless organization involved.

But in the case of leaders of parties struggling for office in an election, the issue is not so clear. The interviewer could well say to himself, 'I am providing a service to the reader in asking for a fuller and more convincing answer, and my business as a journalist is surely eliciting the fullest answers I can.'

On the other hand, isn't the interviewer doing one party political leader's work for him? Is he not acting as an unpaid public relations officer to the party leader, helping him to present himself as more plausible than he would have seemed had the answer been left in its original, brief and unconvincing form?

There is a case in a written interview of this type for trying to get the most complete set of answers possible, but doing what amounts to a cosmetic job on the answers would not be acceptable. In the ultimate, if the answer is an evasion or even a patent lie, it must be allowed to stand so that the interviewee may be judged on the basis of it. Too much adding here, subtracting there, and rephrasing somewhere else can amount to collusion rather than reporting.

An interviewer using written questions and answers should decide at the outset, or allow the executives above him in the hierarchy to decide, what his policy will be. Will he rigidly use the answers as given, offering no opportunity for the interviewee to improve them, or will he take part in a dialogue to produce what he thinks, as a journalist, is the most informative result? There may be a case for the latter course, but the former is simpler. The interviewee bears the complete responsibility for his answers; if they are incomplete, crass or even fraudulent (I am not of course suggesting that Tony Blair's were), then the blame rests squarely on the interviewee's own head.

The reader, however, may be left with a feeling of irritation at both the interviewee and the newspaper over what he sees as inadequate answers. That may be an unavoidable danger with the written interview when the interviewee is a contending politician.

Another danger illustrated in the *Evening Standard* written interview was that of repetition. This may seem paradoxical. Surely an interviewee is more likely to repeat himself in face-to-face conversation than in writing where repetitions should be immediately detectable? Apparently not. Few people, at least when sober, can bear to repeat themselves in conversation, realizing that it is likely to characterise them as bores. There is no such compunction when faced with a sheet of paper. On the contrary, repeating oneself verbatim may seem to be an act of stylish nonchalance, the mute equivalent of saying, 'Ask me a similar question and I'll reel off a similar answer.'

In this case, Tony Blair gave precisely the same answer to two questions and almost precisely the same answer to a third. Asked as Question Thirteen, *Will Labour abolish tax relief?* he replied: 'Labour has made clear our central tax announcements. No Chancellor or Shadow Chancellor can go further. Indeed Kenneth Clarke cannot match our proposals.'

Asked, as Question Fourteen, *Will Labour change tax allowances, like every government before it?* Tony Blair replied: 'Labour has made clear our central tax announcements. No Chancellor or Shadow Chancellor can go further. Indeed Kenneth Clarke cannot match our proposals.'

The impression of conversing with an out-of-order Dalek was very strong at this point. It was enhanced by Question Twenty-four. Asked, *Will Labour tax pension funds?* Tony Blair replied: 'Our public expenditure plans require no extra taxation. Labour has made clear our central tax announcements. No Chancellor or Shadow Chancellor can go further. Indeed Kenneth Clarke cannot match our proposals.'

It may be argued that the written question approach worked in this case because it enabled Tony Blair to reveal himself as a man with a rigidly disciplined set text. But did it? Did it, rather, merely draw attention to another snag with the written question and answer interview – the danger of projecting apparent personality but actual anonymity? Tony Blair's name was on the interview, and he may have okayed it, but was it really him talking, or only a committee in his office?

This is a possibility that may well worry the reader of an in-writing interview. Is it really a human being talking, or is it an example of group-think? Cynics may say that if the reader is still awake at the end, it may well be a human being talking. In the case of a prime minister or a leader of the opposition, it may effectively not matter (except in terms of readability) whether that functionary or a group of rather less exalted functionaries is talking: the leader is bound by what appears under his name, so the reader can rely on it.

Nevertheless, the impression of a hand, or hands, inside a glove puppet does not make for a satisfactory interview from anyone's point of view. It suggests to the reader that the interviewee may be somehow invalid, which may be quite unfair to him, and it suggests that the interviewer (or the newspaper if, as in this case, no individual interviewer's name was given) has not done his job properly, in that he has not penetrated to the heart of the interviewee or of the matters being discussed.

But the negative side of in-writing interviews applies chiefly when it is applied to high-level controversial figures such as politicians in an election. For less controversial figures, where the extraction of factual information is the object of the exercise, there can be advantages. The interviewer has plenty of time to devise and polish his questions. The interviewee does not have to carve an hour out of his working day to face an interviewer, but can supply the answers piecemeal to suit himself.

On the whole, however, and as a personal footnote, I am rather against questions in writing. My first attempt at it in local journalism blew up in my face. In the paper's area was a Borstal institution from which boys regularly absconded. At a particular time, this outward flow became a deluge. I was then a very junior reporter. I addressed twenty written questions to the governor of the Borstal, about what was happening and how it could be put right. He didn't answer but sent the questions to the Home Office as the ultimate authority. The Home Office returned them to the editor unanswered. I had not consulted the editor before forming and sending the questions, hoping to astound him with the results. Instead of being praised for my initiative, I was called over the coals for being young and irresponsible.

The experience taught me two things. One, when the ceiling in any particular job seems to be too low, get ready to move on as swiftly as you can. Two, before setting up any sort of interview, but especially one involving the formality of questions and answers in writing, get the backing of the hierarchy above you. Being themselves involved, they will be sure your idea and intentions are thoroughly worthwhile, if not bordering on sheer genius.

There is a further danger with in-writing interviews which was brought home to me by my own sad experience. As a teenager, before my first newspaper job, I wrote freelance material for a yachting magazine. I wanted to interview the then best-known yacht designer Uffa Fox, a friend of Prince Philip. At that time I lacked the confidence and the cash to telephone him at his south coast boatyard and to suggest that I travel down from my east coast home to interview him. Faced with little more than a schoolboy, he might not have taken me seriously. So I addressed a series of written questions to him, explaining my connection with the magazine. I never received an answer. Uffa Fox was known to be unpredictable and none too keen on what would now be called the media, but I felt the rebuff keenly. When decades later I read of his death, I am afraid it was the painful snub that first came to my mind.

But of course it was my own fault. An interviewer cannot bypass the need for personal self-confidence. I should have telephoned him from a public call box with the aid of a large pile of coins and pestered him until I had at least got him to agree to consider either a telephone interview or a written interview. That approach would have been more difficult to ignore.

The Internet and all that notwithstanding, there is no wholly satisfactory substitute for personal involvement between people in any undertaking, especially interviewing. In-writing interviews can be justified only in specific circumstances which completely rule out personal contact.

Chapter 23

Seeing Significance

Quite often a broadsheet journalist (and even more often his employers) may be tempted to interview a popular artist – actor, singer, television personality – purely in the belief that the interviewee's name on the front page may do wonders for sales. Here the motive may be questionable, if understandable.

Quite often, however, a broadsheet journalist may wish to interview such a popular personality not out of any venal motive, but because he believes that even serious newspapers and periodicals should deal with the whole of life, not merely the more highbrow parts of it.

In either case, it will help if the interviewer can visualize the interviewee as having a significance beyond his obvious popular adulation. What does the interviewee signify in political, social or aesthetic terms?

The principle will serve for non-celebrities as well as celebrities. People who might be thought not worthy of serious consideration as individuals can be made worthy of it if their broader significance can be shown. I once interviewed a pawnbroker in the town in which I then worked. His was the last pawnbroker's shop in the town, and he was closing it in the prosperous late 1950s – there was no longer any call for pawnshops. I made the pawnbroker a representative figure in a changing society, paradoxically bemoaning the fact that people were now more prosperous. Years later when I was on *The Guardian*, I interviewed the first pawnbroker to open up again, in a town which had been pawnshopless, encouraged by the increasing relative poverty among the new underclass of the 1980s. Neither shopkeeper was in himself worth interviewing in a local, let alone a national, newspaper but as a social phenomenon, a pointer to the way society was moving, both interviews earned their place.

The same treatment can be applied to celebrities who do not immediately spring to mind as being worthy of attention in serious media. As long as the sleight of hand in constructing the interviewee as a phenomenon is not too visibly glib, this is a perfectly legitimate technique. An extreme example of it was the interview with the Spice Girls which earned its place in *The Spectator*. That intellectually heavy-weight weekly magazine included the interview by Simon Sebag Montefiore in its Christmas 1996 issue, and trailed it on its front page. As presented by the interviewer, it could have been equally well published in a less frivolous issue.

The Spice Girls, it may be best to explain, are (or were – today's pop icons tend to rise and fall with bewildering rapidity) a group of five young women who sing and dance on television and in live shows. They do – or did –it in a vivid way which owes a lot to presentational aids like constantly changing brightly coloured and idiosyncratically designed clothes; distorting shots; dizzyingly varying perspectives and magnified sound. The shock effect of the act was always undeniable, and the girls were written about in the tabloid press almost as frequently as if they had been misbehaving royals.

'Yes, yes, but what do they *signify*?' was a quite natural question for any intelligent person confronted with them. Nevertheless, for *The Spectator* to interview them could not be accounted the most predictable event of the year.

The interview, which was accompanied by a cartoon by Heath, showing the five Spice Girls with huge out-of-control breasts resembling ten footballs in play on different parts of the pitch, began with a bold declaration of intent:

> Interview the Spice Girls, I thought. But the Spice Girls are interviewed all the time. My interview, however, would be different. I would ask questions that I would ask Mr Major, Mr Heseltine or any other politician. Only one thing worried me about this plan. What if they weren't interested in politics? It was a needless worry. They were completely political. Politics was really their subject.
>
> 'We Spice Girls are true Thatcherites. Thatcher was the first Spice Girl, the pioneer of our ideology – Girl Power. But for now we're desperately worried about the slide to a single currency,' said Gerri, the 24-year-old, husky-voiced, Titian-haired lead singer.

Was it a patrician joke (like the learned judge asking, 'What is the Beatles?') to spell the lead singer's name Gerri when the majority opinion is that it is spelt Geri? I shall maintain the Montefiore spelling Gerri where I quote from his piece, using the shorter form when I refer to her myself.

Treading a fine line between a completely straight face and a visible tongue in the cheek, the interviewer conceded that the politics of the

Spice Girls might be 'somewhat surprising':

> You may, indeed, wonder who on earth the Spice Girls are and why we
> care.

Just so. In an interview of this type, in which significance is being read
into the pronouncements of young popular entertainers, the interviewer is wise to genuflect towards the habitual readers (or listeners or
viewers) in the form of a certain dryness of tone which, whilst not
dismissing the interviewees, who are of course well worth interviewing, nevertheless suggests that the interviewer is perfectly well aware
that their pronouncements may not have the authority of a Confucius
or even a prime minister.

Well worth interviewing? Such an implication has, in an intellectual
magazine, to be defended. The interviewer defended it by pointing out
their impact on the entertainment scene. They had dominated the
culture of those aged between five and twenty-five in most countries.
Their album *Spice* had already sold three million copies. Their song,
'Wannabe' ('an anthem to Thatcherite meritocratic aspiration') had
sold another three million and had remained at number one in the hit
parade for seven weeks. They were number one in twenty-seven countries. They were the most successful popular Western group in Japan
since the Beatles.

But it was not their commercial success that made them interesting,
went on the interviewer. Why did politicians from Tony Blair, leader
of the Labour Party, to Brian Mawhinney, chairman of the
Conservative Party, care so much about Spice? Just like the Thatcherite
revolution, 'it has to do with ideas – the Spice Girls have views on
everything.'

The interviewer went on to discuss ideas, bringing in the names of
Bill Clinton, Ferdinand Marcos, Descartes, Voltaire, Marshal Tito and
Fidel Castro. What had Tito and Castro got to do with it? They were
'on the spot', in control of territories, so the West had to find out
about them. 'It is the same with the Spice Girls – they control the vital
territory of the young, apparently apolitical voters who do not even
vote.'

At the end of the first page of the interview, only the two sentences
previously attributed to 'Gerri' had appeared as direct quotes from any
of the five Spice Girls. The rest of the page was filled by the cogently
and amusingly argued case in favour of their being interviewed at all.
Surely, by the time the Spice Girls got to speak more for themselves on
the second page, no one could be in any possible doubt about the legit-
imacy of the proceedings? If they were, it was through no fault of the

interviewer. It would have taken half an hour to argue back against the points made to explain the validity and significance of the interview.

And so to the serious issues. Would Britain ever join a single currency?

> At first, the Spice Girls adopted the John Major/Kenneth Clarke formula of refusing to rule out joining. But Victoria, 'Posh Spice' forced through her anti-European free-market policies: 'The whole European federal plan is ridiculous. We are patriotic. The single currency is an outrage. We want the Queen's head – or the King's head if we have a King – on our own coins.'

The interviewees were then given a commendably free rein on issues such as the royal family ('The best soap opera in the world' – Geri, Ginger Spice), the possibility of another aristocratic prime minister, such as Winston Churchill ('We shouldn't be prejudiced against any background, poor or aristocratic. The middle class are the worst. We like the aristocrats' – Mel B, Scary Spice, in her broad scouse accent), the importance of fidelity ('In an ideal world – but it's almost impossible because the hormones get so out of control' – Geri, Ginger Spice), Sir James Goldsmith and his Referendum Party which he set up to campaign for a referendum on whether there should be closer ties with Europe ('Is he anything to do with Jemima Goldsmith?' – Victoria, Posh Spice), Sir Edward Heath's role in European integration ('If Ted Heath was the man in power who tricked the English into voting for a federal Europe when they did not mean to, then that's bad' – Victoria, Posh Spice), the complexities of the choice between the two major party leaders (of Tony Blair: 'His hair is all right, but we don't agree with his tax policies. He's just not a safe pair of hands for the economy' – Geri, Ginger Spice; of John Major, 'As for Major, he's a boring pillock. But compared to the rest, he's far better. We'd never vote Labour' – Victoria, Posh Spice), and so on.

The interviewer then resumed a clever inflection which had the effect of justifying taking the Spice Girls seriously while signifying to intellectual readers that he did not necessarily fully accept them on the highest intellectual plane:

> On the question of what creates the moral man, education *v.* genetics, the Spice Girls took a more Platonic than Rousseauesque view: 'We don't think man's born as a blank sheet of paper, innocent and noble.'

The Spice Girls interview was legitimate as Christmas entertainment, especially when handled with a mixture of comically patrician condescension and straight reporting skill that fully justified its space. Seeing significance is not, of course, useful only when dealing with national or international celebrities who perhaps require an intellectual fig leaf. It can not only enrich an interview but also determine whether the interview is worthwhile in the first place. Consider the specific medium for which you work and ask yourself whether there is an interview for you in any names which, for any reason, flash before your eyes. Can you see a particular significance in any of them – something that opens up a subject or an issue as distinct from promising only a straight personal history?

Interviewers who work for local newspapers or radio and television programmes should certainly bear this in mind. For instance, is there a local significance in any piece of music, play or novel just published or performed or about to be published or performed? If you work for *The Scotsman* and a Scottish author has brought out a new novel, there is an obvious case for interviewing him, but some significances can be less obvious.

When my first novel *Candidate of Promise* was published, Neville Miller, working for the *South Wales Argus*, rang me up to do an interview. My own personal history, since it in no way included Wales, would have been of little interest. His first question, indicating where he had spotted the significance for his own paper, was why I had made my main character, a plausibly eloquent and ambitious working class Conservative Parliamentary candidate fighting a well-off Labour MP, a Welshman rather than an Englishman.

That made me think harder about why I had done so. At the time I wrote it I had just, almost instinctively, felt that it 'played better' that way. The line of questioning produced a readable piece about Welshness and the great number of orators who were Welsh, rather than just the usual elements of an author interview.

Seeing a possible significance which is at first not necessarily obvious is an enormously useful interviewer's basic skill. It gives the interviewee a wider context and, unless it is visibly contrived and strained, doubles the possible interest of the final result.

Chapter 24

The 'Magazine' Approach

It is undesirable for an interviewer, especially of politicians, to be unduly influenced by his own personal views on the merits of the interviewee and his opinions. Being influenced by his assessment of the circumstances in which the interviewee finds himself at the moment of the interview is more legitimate, even though no interviewer should assume that temporary circumstances, such as public praise or condemnation, will be permanent.

Circumstances will inevitably condition if not dominate the *tone* of an interview. It is legitimate to give a more combative grilling to a politician who has been in office ten years than to one who has been in office for ten minutes; not legitimate to give one politician a harder time than another because the interviewer doesn't happen to share his views.

In other words, one must say a hearty 'yes' to an assessment of where the interviewee stands in the public's consciousness, a hearty 'no' to an assessment of whether you as interviewer happen to agree with the interviewee, like the interviewee, dislike the interviewee, like or dislike the praise/blame he seems to be encountering at the time of the interview.

Usually the public deserves light rather than heat from an interviewer.

That has been one of the interviewing strengths of Sir David Frost in his Sunday morning BBC1 *Breakfast With Frost* television programme. Though he can be accounted a celebrity, David Frost's questions are seldom 'celeb' questions, seldom 'expert' or in any way hoity-toity: he asks the sort of questions the average member of the public would like to ask for himself if he had the chance; and he appears to listen to the answers, interrupting only when the average viewer would like to interrupt. He has an all-round affability.

If this is sometimes seen as a 'magazine' rather than hard news approach – allowing rather than forcing things to get said – at least David Frost does not give the impression of being a pushy oaf so

149

pleased with himself that he imagines his own prejudices to be divinely inspired, and the views of the interviewee to have a right to exist only as the butt of his own superior being.

In his two programmes immediately following the 1997 general election and the historic Labour landslide, the biggest since the Second World War, Sir David was face to face with, amongst others, the ex-Home Secretary Michael Howard, John Prescott, Deputy Prime Minister and transport, environment and regions supremo, Martin Bell, the former BBC war correspondent who stood at Tatton on an anti-corruption ticket against the sitting and embattled Conservative MP Neil Hamilton, both Labour and Liberal Democrat parties offering no candidate.

This line-up did not precisely constitute a political balance, but their selection was justified in news terms: in other words, in the circumstances of the moment. Bell was a curiosity attached to no party whose future in the House of Commons was a matter of general interest. John Prescott was obviously a well-placed source of information on the new government's future attitudes, and Howard, a contender for the Conservative Party leadership, had just been said by a former Junior minister under him, Ann Widdecombe, to have 'something of the night about him'.

The tone adopted to them all was uniform: a friendly but not sycophantic impartiality, in which the interviewees were largely allowed to make their own points. This open-armed technique got the interviewees to open up more than a more hectoring style might have done. If one or two points that escaped from at least two pairs of lips were potentially compromising, or at least revealing, and yet were not followed up, it could well be claimed that any intelligent viewer was well able to spot the points for himself.

The tone was especially justified at a time when the political stage had been tilted, when the politicians were all in new roles, and the public still did not know what they thought and what they were going to do in those new roles. Too much hectoring at such a point would have been like interrupting a college lecturer with a hostile question when he was only two sentences into his lecture. With more familiar figures, later in an administration, a more demanding and critical style of questioning could be defended.

'Here he is in the trademark suit that has become legendary,' Frost introduced the white-suited Martin Bell, and followed up with his first simple, brief question, 'As you look ahead, what do you most want to do in the House of Commons?'

This is just the sort of question that the smash-and-grab school of interviewing despises. It could be asked by anybody, expert or non-expert, political sophisticate or political innocent. It carries no hint of a political attitude on the part of the interviewer. It simply opens up an arena in which an honest campaigner against corruption in public life could show his mettle or provides an unfenced pit into which a man not clear about his intentions could fall. It carries no warning signs reading in invisible but tangible writing, 'Danger! Beware!' as so many clever-clever questions do.

Bell replied by saying he wanted to be as good a constituency MP as Tatton had ever had. He wanted to do his bit in cleaning up politics and he wanted that to be his focus early on.

The second question was couched in terms that added to the illusion of relaxation: 'And you would like to get on the relevant committee, I read somewhere?' Bell replied that he would like to but normally its members were very senior Members of Parliament so he would just have to see 'how that plays'.

The third question was also disarmingly simple: 'What about where you are going to sit; there is not a crossbench, is there?' (As in the House of Lords for non-Labour-or-Conservative peers.)

Imagine the more 'vigorous' way of asking this question: 'There aren't any crossbenches in the House of Commons, so haven't you got to make up your mind whether you belong on the Labour or Conservative benches?' This is either more 'challenging' or more rude, depending on one's point of view; but it is certainly not more likely to produce an intelligible answer. And Frost's, '. . . is there?' suggesting he might not be absolutely sure whether there were crossbenches or not in the House of Commons (a rather unlikely ignorance) is the sort of charmingly diffident technique that often produces results.

Bell replied that he would have liked a crossbench but that, to some extent, the problem had been solved for him by the mathematics of the election result. There were more Labour MPs than there was space for them so they might have to drift round towards the Opposition side. He could see a place for him between them and the Liberal Democrats. It might place him comfortably or uncomfortably close to Dr Ian Paisley.

DAVID FROST: I have never seen the two of you together before. What about voting? I suppose you will vote sometimes for the Conservatives, sometimes for Labour?

Again, this was an example of 'magazine' interviewing technique, giving the appearance of easy conversation by devoting one sentence to the interviewee's last remark and then passing immediately to the next question. There was no needling, just an invitation to enter the arena. Bell said he was pledged to be non-party and would be non-party. It depended on the interests of the people of Tatton and his own beliefs and conscience.

Next, David Frost asked if, as the result of this baptism in politics, he had ended up with more or less respect for politicians. This was, of course, a vital though apparently simple question. It is all very well for a journalist like Martin Bell to condemn corruption in politics; but faced with the reality of politics and political pressures, did the attitudes of some politicians become more comprehensible? Did Bell's practical experience of politicking so far give him contempt or greater tolerance of politicians in general or particular? Did he now see his anti-corruption crusade as more necessary in politics as a whole, or did he see it as exaggerated, even priggish?

Asked any of these questions in so many words, the average interviewee might have assumed there was some sort of hostile intent; the open question enabled the interview to spread himself as he wished.

DAVID FROST: 'They voted for a vacuum,' claimed Mr Hamilton, in his not altogether congratulatory comments. You are not a vacuum; what are you actually going to concentrate on in terms of issues?

It would be possible to argue that an interviewer should not have presumed to adjudicate on whether Martin Bell, given his lack of a political party, was a vacuum or not, but simply have confined himself to questions. Yet, seen in terms of David Frost's usual demeanour, the remark can be seen simply as a pleasantry.

One way or the other, Bell replied that his experiences had given him a concern for the welfare of servicemen's families. There was a rising divorce rate as servicemen went on six-month unaccompanied tours. There were very few MPs who had ever served in uniform, so he saw himself as being someone who could be a people's champion in that respect.

It is unnecessary, as my focus is on the interviewer rather than the interviewee, to give all Martin Bell's answers. But here are the rest of David Frost's questions:

I read this morning that there is a rumour that the Gordon Downey report [into standards in public life] which is so relevant to your election, may not be published because people like Neil Hamilton are no longer in the House of Commons, and so it is no longer relevant. Would it be a pity, do you think, if that were not published?

That was an amazing moment we just showed when he ambushed you, or they ambushed you? [This was the occasion when Mr and Mrs Hamilton met Bell face to face in the street while canvassing.]

How many do you think, Conservative votes you probably got out of that vast majority?

And in terms of the future? Are you going to buy a house in the constituency?

Well, the star, the other side of this campaign, Melissa (Bell's daughter). Will she continue to work with you in the House of Commons?

Only one term, you said. But you could be prevailed upon. People who get into politics find it is a drug, Martin. Can you really fight that drug? [Answer: 'You mean like people who get into television?' Touché.]

[And a final observation:] Martin, marvellous, and thank you very much indeed.

It may be argued that that wind-up was plainly partial in its tone. 'Marvellous'? In general, all interviewers may be wise to avoid such exclamations of enthusiasm when dealing with political or other contentious matters; but in the case of Sir David it was so much par for the course, so much part of his usual showbiz-conditioned (but not showbiz-submerged) style, that no one would be likely to mistake a pleasantry for a political commendation. It has been argued that a gentleman may be habitually polite or habitually rude to duchesses and to girls who sell flowers in the street; the important thing is that his manner is the same – rude or polite – to both. Much the same thing may be said of interviewers, with the proviso that the interviewer must be so well known that viewers, listeners or readers will know his style and can budget for it.

John Prescott was a different proposition. As a representative of what some saw as Old Labour among the shoals of Tony Blair's New Labour, he had kept well away from the centre of the stage in the election campaign. In Lowestoft with his campaign bus, he told the *Sunday Times* interviewer A.A. Gill 'off the record' that everyone knew that a national minimum wage which Labour was promising would mean more unemployment in the short term. Gill, usually deployed as a highly readable television and restaurant critic, reported it anyway. As the result of this report, John Prescott did not seem like a man frightened of thinking or voicing unpalatable truths. Viewers, listeners and readers were therefore obviously interested in what, the election won, John Prescott would say next.

Sir David Frost asked him thirty questions, roughly double the number he put to Bell. These proportions were what the circumstances suggested: Prescott was not only an outspoken man, he was Deputy Prime Minister and therefore in a position to do more than merely speak. It is almost always more interesting to hear what a politician is going to *do* than what he thinks. Sir Isaiah Berlin, Mother Teresa or Confucius might be interesting sitting in an armchair talking about life. Few politicians are: except for their fingers on the controls, they may be quite negligible. It was therefore appropriate, and in no way necessarily suggestive of political bias, for John Prescott to be in the star position with double the number of questions.

Big and gravel-voiced, Prescott radiated bluff good humour while Frost's body language, in counterpoint to Prescott's, was rather like that of a priest at a domestic fireside, encouraging someone who had just come into money to talk about his hopes and fears. Respect for the office was suggested, as was a cool, well-disposed amiability towards the man, who he called 'John' at the end of his questions.

Gently prodded by David Frost, John Prescott gave what Frost later called '*a tour de horizon*' of Labour's policies and intentions in government. So gentle and unforced was the Frost manner that when he in fact put the victorious politician on the spot with his questioning, it seemed to everyone (except perhaps Prescott) that nothing of the sort could possibly be happening. This was in complete contrast to the more aggressive type of questioner whose arrogance often produces too little illumination and too much public sympathy for the interviewee.

David Frost let John Prescott set out the new government's intentions by asking him straightforward questions about the Labour party's divisions over Europe, their specific priorities in dealing with devolution, the Welsh Assembly, freedom of information, a Bill of Rights, a referendum on the regions and so on. What did they plan on the issue of a referendum on proportional represenation, especially as their majority of 179 under the present system had served them well? What about roads? Motorway tolls? Railways? Could he help over 'confusion' about Gordon Brown's coming budget: would it be about previously announced welfare-to-work measures and the cutting of VAT on fuel to five per cent or would there be other things?

'I wouldn't even expect you to necessarily even know what they would be now,' said David Frost teasingly (no one likes being seen as someone kept out of the inner counsels, and it just might therefore have goaded the interviewee into a revelation.) 'But is it just within that confined brief or are you looking at other things to include in that budget?' The reply, that the Chancellor was Gordon Brown, and that he would do the things promised in the election campaign, may have been entirely predictable, but it would almost certainly have been the same answer however assertive the interviewer had been in his manner. A persistent interviewer would almost certainly merely have wasted air time by getting the same answer repeatedly.

David Frost's manner was its most silky when he pressed John Prescott, like a man enquiring about the quality of a product at a DIY store, for undertakings about delivery dates of the things that Labour had promised. The atmosphere of the ensuing dialogue was rather like an affable chat in clubland about the virtues of a new car.

DAVID FROST: A hundred days, they used to talk about in the Kennedy era, about JFK. What would you have liked to have achieved after a hundred days, just a hundred days?

JOHN PRESCOTT: I'm not going to pick out things, except we're going to . . .

FROST: None of those things are going to slip that we see here . . .

PRESCOTT (*picks up small white card, resembling a credit card, from the table and waves it about*): That's the card, as you know. Come back in five years, tick me off on it, David. Jobs, education—

FROST: Class sizes, fast track punishment, we know, cut the NHS waiting list – everyone wonders how you could do that—

PRESCOTT (*points to card, which he has put back on the table*): Devolution in Scotland and Wales—

FROST: The windfall tax, government spending and borrowing, ensure low inflation, strengthen the economy. . . . Do you have to achieve *all* those?

PRESCOTT: That is what we have set out to do, and that is what we are going on about with the contract to the people; you want things done, we have to get them done; judge us on the delivery of our promises in five years.

FROST: George Brown [a former Labour Deputy Leader] once said to me, 'If a politician can achieve six right out of ten, he is doing well.' You are not going to get ten out of ten.

PRESCOTT (*pointing to card*): You have six there and it is ten promises. . . . Ha, ha—

FROST: Ha, ha. And you have got one special responsibility always, that is unemployment, isn't it?

PRESCOTT: Yes, jobs, and better quality services and having, people having, a say in decision making. I think decentralization of decision making, whether it is devolution in Scotland or Wales or decentralization of the English regions, is an important move towards having people have more say in their own lives and better quality life.

FROST: John, thank you very much indeed for that *tour de horizon* this morning, we greatly appreciate it. Good luck on behalf of Britain in the days ahead . . .

Was this approach over-avuncular, not probing enough of the number two in a new government? That is a matter of opinion, but David Frost is even-handed in affability and so cannot be accused of political bias. Nor is he frightened of thorny questions, though he is usually careful to finesse them in such a way as not to gum up the interview.

Often it is wise to defer asking the most provocative question until the interviewee has warmed up a little. But often it is wisest to get the difficult question over first, so that the interviewer will then feel able to talk freely, without the fear of ambush on that difficult question.

Which path to choose for any particular interview is a matter for the interviewer's judgement and experience. (In practice, though it may not be easy, the interviewer can return to the sensitive point later, if mentioning it first produces an unsatisfactory result.)

Frost took the second course, choosing as his first question to put to the ex-Home Secretary Michael Howard, a contender for the Conservative Party leadership, the most contentious. There were obvious arguments for this course. From the interviewer's point of view, it established from the first that the vital point would be tackled; from the interviewee's point of view, it got the most difficult question 'out of the way' so that he would hope that the rest of the interview would be devoted to topics more favourable to his leadership chances.

Ann Widdecombe, the former junior minister responsible for prisons, working under him at the Home Office, had just publicly criticized him over his sacking of Derek Lewis, the man recruited from commerce to be director general of prisons. After a series of escapes and other mishaps at prisons, Michael Howard, as the Home Secretary ultimately responsible for prisons, had been criticized inside and outside the House of Commons. He dismissed Derek Lewis as the man with operational responsibility.

Lewis, who subsequently wrote a book which dealt with the controversy around his dismissal, said that Howard had interfered in operational matters. After mentioning his intention to appeal to an industrial tribunal about his dismissal, he was awarded over £200,000 by the government for loss of office. Days after Michael Howard announced he was a candidate for party leader, Miss Widdecombe said she had been opposed to Lewis's dismissal and said of Michael Howard that he had 'something of the night' about him. That was the situation immediately before the Frost interview.

Frost opened the interview by saying that when Ann Widdecombe had used the term 'something of the night', he had thought a letter 'k' must have been dropped off, but it seemed to be deliberate.

Michael Howard responded with a strong disclaimer, saying that he had had to overrule Ann Widdecombe over the dismissal because there had been a series of mishaps:

MICHAEL HOWARD: Ann and I disagreed about a very important decision, the dismissal of Derek Lewis as head of the Prison Service. I had to overrule her because there was an independent report which made very serious criticisms of the Prison Service management from top to bottom. Ann felt very strongly about that. We disagreed. I am convinced the decision we made was the right one and of course few decisions have been more subject to Parliamentary scrutiny, including a debate on the floor of the House of

Commons, than that one.

DAVID FROST: And so you reject what she says and hope she doesn't write to John Major.

HOWARD: Well, that is entirely a matter for her. But we disagreed on that and she felt and still feels strongly about it.

FROST: Now tell me, John Redwood says that the party should, quote, 'show humility' . . .

David Frost may have been consulting his notes when Michael Howard uttered the words, 'from top to bottom', and may therefore have missed the look that flickered behind the eyes of the former Home Secretary. To at least one viewer this appeared to be the look, always worth keeping a vigilant eye out for, which silently says, 'Oh God, what have I said? Will he pick me up on it?' Because of course the very 'top' of prison management was the Home Secretary himself. There seemed to me little doubt that an interviewer more like, for instance, Sir Robin Day would immediately have said: 'But weren't you ultimately responsible as Home Secretary at the time, Mr Howard, and wouldn't your own resignation have been more appropriate?'

Who would have been more right – Day for picking up on it or Frost for leaving it alone?

There are respectable arguments on both sides in such a case. The fact was that Michael Howard had been plentifully criticized at the time for not accepting ultimate responsibility and not resigning. Would any useful purpose have been served by raking up the same point again? Those of the more aggressive school might say yes, there was a point: here was a man who was putting himself up as a possible leader of his party, which was a new situation. Those who see the point of the looser rein of David Frost would argue no: everyone, certainly the people who were about to choose a new leader of their party, would remember the controversy over the dismissal of Derek Lewis; and it was now time to look into the future attitudes of the Conservative Party, which was what David Frost proceeded to do.

David Frost's two weekly programmes directly after the historic 1997 general election were, as ever, an illustration of the uses and limitations of gentle 'magazine' techniques translated to television. They may or may not demolish the more intractable toughies; but truths somehow tend to emerge, which after all is the object of the exercise.

Chapter 25
Pressing Hard

It is not unusual for a determined interviewer to press a stone-walling interviewee three or four times for an answer to a question. It is unusual for an interviewer to put the same question fourteen times, plus three related questions amounting to the same thing.

Jeremy Paxman, not to mention the interviewee, Conservative Party leadership candidate and former Home Secretary Michael Howard, probably set a record on the *Newsnight* programme on BBC2 just after Howard had ceased to be Home Secretary following the Labour landslide in the 1997 general election.

The public makes its judgements on general impressions of public personalities rather than their performance in specific circumstances, but it is the job of the interviewer to explore specific circumstances: a catalogue of specific circumstances fosters the vital general impression. The particular circumstances of this case must be stated in more detail if the pros and cons of Jeremy Paxman's interview with Michael Howard are to be at all clear.

The previous chapter gives a basic account of the controversial dismissal of Derek Lewis, and of Ann Widdecombe's 'something of the night' response to Howard's candidature for the party leadership. More specifically, Miss Widdecombe said that Lewis had refused to suspend the governor of Parkhurst prison and that Howard had threatened to overrule Lewis. Howard denied threatening to overrule him or in any way exerting improper pressure in an operational matter. The denial of the threat to overrule emerged as the central point.

Following Miss Widdecombe's attack on Howard, the *Daily Mail* carried a story alleging that Lewis had wooed Miss Widdecombe with chocolates and flowers, the implication being that her interest in preserving Lewis's job had been personally inspired rather than in the public interest. The group lobbying for Howard as leader denied any part in the appearance of this story.

That was the backcloth to the appearance of Michael Howard on Jeremy Paxman's *Newsnight* programme.

Paxman has a deserved reputation as one of the most assertive and tenacious of television interviewers. But his strength, like that of his apparent reverse pole, Sir David Frost, is that his manner is usually extended impartially to every interviewee. Before interviewing Howard on the BBC2 *Newsnight* programme under discussion, Paxman interviewed Ann Widdecombe, who was in the BBC's Westminster studio. This was the correct playing order: accusation first, opportunity for rebuttal later. The reverse order would have implied that Paxman and *Newsnight* had given Widdecombe the last word because they believed her accusations more than Howard's rebuttals, and were choosing to leave them fresh in the public's mind.

JEREMY PAXMAN: I'll be talking to Michael Howard in a moment, but first Ann Widdecombe joins us from Westminster. Ann Widdecombe, it is clear what the implication is in these stories about the chocolates and dinners and flowers and so on. Were you in love with Derek Lewis?

No one, from Michael Howard to Miss Widdecombe herself, could complain that this opening question lacked directness. Previous discussion of the subject by other interviewers and commentators had been on more pussyfooting lines. There is much to be said, in situations where personal motives are under discussion, for questions to be direct rather than prissy. Jeremy Paxman put the question in a firm but uninflected, essentially neutral voice and received an answer in an equally firm and obviously not unamused voice.

ANN WIDDECOMBE: Certainly not, and let me say very clearly, there were no chocolates, not a Commons dinner, not a petal of flowers all the time Derek Lewis was in charge of the Prison Service. As I said, the only flowers to exchange hands at that time were from me to his wife on the day of his sacking.

PAXMAN: And you say for that the Home Secretary at the time, Michael Howard, bawled you out?

WIDDECOMBE: Perhaps bawled me out is more metaphorical than literal but he certainly expressed extreme displeasure and gave me a ticking off.

PAXMAN: Now you said his actions were unsustainably defended when you talked about it in the House of Commons. What did you mean?

WIDDECOMBE: I am not prepared to make any allegations I may make across the airways. So I want to establish the proper route to do it and to establish the proper way to do it, I shall make sure Michael Howard has due notice before.

PAXMAN: Why do you think these allegations have been made now about you and Mr Lewis?

WIDDECOMBE: I have no idea. Very clearly an attempt to discredit me. But the fact that they have been specific and have talked about things that didn't happen I think is central to our hand and has all been very helpful.

[She added that today she had planned to go to Scotland to be interviewed on something completely different, but had stayed all day to counter the allegations.]

PAXMAN: Do you know where they came from?

WIDDECOMBE: No, I do not know where they came from. It is certain they are Mr Howard's allies and I don't know who those allies are.

The interviewer could and perhaps should have put another question at this point, since it bore directly on her motives. While accepting that there had been no chocolates and dinners, or indeed anything in the least discreditable, could it be true that she had simply liked Mr Lewis personally and that her private liking had clouded her judgement on an essentially public issue? Instead the interviewer opted for an equally valid but different question touching on the interviewee's behaviour.

PAXMAN: Now you have explained why you didn't resign out of what you now considered to be perhaps a misplaced sense of loyalty to the Prime Minister. Presumably you now regret that?

WIDDECOMBE: I do regret not having resigned. I wish I had. What I am doing now is deeply painful to me although Michael may not realize that. It is not an easy thing to do, I wish I had resigned at the time. But, all I can say is, I believe that the dissensions which were within the party pretty well destroyed us. I would not have wanted to be one of those dissenters either before or during the general election and I only wish that most of my colleagues had taken the same view.

PAXMAN: But what a lot of us find hard to understand is why you didn't resign then, while Mr Howard had the power directly over the lives of prisoners throughout the country, police officers, every citizen of the country really, in a way? I mean if he really had something of the night about him, as you say, why didn't you act then instead of when he is merely running for the leadership of your party?

WIDDECOMBE: Look, let me make it very clear. My objections to what Mr Howard did were not all-encompassing directions in the way he ran the Prison Service. . . . As far as I am concerned Mr Howard and I had policy agreements almost continually throughout his term of office. And I have to say, and I have said it in the House and I will say it again, he was a very, very able Home Secretary in terms of executing his policies—

The interviewer got the interviewee away from all the issues on which she and the former Home Secretary had agreed and back on to the central, contested, issue. This was quite justified: the public wants to know about the one occasion when two cars crash, not the million occasions when two cars don't crash.

PAXMAN: Is he a man the public can trust?
WIDDECOMBE: That is for the public to judge. I have merely put what I know in the public domain. That sort of judgement is for others, not for me.
PAXMAN: You say he has something of the night about him.
WIDDECOMBE: What I have put myself on the record I am prepared to elaborate on, what I have said privately . . . I don't think I want to elaborate on—
PAXMAN: What does something of the night mean?
WIDDECOMBE: I have just said to you, I don't want to elaborate on that.

Jeremy Paxman would have been perfectly entitled to ask her again precisely what she had meant. The phrase presumably suggested that there was a dark side to Michael Howard. There could even have been an oblique suggestion of dark forces in a haunted house on the lines of a Hammer horror film. The interviewer could well have asked her point-blank, and kept on asking fourteen times (the same number of times he was later to put a question to the former Home Secretary) what exactly she had meant by an elliptical phrase which, after all, she had uttered in public. If she had still refused to elaborate he could have asked her whether her choice of enigmatic rather than clear words was because she wished to wound but was afraid to strike. He did not do so.

Was he right not to do so? He would have been perfectly entitled to justify the omission on the grounds that the crucial issue was whether Michael Howard was fit to be leader of the Conservative Party, not Ann Widdecombe's motives in choosing the phrase she had done; she, after all, was not a candidate for the leadership of the chief Opposition party. The interviewer's next question was aimed direct at this point.

PAXMAN. But you wouldn't trust him to lead your party?
WIDDECOMBE: I am not supporting his candidature . . .
PAXMAN: Thank you.

Paxman then turned to Michael Howard, whom he physically faced in the studio. The first few questions concerned the *Daily Mail* story about the alleged presents rather than the substantive matter, and in the course of answering these Michael Howard distanced himself from the story.

PAXMAN: Mr Howard, do you condemn these stories about flowers and dinners and chocolates?

HOWARD: Yes, and they do not come from my campaign team, let me make that absolutely clear. And my understanding is that the journalist who wrote the story in the *Daily Mail* to which you have referred has confirmed that he did not speak to anyone in or near my campaign team before he wrote that article.

PAXMAN: Clearly they came from somebody sympathetic to you, though.

HOWARD: Well, not necessarily at all, I have no idea who they came from. If you look at the article as a whole it is not a particularly sympathetic piece.

PAXMAN: Would you agree that such stories are cheap and nasty and bring shame on anyone who spreads them?

[This was delivered as a statement rather than a question.]

HOWARD: I don't think we should be wasting anybody's time talking about stories like that. I don't think they should ever have appeared in the public prints and I don't think we should waste our time talking about them. There are serious issues to be discussed since they have been raised about the dismissal of Derek Lewis as head of the Prison Service, a decision which I had to take in the light of an independent report, not mentioned in your introduction, which came to the conclusion that there were inexcusable weaknesses in the management of the Prison Service from top to bottom.

PAXMAN: Why did you bawl out Ann Widdecombe for sending flowers in what she thought was a Christian gesture to Mrs Lewis?

HOWARD: I didn't, as indeed she has just confirmed.

PAXMAN: She said you were extremely—

HOWARD: She said I didn't bawl her out.

PAXMAN: She said she objected to the words 'bawl out' but she said you were extremely agitated about it.

HOWARD: I thought it an inappropriate thing to do, given that I had just dismissed Mrs Lewis's husband. But I hope we are not going to spend all this time talking about flowers and things like that.

PAXMAN: Mr Howard, have you ever lied in any public statement?

HOWARD: Certainly not. I gave a very full account of the dismissal of Derek Lewis in the House of Commons Select Committee and in the House of Commons itself in a debate that took place. There can have been few decisions that have been subjected to more close and minute scrutiny in recent years than that decision. It was a decision that it was necessary for me to take after the terrorists had escaped from Whitemoor, other dangerous prisoners had escaped from Parkhurst and an independent report had found that there were serious weaknesses in the management of the Prison Service from top to bottom.

PAXMAN: Is there anything you would wish to change about your statements to the House of Commons or any other public statement you made about this matter?

This question is often a useful preliminary to tightening the interviewer's noose. Ostensibly, it enables the interviewee to change his position on any matter if he thinks that truth or technique requires it. In fact at that point it would have been very difficult for the interviewee to do anything other than maintain that there was nothing he had said that he wished to alter. The obvious next (dangerous) question after this particular one has been answered with a fairly predictable 'no' is, 'Then how do you explain so-and-so?'

HOWARD: No. Nothing. I gave a full account of what had happened in relation to my decision.

PAXMAN: Right. Can you help us with this, then?

This is a useful phrase to precede a body-blow question or series of body-blow questions. It has the flavour of an advocate in court, suggesting that naturally a witness is willing to help the court in any way he can. In this case, of course, there was no court, only one man interrogating the interviewee and no defending counsel, but an atmosphere had been established in which it was very difficult for the interviewee not to 'help'.

PAXMAN: You stated in your statement that the Leader of the Opposition had said that 'I' – that is you personally – told Mr Lewis that the governor of Parkhurst should be suspended immediately, that when Mr Lewis objected, as it was an operational matter, 'I threatened to instruct him to do it.' Derek Lewis says, 'Howard had certainly told me that the governor of Parkhurst should be suspended and had threatened to overrule me.' Are you saying that Mr Lewis is lying, then?

HOWARD: I have given a full acount of this and the position is what I told the House of Commons and let me tell you what the position—

PAXMAN: So you are saying Mr Lewis is lying?

This was a hard question to answer – it is never easy to call another human being a liar – but a quite legitimate question to ask. Had the Home Secretary threatened to overrule the director general of the Prison Service or not? If he had not, then by definition Derek Lewis was either lying or in serious and inexplicable error.

HOWARD: Let me tell you exactly what the position is. I was entitled to be consulted—

PAXMAN: Yes.

HOWARD: And I was consulted. I was entitled to express an opinion and I did express an opinion. I was not entitled to instruct Derek Lewis what to do and I did not instruct him what to do.

But the interviewer tenaciously held to the essential point that the director general had a differing view of what had happened.

PAXMAN: Well, his version of it—

HOWARD: And you will understand that, withal, Mr Marriott [the governor] was not suspended. He was moved and Derek Lewis told the Select Committee of the House of Commons that it was his opinion – Derek Lewis's opinion – that he should be moved immediately. That is what happened.

All had appeared to be comparatively plain sailing so far, but the preliminary questions, as we have already seen, had been put in the form of a net which was now tightened. Jeremy Paxman continued throughout to ask his questions in a quiet, reasonable, persistent but non-hectoring tone. No personal hostility came across, however probing the questions became. If the interviewer had been as aggressive in manner as his questions legitimately were in intent, the subject would soon have ceased to be Howard's behaviour and instead would have been about Paxman's – a digression every interviewer must always do his best to avoid.

PAXMAN: Mr Lewis says, 'I' – that is, Mr Lewis – 'told him what we had decided about Marriott and why. He –' that is you '– exploded. Simply moving the governor was politically unpalatable. It sounded indecisive, it would be seen as a fudge. If I did not change my mind and suspend Marriott, he would have to consider overruling me.' You can't both be right.

HOWARD: Mr Marriott was not suspended. I was entitled to express my views, I was entitled to be consulted.

PAXMAN (*first time of asking the simple direct question*): Did you threaten to overrule him?

HOWARD: I was not entitled to instruct Derek Lewis and I did not instruct him, and if you—

PAXMAN (*second time of asking*): But you attempted to overrule him?

HOWARD: The truth of the matter is Mr Marriott was not suspended.

PAXMAN (*third time*): Did you threaten to overrule him?

The critical question had now been placed in the centre of the arena. Did the then Home Secretary threaten to overrule the director general of the Prison Service or not, irrespective of whether this threat had actually been carried out? This was only the beginning of the long gruelling exchanges over one direct question that did not get answered, and which the slowest-witted viewer could see, well before the fourth repetition, would never get answered.

HOWARD: I did not overrule Derek Lewis.

PAXMAN (*fourth time*): Did you threaten to overrule him?

HOWARD: I took advice on what I could or could not do and—

PAXMAN (*fifth time*): Did you threaten to overrule him, Mr Howard?

HOWARD: And I acted scrupulously in accordance with that advice.

PAXMAN (*sixth time*): Did you threaten to overrule him?

HOWARD: I did not overrule Derek Lewis—

PAXMAN (*seventh time*): Did you threaten to overrule him?

HOWARD: Mr Marriott was not suspended.

PAXMAN (*eighth time*): Did you threaten to overrule him?

HOWARD: I have accounted for my decision to dismiss Derek Lewis—

PAXMAN (*ninth time*): Did you threaten to overrule him?

HOWARD: – in great detail before the House of Commons.

PAXMAN (*tenth time*): I note you are not answering the question, whether you threatened to overrule him?

HOWARD: Well, the important aspect of this, which it is very clear to bear in mind—

PAXMAN (*eleventh time*): Okay, I'm going to be frightfully rude, but—

HOWARD: Yes.

PAXMAN (*twelfth time*): But I'm sorry, it is a straight yes or no question: did you threaten to overrule him?

HOWARD: I discussed this matter with Derek Lewis. I gave him the benefit of my opinion. I gave him the benefit of my opinion in strong language. But I did not instruct him because I was not entitled to instruct him. I was entitled to express my opinion and that is what I did.

PAXMAN (*thirteenth time*): With respect, then, it is not answering the question of whether you threatened to overrule him.

HOWARD: It is dealing with the relevant point of what I was entitled to do and what I was not entitled to do. And I have dealt with this in detail before the House of Commons and before the Select Committee.

PAXMAN (*fourteenth and final unavailing time*): With respect, you haven't answered the question of whether you threatened to overrule him.

HOWARD: You see, the question is what was I entitled to do and what wasn't I entitled to do. I was not entitled to instruct him, and I did not do that. I—

PAXMAN: We will leave that aspect there and move on to this question of
whether you are fit for the leadership of the party. Wouldn't a reasonable
person conclude that someone who is unable even to unify a very small
ministerial team in less than two weeks of losing office is quite incapable of
unifying a party?

The former Home Secretary replied that there were many of his
colleagues who felt differently; and the interview proceeded on other
lines, leaving the question of whether Michael Howard had *threatened*
to overrule Lewis unanswered.

Should the interviewer have asked the same question yet again – or
had he already asked it many times too often?

There are valid arguments on either side. It might be argued that if
the interviewer had continued to persist, the interviewee might have
lost his temper and blurted out something revealing. This would have
been a remote gamble: Michael Howard's tone had remained glacially
calm throughout. The atmosphere between the two men was not that
of a boxing ring but of a chess game between masters. The manners of
both men were exemplary. Jeremy Paxman, though displaying the
tenacity of a bulldog, always spoke in the lightest and most polite of
tones, as if questioning an injured person about a street accident. He
certainly could not be accused of harassment, except in the sheer
number of times he asked the coolly put question. If criticized for his
persistence he would have been perfectly entitled to point out that he
would not have needed to put the same question fourteen times if it
had been answered: for the interviewee repeatedly to deny having in
practice overruled his director general of the Prison Service was no
answer at all to the question of whether he had threatened to do so.

The argument that fourteen times was several times too many has a
certain appeal. Every interviewer must always be on his guard against
the danger of being merely gladiatorially vainglorious without regard
for what this will actually achieve. By the third or fourth time of
asking it was perfectly obvious that the interviewee was going to
decline to answer the question, and the average viewer might well
already have formed the view, right or wrong, that the former Home
Secretary was not answering the question because the true answer was
that, yes, indeed, he must have threatened to overrule the director
general of the Prison Service, as the director general had himself
alleged.

Public relations consultants would almost certainly advise that
evading or refusing to answer a question is nearly always a mistake,
because evasion always gives the worst impression possible, justified or
not. Far better to say exactly what happened, and to give a full expla-

nation of why it happened. You and I were not at the crucial meeting and do not know for certain what really happened. In the case of a purely fictitious former Home Secretary, an interviewer with a different approach might well have put to him something like this: 'Mr Blank, wasn't it the case that escapes of dangerous prisoners from jails was becoming a public scandal and the moment came when you advised the director general of the Prison Service to suspend the governor of Blank prison, and when he refused you became very angry and said to him, "Look, don't you understand something decisive has got to be done and seen by the public to be done damn quickly? If you don't get off your backside and do something about this ludicrous situation of prisoners walking out all over the place, I will!" And then you realized that constitutionally, although you could advise the director general, you couldn't in effect threaten to overrule him, and that what you had said could be interpreted in that way, so you have tended to evade questions on it?'

If such a fictitious former Home Secretary had 'come clean' with that explanation, he would probably have satisfied interviewers and the public more. He would probably have ended up with more rather than less public sympathy: the fellow, it would have been thought by the public, was merely trying his best to end a wave of prison escapes and he deserved sympathy if in the course of trying to get something done he had temporarily lost his cool and said more than he should have done.

But to say anything of that nature would have taken a different interviewer and a different interviewee. Probably neither Jeremy Paxman nor the rest of us will ever know what really happened over the dismissal of Derek Lewis as director general of the Prison Service. Nor will we ever know what would have happened if an interviewer had put a question on the lines I have just indicated. What we *did* discover from the interview, a discovery valuable in itself, was that a prospective leader of a major political party was a man who could coolly evade a direct question fourteen times. It said much about his composure and determination, but it also said other things.

For that reason alone, Jeremy Paxman's *Newsnight* confrontation was a remarkable and professionally instructive example of the craft of hard-pressing interviewing technique. It is not a technique for all seasons, but it has a lot to be said for it when dealing with political heavyweights who are perfectly capable of looking after themselves in a critical situation.

Chapter 26

Recreating the Moment

There are occasions when it may not be the ideal time to produce the ideal interview, yet the interviewer nevertheless has to conduct it at that time.

Ideally, let us say, the interview should have been conducted three weeks ago, when the interviewee, an overseas entrepreneur, first arrived in this country with his business plan for buying all the royal palaces, allowing the present incumbents to occupy suites in them and converting the rest into luxury hotel accommodation.

Perhaps the significance of his arrival, bearing scale models of how the palaces would look after conversion, was not sufficiently appreciated at the time for an interview to be sought. Perhaps no one took him seriously. Perhaps his arrival was not announced. One way or another, the opportunity was missed.

Obviously the next logical time for an interview, the next logical news peg, would be when he leaves in another three weeks with his scheme either accepted or rejected. But editorial pressure, perhaps itself under competitive pressure from other media, may be to produce an interview here and now to stand beside inconclusive news stories about his visit, the result of which is still uncertain.

The answer may be a composite, a blend of on-the-spot interview with background facts and reflections, designed to recreate a moment (his arrival at Heathrow with his scale models) which has now passed.

Normally, the fewer background facts shovelled cold into an interview the better. There is no point in meeting someone for an hour in order to regurgitate material you already had in your cuttings file or notebook: the occasion, not your memory of past facts or your notebook, should be the thing that is milked. But when the time is wrong for an ideal interview but right in terms of something else – let us say the publication of a book or the release of a film which will be an ideal news peg – a composite of immediate impressions and background facts may be the only productive way forward.

I have mentioned a fictitious case by way of illustration. Perhaps a real one, though less potentially momentous, will be an even better illustration. Researching his novel *Felix In The Underworld*, John Mortimer spent substantial amounts of time with those unfortunate homeless people sleeping out in cardboard boxes behind the Savoy Hotel in London between Lincoln's Inn and Shell-Mex House. These residents of so-called Cardboard City must have had uneasy and genuine resonances for a man who was a successful barrister as well as a writer and a card-carrying liberal who could safely be predicted to be on the libertarian ticket except on hunting (his wife hunts). It would have been a wonderful piece had he been interviewed in his cashmere overcoat, talking to the Cardboard City citizens and they had been interviewed after talking to him.

But between the researching of a novel and its publication there is a gap of many months. The ideal thing would have been for an interviewer to go with John Mortimer on his Cardboard City travels, freeze the resultant copious notes for a few months and then integrate them into the final piece produced at the time of the publication of the book.

Real life journalism is not like that. No journalist would want to put work in cold storage for use at a much later date. What if someone else in the meantime published in essence the same interview as the one for which the notes had been taken? There is always a pressure on journalists to produce, and to produce *now*.

'What are you doing today, Smith?'

'I am spending all day and all night interviewing John Mortimer and some citizens of Cardboard City.'

'When do we get the story?'

'In nine months' time.'

'You're fired.'

That conversation is easily imagined.

The solution in *The Times*, on the publication of *Felix In The Underworld*, was a large picture of John Mortimer in his elegant overcoat under a collonade frequented by those sleeping out (but none of them in view in the photograph), accompanied by an interview by Valerie Grove.

Valerie Grove is one of the most consistently successful interviewers in the business, displaying both expert technique and innate intelligence, so that form and content are in happy alliance. It is entirely possible that she asked John Mortimer if she could accompany him on one of his night rounds and that he declined because he did not want the homeless people to whom he was talking to think he was disrespectful of them. Or she may have judged that an interview would be most suitable just after the publication of the book, and therefore have ignored the author's visits to Cardboard City.

The author's novel had as its main character a respectable middle class novelist, not entirely unlike himself, who eventually finds himself sharing the plight of the homeless.

Not seeing the author in action for ourselves, as it were, was a pity from the point of view of the effectiveness of the interview. There would certainly have been more immediacy if the interview had been conducted while John Mortimer was in Cardboard City. But the interviewer made up for the omission by coupling what was in essence a 'straight' interview with the author, which could have been conducted anywhere (but was in fact conducted at the Garrick Club, with Melvyn Bragg and Sir Jeremy Isaacs sitting nearby) with the technique of throwing the emphasis more or less constantly on to the homeless. They were never actually shown to the reader at first hand, but their presence was always strongly felt.

The intro to the interview, which was entitled 'A Voyage Round Cardboard City', powerfully and immediately set the scene:

> The homeless beggars in cardboard boxes behind the Savoy have become accustomed to finding John Mortimer looming alongside them.

Was there an element of gentle sardonic humour? John Mortimer is a large, well-fed and well-clothed man; there is certainly something of an anomaly in his presence among beggars, an anomaly he would be the first to recognize and which was one of the points of his book.

> 'Nice, gentle people,' he says – Mortimer is incapable of an illiberal thought – 'who talked about Rumpole, and read the *Evening Standard.*'

The interviewer swiftly followed up by describing the nature of the contact between Mortimer and those he had come to observe.

> Mortimer is now friendly with several of the characters who sleep out between Lincoln's Inn and Shell-Mex House, guarding their territory and setting out their possessions as carefully as sailors or monks. He says apart from the young, who may be drug addicts and prostitutes, and a few 'totally mad old women,' they tend to be 'confused middle-aged men who just can't cope after their families fall apart. Or young soldiers so institutionalized after the Army they can't look after themselves.'
>
> One businessman he met, said the author, couldn't face the back-tax he owed, and slept in the doorway of the Inland Revenue in Kingsway.

Citizens could make £30 a night, and if they spent it on a six pack of lager, he didn't mind. It was a perfectly honourable profession, begging; and he had never found them at all threatening. 'I'm very much in favour of giving money to beggars; I feel no moral outrage. After all, I beg the entire time. For the Royal Court I'm holding out my hand for £5 million.'

It would have been easy for the interviewer to point out the difference between helping an appeal for a celebrated theatre and begging crumbs on one's own behalf, but the interviewer was subtle enough to steer clear of any overt comment. She allowed him to talk on, alleging that politicians from the American President Bill Clinton to the British Home Secretary Jack Straw were telling the rest of us that we lived 'inside a stockade of property-owning, law-abiding decent people. Outside are the ravening hordes of alien beings who must be kept at bay. I wanted to show how we're all part of the same society, and how Felix could be reduced to living among them.'

It is as well to vary the tone in any interview, especially perhaps in the case of interviews on downbeat subjects, otherwise compassion fatigue may set in.

The rest of the interview was an attempt to recreate the atmosphere of Cardboard City only in the sense that, though it dealt with matters more usually discussed in author interviews, those matters tended to be involved in some way with social concern. The subject matter moved on, but the mood cunningly remained.

Readers were first treated to a discussion of the compulsions that drive a writer and the recent products of those compulsions. An updater on work in progress is a virtually obligatory element in an interview with a writer or other artist. The author had completed a new play and a film script for Franco Zeffirelli, *Tea With Mussolini*, and a film of Jessica Mitford's *Hons and Rebels*. He was also writing a *Paradise Postponed* update in which the Conservative MP of humble origins, Leslie Titmuss, now Lord Titmuss, colludes with Labour to defeat those who overthrew Mrs Thatcher as Prime Minister.

The interviewer then gave a quietly amused and amusing glance at the author's other activity: performing his anthology, *Mortimer's Miscellany*, in 'improbable venues'. Mortimer himself was quoted:

The adrenalin, the relief when it's over, no drug could produce the sensation. Like delivering your final speech in a murder trial – when you know the jury will do the rest. Back we go into the car drinking champagne and eating petrol-station sandwiches.

Again there was no attempt at derision, which was just as well, because the proceeds of the readings went to Turville Village School, bought for £220,000 and now run as a nursery school which was open in the holidays to deprived inner city children.

The picture of Mr and Mrs Mortimer on 1997 general election night added to the portrait. Before dancing with Labour Party workers at the Royal Festival Hall to celebrate their victory, they had gone to see Ian Holm's King Lear. Mortimer was quoted as saying, 'I took off my glasses when he took off his clothes', a droll reminder that even libertarians have to acknowledge contradictions in their position. But he had 'never seen so many pleased Conservatives', which must have helped.

Valerie Grove asked him about his support of fox-hunting but did not, perhaps, press him as hard on the subject as she could have done and the anti-hunting lobby would have liked. She did, however, draw an amusing picture of the bulky author's delicate situation: he was against the current fox-hunting Bill; had never hunted himself though his wife ran a campaign called Leave Country Sports Alone that led to them receiving disgusting things through the letterbox; and was aware that his position on hunting meant he was unlikely to become Lord Mortimer under the new Labour government.

> The Bill suggests authoritarianism, political correctness, a tendency to believe that you should send people to prison just for doing something you don't like. Labour is footling about with things that don't matter. Fox-hunting doesn't matter a twit, does it? If liberty means anything, it means tolerance of people who do things you don't approve of, like smoking and fox-hunting.

Faced with any argument that is as leaky as a sieve, an interviewer must quickly make up his mind: is he going to pursue the matter or not? It is tempting to do so.

Valerie Grove could have asked whether the important point was not whether hunting was likeable but whether it was cruel. She could have asked at what point cruelty and the enjoyment of cruelty ceased to 'matter'. Did cruelty to children 'matter'? To domestic pets? To stray animals? Did teenage gangs kicking a wild rabbit to death for fun 'matter'? Would it 'matter' if you came home and found your child pulling the wings off houseflies (undesirable pests, like foxes) for fun? If so, why did it not 'matter' when human beings had foxes torn to pieces for fun?

The interviewer in this case was, in my view, probably right to leave the questions unasked. The whole subject had been argued over almost to extinction. Every reader was likely already to know the for and against fox-hunting arguments by heart, backwards and forwards. No new argument or insight was likely to be produced by asking further questions. In any case the subject (except in so far as it was one aspect of the interviewee's social concern) was not central to the interview. It was far better to let the direct quote from the interviewee stand unchallenged, leaving readers to decide for themselves whether the interviewee's position was tolerant or self deceiving, and move on.

In this case, the interviewer moved on by adroitly pointing out that the interviewee was good at keeping self-revelation at bay. Even his autobiographies were 'masterpieces of non-revelation, written to amuse'.

She quoted him as follows: 'An interview is a work of fiction really. People say only as much as they want, and invent roles for themselves.'

Perhaps the interview, a vivid example of how to create an atmosphere (Cardboard City) without being there, and a view of a person without excessive comment and finger-pointing, should have ended there. As it was, it ended shortly afterwards with a comment about how Chekhov had behaved to his women like a cheetah behaved to its mates: having them once and then passing on. John Mortimer said he would have 'preferred not to know' this. Though it was a revelation of character, it was not quite so relevant to the terrain of the whole ingeniously mixed piece, a piece which effectively recreated events – Mortimer among the homeless – which were in the past.

Chapter 27

Only as good as . . .

All the interviewing dexterity in the world cannot compensate fully for a dull interviewee, whereas even simple unselective shorthand note-taking will reveal a great deal if the interviewee is an interesting enough person and a merely adequate conversationalist. It is a thought which should induce a degree of humility in even the most egotistical interviewer.

To claim that an interview can be only as good as the interviewee would be too discouraging, though not a few interviews appear in which the case for interviewing the person at all does not become overwhelmingly clear. The claim is almost true, but not entirely. It would be truer to say that an interview can be as good only as its inter-viewee, plus perhaps thirty to forty per cent.

With skill, an interviewer may produce an interesting piece of writing, radio or television out of a dull interviewee. But in such cases, the result may be less an interview proper than an essay by the interviewer with some material produced from what the interviewee occasionally said.

On television, Sir Robin Day, a star by temperament (i.e. I imagine always happiest when centre-stage, even if prepared to yield it as a professional necessity), was able to make it seem that many a charac-terless interviewee was interesting. Indeed, many politicians and other representatives of power groups on television and radio might have had all the properties of a general anaesthetic had it not been for his colourful goading. But the result was really a visual and audio illusion: chop out the footage involving him, leaving only the footage involving the interviewees, and the result would have been dire.

For an interview to be interesting as a whole, the interviewee has to be interesting or potentially interesting if handled in the right way. Comparatively dreary interviewees require more thoughtful handling than clever, articulate and characterful ones who have something to say and the ability to say it.

The point is most easily made by comparing a number of interviews conducted by the same interviewer. It will readily be seen that an open style of interviewing, in which the interviewee is given the nod to talk as he wants, works most effectively when the interviewee has interesting powers of thought and is accustomed to putting them across. The gaps in the finished result when the interviewee is not so full of ideas and the interviewer, understandably but wrongly, loses heart or interest and fails to press home questions in such a way that the result is more interesting, also becomes more clear.

The collection of interviews with contemporary British film makers, *Talking Pictures*, conducted by Graham Jones, edited by Lucy Johnson and published by the British Film Institute, is a useful illustration of the point. The same sort of questions produced greatly differing results, depending on the expansiveness and 'give' of the interviewees.

To some extent all the interviews made depressing reading, since conditions in the contemporary British film industry favour hucksterdom over creativity. True, the British film industry has been precarious throughout my lifetime, despite the efforts of financiers and creators like Alexander Korda, J. Arthur Rank, Michael Balcon, Richard Attenborough and Bryan Forbes. If I had £10 for every news story I have written about the parlous state of the British film industry, I am tempted to think that I would be considerably richer than the industry itself. I had a front row seat at one of the funerals when in the late 1960s I scripted my novel *Candidate of Promise* for Bryan Forbes to make after he took over Elstree Studios with the intention of restoring the British film industry with a slate of studio-based films, only to find that he fell victim to his own money men before it and several other planned films could be made.

The great days of the British film industry were just before the Second World War, during the Second World War and in the decade immediately after the Second World War, followed by a boom in the 1960s and 1970s when many films were made in and around swinging London with American finance. When swinging London ceased to be the international flavour of the month the Americans withdrew. There followed a Dark Age in which several British film studios closed down, Beaconsfield became the National Film and Television School, Shepperton became a 'four walls' studio with hardly any staff, producers being required to bring in their own; and Rank's Pinewood, the flagship of the British film industry, specialized almost exclusively in hiring out its excellent facilities to American producers.

Out of this situation, and the National Film and Television School, grew a generation of younger British film makers who were prepared to work for little or no money in order to put their films together for themselves.

Such is the background, certainly of interest to a wider audience than the participants themselves, against which Graham Jones produced his book of interviews. It could be argued that the obvious first question was: why did these young film makers bother? That question was not quite answered in *Talking Pictures*, in which the interviewees talked, and were allowed to talk, more at length about the 'how' rather than the 'why', more about how they had had to scour for funds than about the passion and artistry which alone could give the cash-scouring operation a point.

This interviewing stance could be excused on the grounds that ways and means were the things uppermost in the young film makers' minds and that the book amounted to a primer for young producers on how to survive. Yet, faced with an interviewee, it is usually if not always better to try to explore *why* he is doing what he is doing, if only to make the final result of more interest not only to the core audience but also to a lay audience who might conceivably be interested if human motives as well as technical means were explored.

Graham Jones is himself a film maker; he directed *How to Cheat in the Leaving Certificate*. As a participant, perhaps he thought the simple question, 'Why bother?' was redundant. Similarly, though the films made by the twenty-nine interviewees were mentioned, they were not described. Many of them were shorts or other films which might not have been seen on general release by the average reader. It was not possible to judge from the interviews alone whether the films mentioned were worth making or were catchpenny (or catchcent) trash. This was a pity.

When the interviewee was the sort of person able to produce sharp perceptions, the easygoing style of questioning could deliver the goods. For instance, Jones obviously asked Elisar C. Kennedy, director of *Demonsoul*, producer of a horror movie, *Virtual Terror*, and a worker in the film industry since the age of seventeen, at least one opening question about the crisis in the British film industry. But he expunged it from the page, allowing Kennedy to talk without apparent prompting.

The result was virtually an uninterrupted essay on the virtues of the non-academic approach to film making:

> It's like anything creative. . . . It's not going to a school and passing an exam and having a qualification. You don't need any qualifications for film making. That's probably why I knew while I was studying my A levels I wasn't going to go to university. I didn't feel I had to; I knew I wanted to work on film. . . . I didn't want to do film school partly

because I've volunteered on films at the National Film School, and I've seen students who have been hanging around there for years on end. It's supposed to be a three-year course, but you see students who are there five, six, seven, eight, nine or even ten years later and they still haven't left. They feel there's no reason to go outside the film school. They can't get out, because outside in the real world it's very cruel.

And so on. The interview (if not openly the interviewer) contrasted this with the low budget independent movies he had been working on in the USA costing about £350,000. He carried on talking for presumably over four minutes, producing over 500 words before the interviewer cut in with another question, about whether the independent film maker Roger Corman was 'somone we can all learn from'.

The deft interviewee replied, 'I think so,' and then resumed talking about his own ideas.

The result was that an interview taking perhaps half an hour was supported on only six visible questions, and yet was interesting and revealing.

In contrast, Paul Hills, a member of the New Producers Alliance (which other interviewees attacked as too cosy) and writer, producer and director of the feature film *Boston Kickout*, was almost monosyllabic. Twelve questions were needed – double that of the Kennedy interview – to support an interview of half the finished length.

Perhaps the interviewee just did not have much more to say? This can be a lazy assumption on the part of an interviewer. The more an interviewee comes across as a man of few words, the more an interviewer should, first, stand back and ask himself why this should be so, and then advance boldly with a new approach designed to prise more information and comment from the diffident mind and reluctant lips of the interviewee.

Here the interviewer's first question was a statement, never the wisest course to adopt with any interviewee unless you know beforehand that he will talk readily given the slenderest cue or no cue at all:

You've only just finished shooting *Boston Kickout*.

Was the interviewee really supposed to reply: 'No, I finished it ten years ago.'? Or, 'No, I shall not finish it for another ten months.'? If the interviewer knew that Paul Hills had only just finished shooting *Boston Kickout*, the question was at best redundant. Plainly as a potential trigger to any interviewee who tended to answer questions literally, it was also a turn-off. An interview conducted all on these lines could proceed as follows:

INTERVIEWER: You have got another film lined up.
INTERVIEWEE: Yes.
INTERVIEWER: You found it difficult getting the finance together.
INTERVIEWEE: Yes.
INTERVIEWER: That discouraged you.
INTERVIEWEE: Yes.
INTERVIEWER: You have never thought of giving up film making altogether.
INTERVIEWEE: No.

This is of course a gross exaggeration of the quite useful Jones-Hills interview, an interview which could nevertheless have been even more useful if the interviewer had wheedled a bit more, instead of apparently respecting as sacrosanct the monosyllabic utterances of the interviewee.

The interviewer, instead of merely firing at the interviewee something he already knew (i.e. that he had just completed shooting his film *Boston Kickout*) could have put quite a number of questions that might have got the interviewee talking at length. He might have asked, 'Having just completed the shooting of *Boston Kickout*, are you happy with the result?' He might have asked, 'Was the shooting of *Boston Kickout* more difficult than you had anticipated?' He might have asked, 'Having completed the shooting of *Boston Kickout*, how do you rate the commercial chances of the film?'

It might be thought that the question/statement in fact was just as good, because if the interviewee had had anything to say about his happiness with the result, the difficulties he had encountered, or the commercial prospects of the film, he could have voiced them whatever the question asked.

This might be true of some interviewees, but not all. Some would tell you what was on their minds whatever question you asked, but some would cautiously regard themselves as bound by the question actually asked and would give an answer strictly according to the wording of the question. These are the sort of interviewees who, asked, 'Have you enough American and British private finance to make your next film?' would reply, 'No', but fail to add, 'But we have enough Japanese and Asian finance to make the film.'

When handling a reticent interviewee, the more precise the questions the better. The aim should be to sculpt the questions in such a way that the interviewee feels that they are easy to answer. He should not be in any doubt about what the question is, or what is expected of him. The more 'difficult' or inarticulate the interviewee, the more important it is to remember this rule.

The interviewee in fact responded to the opening statement/question, 'You've only just finished shooting *Boston Kickout*' by replying:

> Yes, last Sunday. There was a scene that we had to pick up because we weren't allowed to film it where the film was set. It was a car ramming through the window of a shop. It's a rites of passage film about four young boys growing up in an English new town in Hertfordshire, what happens to them over the course of a summer, how they go their separate ways.

The interviewer then asked, 'How did you get the film together?' Paul Hills replied by citing his track record, including his first full length film, *The Frontline*, to which the interviewer asked, 'Did you actually get it released?'

Jumping from subject to subject because a monosyllabic interviewee does so is dangerous for an interviewer: either, or both, subjects can simply get lost. In this case, the interviewer did not allow this to happen; he followed up with questions on both *The Frontline* and *Boston Kickout*. But he did ask the overworked, 'How did you feel?' question:

JONES: How did you feel coming up to the first shoot?
HILLS: I felt more stressed on the night before the first day of shooting than I'd ever felt in my life. I couldn't concentrate on anything apart from the set-ups, the shots, the lenses.

The interviewer then had to ask the question that would already have been answered by a more forthcoming interviewee:

JONES: How did you approach shooting on the first day?
HILLS: I tried to shoot it as chronologically as possible. It was a long day, eighteen hours, twenty-seven set-ups: trying to make it look sunny when it was raining.

The interviewer, perhaps judging that he would get little more water out of this particular pump, then asked, 'Would you describe the role of line producer?' He could, and arguably should, have persistently asked for more information about the interviewee's feelings and actions on the first day of the shoot. The 'What did you feel?' question is a cliché, but having asked it, the interviewer might as well get as much out of it as possible. It may have been an instance where a professional journalist and interviewer would have fared better than a fellow film maker.

Interviewing is a technique as wide-ranging and yet as specific as that of the film maker. Those trained for it and experienced in it are likely to make fewer mistakes than those who aren't. This fact is most apparent when the interviewee is either reticent or when he is a blabbermouth who is not easy to stop or guide. Interviews of different people by the same interviewer, especially a non-professional interviewer, tend to bring this point out.

All interviewers must face the fact that a less than satisfactory interviewee cannot be made wholly satisfactory. Yet that fact should certainly never be made an excuse for not *trying* to make the interviewee interesting to the reader, listener or viewer. In such cases the interviewer should try even harder.

Part Three:
How Not to Interview

Chapter 28

Celebrity Prattle

CELEBRITY INTERVIEWEE: I am going to reveal something I have never revealed before– when I was nine I tried to murder my mother because my favourite colour was blue.

CELEBRITY INTERVIEWER: My favourite colour is yellow. Why do you like blue so much?

INTERVIEWEE: Well, I suppose the school uniform was blue and the armbands of the People's National Radical Movement, of which my father was then a leading member – this was of course before it was banned after the riots – wore blue; and he used to dress me up in these from the age of three, so that when my mother went out and bought me a brown frock instead of a blue one, I fetched a meat cleaver from the kitchen and—

INTERVIEWER: I remember being so disappointed when I wanted a railway set for Christmas and my mother got me a doll's house. These things are so traumatic, aren't they, I mean, especially when you are young, like you are as a child? Can you remember or recall any other interesting memories from your recollections of childhood?

INTERVIEWEE: There was a brief time when I was eleven and my father changed his sex as a result of, he said as he hit me with the handbag, being struck by a cricket ball at Lords. Later he reverted to being a man.

INTERVIEWER: I used to hate playing with a big hard ball when I was at school! I shall never forget one afternoon in June or it may have been July or August – it was at any rate quite hot, or would have been if the sky had not been overcast – I was wicket keeper at cricket. Oh, how I hated that! – And we had a huge great chap called Leonard (or that could have been someone else) and he used to bowl at enormous speed. I quite literally died of fear, literally! I shall always remember that last over. He went back at least thirty paces from the crease and then raced forward like a racing car or race horse or something like that, and his face was huge and red, and his big black eyes were glaring and he hurled the ball right at my face! It could have hit me, but it didn't. How old were you when you went to acting school?

INTERVIEWEE: I was telling you about how I came to try to murder my mother and my father became a woman—

INTERVIEWER: I can't let you get away with dodging the question! How old were you when you went to acting school?

INTERVIEWEE: That was after I had been bound over to keep the peace for putting a home-made firebomb – I have never talked about this before – into the letter box of the Socialist Union, just in order that I might have something to boast about to my father.

INTERVIEWER: When you went to acting school, did it ever occur to you that one day you would be the successful, charismatic, powerful, brilliant, rich and altogether intoxicating star of stage and screen you are today?

INTERVIEWEE: Well, certainly not at that time; that was later. The thing I first remember about drama school is Laurence Olivier coming to talk to us . . .

INTERVIEWER: Did he come by car? What was his car like? He must have had a very expensive car.

INTERVIEWEE: I don't remember. I shall always remember the suit he wore that day, when I first saw him. It was double breasted, or at least I think it was, blue with wide chalk stripes. But the thing I remember most is that he was also wearing open-toed sandals. I asked him why.

INTERVIEWER: I only met Laurence Olivier once and it was unforgettable. I can't remember when, but I do remember his memory was already failing, because he didn't know who I was. He had a terribly glazed look in his eyes, I remember, when we were being introduced. I felt so sorry for poor Larry, as I called him when he didn't know who I was, just to show him there was no ill-feeling. Did you ever meet Charlie Chaplin?

INTERVIEWEE: No.

INTERVIEWER: No?

INTERVIEWEE: No, because he died before I was born. But my father did. It was a Lord Mayor's Banquet, I think, or so he told me, and my father, who was also a guest, got hold of the lapels of Charlie Chaplin's dinner jacket, one of which began to come off, and bounced him up and down in his chair and told him he was a commie bastard who should be sent back to where he came from. He had momentarily forgotten that Chaplin had been born in England. The police had to be called to separate them. It never got into the papers, so my father said, because the reporters there were as drunk as everyone else. I asked myself then how much my father was a fantasizer, and came to the conclusion—

INTERVIEWER: My, we all used to knock it back in those days, didn't we? You must remember all sorts of embarrassing incidents, eh, after you'd had a few?

INTERVIEWEE: No, I'm a lifelong teetotaller. I vowed to be a teetotaller after seeing my father giving the Radical National Party salute outside the House of Commons on the twenty-fifth anniversary of VE Day, in the company of a woman he claimed was his third wife, although it was actually number eight . . .

INTERVIEWER: Well, that was fascinatingly fascinating, Miss Er, Er, but I'm afraid we have run out of time, and very fascinating it has been too, absolutely fascinatingly stunning. On my next programme I ask the Archbishop of Canterbury what he thinks of astrology . . .

Analysis

This fabricated interview was intentionally exaggerated wildly in order to make the point crystal clear. It was just about the worst possible example of the 'Celebrity Prattle' interview, in which a celebrity interviewer with no evident journalistic credentials gains airtime by failing to follow up interesting leads practically handed to him on a plate, preferring instead to prattle on about whatever happened to be at the forefront of his head, which was always self-centred waffle about minor and expendable points.

This type of interviewer would fail to be entertaining even before a late-night television audience which might legitimately be unprepared for any very mentally taxing material. It would be unfair to say that this is the type of interview that is likely to happen when an actor rather than a journalist conducts it. Many actors could do much better, but only if they followed at least some of the journalistic rules for an interview.

Until the 1950s, interviewing technique was based on newspaper practice and was practised mostly by newspapermen who had moved into television – Richard Dimbleby and Fyffe Robertson immediately spring to mind. They knew that the object of a question was simply to get the most revealing answer; nothing else mattered. Once television had become the dominant mass medium, the physical appearance of the interviewer became as important. This ruled out many fine journalists, including Sir William Connor (the columnist Cassandra of the *Daily Mirror*), whose bald head, spectacles and high-pitched voice, irrelevant in a print journalist, disqualified him from the medium of appearances.

There was a knock-on effect. The question asked by the interviewer became itself an art form, a public performance which had to withstand public scrutiny, unlike a newspaperman's question. Actors and those with actors' skills and qualifications moved into what had previously been regarded as a purely journalistic province. They had to be concerned with how they appeared in profile as well as with the interviewee and what he might have to say. If they had a few hairs out of place, viewers might jam switchboards with their complaints.

The interviewers could not help this. But, insidiously, the more vain of the new brand of interviewers were able to feel that they themselves were as important, if not more important, than the interviewees and the answers they were giving. They were wrong. They are wrong. The answers are what counts in an interview, even if an answer is no more than an evasive silence.

The point is not one of personal pique on the part of a newspaper journalist. If it were, it might not be worth making. If the 'acting school' version of questioner were really doing the job of a journalist, the public would not suffer. But sometimes they are not doing it in any meaningful sense; they are *failing* to do it.

In this particular interview, no journalist worthy of the name, whatever his background, could possibly have missed so many opportunities of following up points that mattered in favour of conducting a vapid 'two social equals conversing' chatter that led nowhere. Certainly it did not lead to increased knowledge of the interviewee, who was dying to explain why and how she had murdered a father who had led an extremist political group, changed his sex and generally deviated picturesquely from the norm.

Perhaps the interviewer was on a late show and simply trying to keep the tone a light one?

This defence will not do. A media interview of any type, whether for the printed page, radio or television is not a conversation, even though it may have a superficial resemblance to a conversation: it exists to extract information or truths. When serious matters are raised they must be addressed seriously. They must certainly not be ignored because they are outside the thinking processes of a 'celebrity' who may be preening himself in a journalist's chair but is not doing a journalist's hard job.

When press conferences for print and electronic media journalists are screened on television, it may appear that some of the questions asked by print journalists are not very good either. The truth is that newspapermen nowadays are sometimes reduced to the role of bit-part players in a public performance staged in and around a press conference, in which radio and television reporters as much as the interviewees are the star players. As bit-players, print journalists may be tempted to shout out banal questions like, 'How did you feel when the double decker bus hit you?' merely to show they are still there.

Some print reporters on such occasions use a cassette recorder rather than a notebook, perhaps because it makes them feel they are more part of the electronic age. It can be a self-deceiving measure. The tape recorder, like the sound camera, is itself a brainless idiot that will record nothing of value unless the right question has been posed by a skilled human being and a useful answer elicited. The discipline of a notebook, pen and cold words on paper will show you immediately when the answer amounts to little or nothing of use. An angry or flamboyant unrevealing answer may be 'wonderful television' in the mind of a producer, but in real terms it means nothing. At their worst, some television soundbites add up to little more than nothing. The television interviewer, more than the print journalist who can look at his notebook and see for himself that the answer amounts to nothing, needs to keep track of the point and not to allow the surrounding psychodrama to take over. A dramatic close shot of the Prime Minister's dilating nostrils as he dodges a point may disguise on television that the interviewer has failed to get a worthwhile answer; it will not disguise it for a newspaper reader.

The central difficulty is this: a television interview in a media-sophisticated age may be bland but it must not, except in extraordinary circumstances, be too uncomfortable, or else the wised-up powerful, influential and rich simply won't appear.

In the 1950s, before television had reached its present dominance, a distinguished and probing interviewer, John Freeman, himself a media tycoon and former Member of Parliament, interviewed the man who was then described as the first 'personality' to be made entirely by television, Gilbert Harding. It was on the television extended interview programme *Face to Face*, later revived with Jeremy Isaacs.

Harding was a man of Johnsonian incisive mind, a formidably bulky man with unsettling spectacles who became a star as a grumpy panellist on the television gameshow, *What's My Line*. Members of the panel had to guess the occupations of guests from their own maddeningly unclear miming: Harding often became front page news for his tetchy or rude treatment of them or his fellow panel members. When Harding, a repressed homosexual who had been deeply attached to his mother, was himself grilled on *Face To Face*, he was asked whether he had ever wept as an adult. He admitted, through falling tears, that he had wept at the death of his mother. Freeman, who was thought to have known the answer beforehand, was widely criticized for what was regarded as an insensitive approach.

Subsequent celebrity interviews on television, even those conducted with the skill and intelligence of a Michael Parkinson, tended not to probe as deeply into highly personal matters. It became widely recognized, even if not explicitly stated, that television was of its nature a medium which made participants more personally exposed, and that questioning should therefore be less ruthless than some newspaper questioning had been and continued to be, except, perhaps, in the case of politicians. Blandness was better than cruelty.

David Frost, on television live, interviewed Dr Emil Savundra, a confidence trickster who was arrested virtually as he left the television studio. For Frost, this was a professional *tour de force*. He was criticized in some quarters for alleged 'trial by television'. It is less likely today that a Dr Savundra would voluntarily go before the cameras, and even less likely that he would incriminate himself.

Politicians, who are virtually compelled to put themselves on the line, especially at election times, are still regarded as fair game. The public's 'right to know' is held to be more important than the feelings of individual politicians. For this reason, politicians have become much more expert at fielding interviewers' awkward questions. Though media interviewers with (possibly undeserved) blander reputations, such as Jimmy Young, have interviewed prime ministers, it is usually the more hardnosed interrogators, such as David or Jonathan Dimbleby, John Humphrys, James Naughtie or Jeremy Paxman who are let loose on top politicians. Paxman was aggrieved, and some of the viewing public disappointed, when during the 1997 general election he was relegated to what his admirers saw as a too minor role. He was perhaps seen as being altogether *too* different from the bland celebrity interviewer just shown doing his flea-brained work – an interviewer who couldn't even round off the programme intelligently.

Except for a few meaningless, tautologous, 'buzz' clichés by way of sycophantic praise, which had no specific application to the interviewee but could have been equally applied to anybody else ('fascinatingly fascinating . . . very fascinating . . . absolutely fascinatingly stunning . . .') the interviewer simply left the interviewee and the audience in mid-air.

Admittedly for an interviewer to attempt to summarize an interview is a cumbersome and dangerous policy, especially if the electronic media audience is getting restive. But an interview is ended more satisfactorily for interviewer and interviewee (and audience if it is on the electronic media) if the interviewee is encouraged to make a last remark worth the making.

Simply dropping the interviewee and referring to the next person you are going to interview is ill-mannered, since it suggests that the interviewer is now bored with the interviewee and is passing on to the next as if they were a string of sausages. Even by the rules of stage performance, with which one might expect such interviewers to be familiar, this is an anticlimax rather than a satisfactory climax.

Be as little like the Celebrity Chatterer as possible.

Chapter 29

Too Many Questions

INTERVIEWER: Prime Minister, you predicted last year when you reviewed the economic performance of this country and discussed future taxation policy that gross national product would rise in the next year by five per cent and that there would be no increase in income tax. You promised to resign if these two things did not come about. Today you announced that the gross national product had been increased by a figure much lower than five per cent, and that you were increasing income tax by ten pence in the pound. Are you going to resign?

PRIME MINISTER: I fully share your concern that the gross national product has not risen by as much as I would have liked, my colleagues would have liked, the country would have liked, indeed everyone would have liked except the members of the Opposition, who are constantly trying to talk down and undermine this country and our financial policies to correct some of its ills.

INTERVIEWER: But Prime Minister, you said—

PRIME MINISTER: May I just complete this important point? It is true not only of ourselves but of our friends in Europe and, indeed, in the group of seven most developed and wealthy nations of the world that gross national product has not increased according to expectations. I do not seek to disguise or minimize that fact at all. We all dislike it, myself as much or more than anybody, but—

INTERVIEWER: But do you dislike it to the point where you feel bound to—

PRIME MINISTER: May I just enter my qualification, since you asked the question? *But* there is reason to hope that we are in the vanguard of nations whose gross national product is indeed on the increase – though not of course as much as we and most of them would have hoped – and we are confident that if we continue with our policies as outlined that next year I will have a brighter picture to convey to you.

INTERVIEWER: Yet, Prime Minister, at the very moment when prescription charges in the National Health Service are going up again, you have chosen to increase income tax by ten pence in the pound, something which last

year you promised not to do and undertook to resign if you did. So do
you—

PRIME MINISTER: The increase in prescription charges is regrettable, and no
one regrets it more than I do. But if we might just look at prescription
charges now and compare them with what they were under the
Opposition, I think we will find that, taking inflation into account, the
charges, even with the latest increases, are in line with what they were
when the Opposition were in power for many of their wasted years. The
Health Service has been attacked because it is under-funded and yet the
moment the government seeks to obtain more money in ways that do not
have to come out of the taxpayers' pockets – that means you, me and every
taxpayer in the country—

INTERVIEWER: But Prime Minister, you repeated when you were a guest at
the Trades Union Congress six months ago, and were pelted with eggs by
people standing on the pavement as you arrived, and given a cool welcome
inside, that if income tax went up you would—

PRIME MINISTER: I was not surprised when the reception I received at the
Trades Union Congress was a cool one; I was disappointed but not
surprised. It is hard, of course it is hard, when people are enduring hard-
ships in the present to look to the future when our policies, if we stay on
course and are not swayed from unpopular measures by a dishonest desire
for cheap short-term popularity, will lead to a real and permanent increase
in wealth.

INTERVIEWER: So there is no question of your re—

PRIME MINISTER: I would say to the Trades Union Congress: trust us to
meet you halfway.

INTERVIEWER: Thank you, Prime Minister, we've run out of time . . .

PRIME MINISTER: My mood is one of quiet confidence.

Analysis

The interviewer made what is a classic mistake in either print or electronic media interviews. He asked two questions at once, or presented
two trains of thought at once. The interviewee was therefore able to
seize on the easy one and ignore the tough one.

Provided all subsequent questions have this duality, a half-hour interview in front of a camera or a notebook can be survived easily by the
interviewee without his ever having to address a tough question at all.

If the interviewer had initially stuck to the essential point – whether
the Prime Minister was going to resign – and the Prime Minister had
dodged the question, the evasion would have been obvious. But when an
interviewee addresses himself to one half of a question it may well seem

rude if the interviewer then rebukes him for not answering the other half. The interviewee is able to give the impression of cooperation and helpfulness while in fact consistently running away from the vital point.

The difficulty is more pronounced for radio or television interviewers. Face to face with the interviewee, with only a notebook between them, a newspaper interviewer might be able to pull a face at the evasion and butt in: 'Are you going to resign or not?' On radio or television this might come across as graceless, gauche or otherwise 'unprofessional'. And since the radio or television interviewer has to consider his own questions and interjections as part of the whole package, there is a psychological pressure on him to be bland rather than risk apparent rudeness.

At a press conference, especially with a very large number of journalists present, a newspaper interviewer is in a similar position to that of the radio or television journalist. If he attempts to come back after only the 'easy' part of his double-barrelled question has been answered, he risks alienating his rival colleagues by looking as if he wants to hog the proceedings. His pleas that his question hasn't in fact been answered can be ignored by the interviewee, who will be well aware that the interviewer's rivals would rather ask their own question than support a rival in his contention that his question has not been fully answered.

It may be argued that if an interviewer is at a well-attended press conference he may *have* to put a two-part question, because he knows that he is unlikely to have two chances of putting a single question. The reasoning is faulty. It is certainly true that it is best to avoid laconic brevity ('Prime Minister, are you going to resign?') because that may seem to justify an equally laconic answer ('Would you?'), which gets no one anywhere. But though a single question should be put with considered politeness, of the sort which would seem to call for an answer in a similar vein, a two or three part question is almost always a liability. Quite apart from the danger of making it easy for the interviewee deliberately to evade the difficult part of the question, it may simply make it difficult for the interviewee to remember all the points of a multi-pointed question.

The simple, one-point question is sometimes unpopular with journalists, especially at press conferences, because it may make the questioner look naïve. There is some temptation to phrase questions in such a way as to put the questioner in a good light rather than to elicit a revealing answer. It should be resisted. As in any other type of interview, private or in the glare of television lights, it is the answers, not the questions, that matter.

If you doubt this for one moment, consider the next interview.

Chapter 30
Too Big a Question

INTERVIEWER: Hamish MacTavish, as president of the Scotch Whisky Duty Reduction Group, you have seen the fortunes of the Scotch whisky industry rise and fall in past years, principally though not always as a result of government taxation and duty policies, and you have on many occasions been critical of the government, notably in the Geneva customs and excise international conference of five years ago, when the British government claimed that its losses on uncollected duty were possibly as high as one and a quarter per cent of the total product, when the Japanese were asked by the conference by seventeen votes to twelve to make it clearer in their labelling that their Scotch-type whisky was in fact produced in Japan and when you argued unsuccessfully for a graduated duty on Scotch whisky based on the quality and price of the whisky, which would have borne most heavily on producers of Scotch whisky at 43, 46 and 52 per cent alcoholic content, and given some relative relief to producers of the more standard 40 per cent; and you have consistently opposed the views of the Temperance Alliance that higher duty on Scotch whisky would cut excessive consumption that in the past year alone has led to a rise in the number of working days lost due to alcohol abuse from three per cent to four point seven per cent, a conclusion underlined as you will remember by the recent report of the government's public health inspectorate into working days lost due to all causes, in which it was shown that the days lost due to all other causes but alcohol were down on the previous year by almost one full percentage point but that the absences ascribed to alcohol abuse were up by rather over the percentage suggested by the TA report; in the light of the lack of success of many of your own past campaigns, including those to discredit the findings of the Temperance Alliance and the government's public health inspectorate, and in the light of the Japanese government's recently announced protective measures for its own whisky production, would you say, keeping your answer reasonably brief because we are running out of time, that the interests of Scotch whisky would be best served by a completely new pressure group rather than your own?

HAMISH MacTAVISH: No.

Analysis

This is an extreme (and of course quite fictional as to the details about Scotch whisky and governmental and other happenings) example of a question which illuminates absolutely nothing except the interviewer's own knowledge and ego. The interviewee might just as well not have been there.

Once news was reported mainly by general reporters, who did their best to remedy their own ignorance by simply asking questions as any other member of the general public might have done. News is now more often reported, in print, radio and television, by specialists, who tend to carry the title of 'correspondent' or even 'editor' as distinct from mere 'reporter'.

In some ways this is beneficial: improved interrogatory skills based on knowledge should give interviewees a tougher ride. In this, as in every other department of journalism or life, nothing comes free. There is a price to be paid. The price here is that the Imbibing Correspondent or Imbibing Editor (as distinct from mere general reporter), conscious that his job is envied and coveted by his younger ambitious colleagues, will feel tempted to saddle any interview he conducts with far too much of his own technical expertise, thus almost relegating the answers to his questions to the status of footnotes.

This eventually becomes a form of pomposity that gets between the reader, listener or viewer and the subject on which he wants the interviewee's views. The overload of knowledge becomes worse than irrelevant, it becomes an active nuisance.

The interviewer would have done better to ask Mr MacTavish a simple first question like, 'There are people who claim that because your campaigns to reduce drastically the duty on Scotch whisky have not been successful, your Scotch Whisky Duty Reduction Group should be replaced by another organization. Would you regard that as fair?'

If the answer were to be, 'Anyone who knows anything about the history of duty on the Scotch whisky industry would not ask that question', then the interviewer would be quite justified in parading some of his expert knowledge, provided always that he followed it up with questions as penetrating and as short as he could possibly make them. The interviewee would then be faced with the knowledge as well as the questions. He could not easily duck.

In other words, a display of knowledge by the interviewer is best used defensively, not aggressively or gratuitously, when it will only get in the way.

Chapter 31

Over to You

(Transcription of unedited tape)

INTERVIEWER: Seamy Hackman, you have been attacked for alleged bad taste for the scene in your latest novel, *Mummy's Victims*, in which the family have a funeral dinner off their mother's coffin only to find, when they open the lid to extract previously forgotten gold fillings from her teeth, that the coffin contains a headless man wearing a g-string and black leather boots.

SEAMY HACKMAN: You mean the first page. Well, I don't understand what all the fuss is about, really. It is art, you as a novelist yourself must see that. One of the most time-honoured tricks in fiction is that of surprise.

INTERVIEWER: But surely there can't be any surprise in a first chapter. Unless the tone of the book has already been established in previous chapters on different lines to that of your surprise, there can't be any surprise, can there? There can only be shock, of which many critics have accused you.

SEAMY HACKMAN: I think we may be splitting hairs there, Mervyn. Dickens, Thackeray, George Eliot, Jeffrey Archer and that man who used to snort a ton of coke a day, they have all done it. People must be narrow-minded if they object to the second chapter of *Mummy's Victims*.

INTERVIEWER: That's the one in which the family dig up their father's coffin in the darkened churchyard and find it full of the rotting corpses of strangled hamsters, a dismantled bicycle and a surgical truss, but no father. Was that scene really necessary?

SEAMY HACKMAN: It was, to establish the point that even death has no certainty.

INTERVIEWER: And what were you establishing in the next chapter, apart from the shock tactics of which your critics accuse you, when the lesbian daughter, having had an abortion to get rid of the child of her crippled half-brother, climbs to the top of the Post Office Tower and sets fire to herself with vodka?

SEAMY HACKMAN: You as a novelist yourself, Mervyn, will recognize that for what it is, a big set piece, like you remember you did in the last Mervyn Moon novel, *The Innocent Bride*, in which your girl waits at the altar while her relatives set off one by one to see if they can find the bridegroom.

INTERVIEWER: Yes but he wasn't found headless in or out of a coffin, he was found in a broken-down taxi near Wapping, trying to get a lift to the church. I admit that having him late for the wedding at all, thus reversing the usual bride-is-late syndrome, was put in to screw up the tension—

SEAMY HACKMAN: Exactly! And it was a masterly touch, Mervyn, the work of a real pro. And when the bride's father at the wedding reception, having had a glass of bubbly too many, leans forward to pick up his notes and puts his hand into the wedding cake, so that the bride's mother walks out, that was also a set piece that was as memorable as anything any writer could hope for. Did you find that scene in *The Innocent Bride* difficult to do. . . ?

INTERVIEWER: As a matter of fact, it was a very difficult one to get started. I began it from the point of view of the bride—

SEAMY HACKMAN: Interesting to talk to you, Mervyn, but I have to move on now, another interview scheduled. Wonderful to talk to a brother writer. Tell your friends to buy my book as well as yours, eh?

Analysis

This interviewer made the basic mistake of allowing the interviewee to switch the subject of the conversation from himself to the interviewer.

Switching an interviewer from a subject he is pursuing should not be easy, but such is human vanity that switching the subject to himself is one of the most likely ways of achieving that object. In this case the author of what would seem to have been an affected, pretentious and trashy book was able to escape criticism by getting the interviewer to talk about himself as 'a fellow writer'. Would Hitler have been just as successful in switching the subject of an interview by talking about the interviewer as 'a fellow moustache-wearer'? It would fall into the same league. The flattery of inclusion in any brotherhood, be it of writers, musicians, actors, politicians, sportsmen, or the disabled, is dangerous to the truth-seeking process – which is the primary if not the only justification for any interview (entertainment is also allowable and usually desirable.)

It does not follow that any interviewee who tries to get the interviewer to talk about himself instead of the person he has come to interview is being deliberately obstructive. The motive may be sheer courtesy. The manoeuvre must nevertheless be resisted.

The British comic novelist and short story writer P.G. Wodehouse once attempted to turn the tables on a television and radio interviewer worthy of respect, Robert Robinson. Wodehouse disliked talking about himself, especially following his denigration caused by his broadcasts from Germany during the war. Robinson was interviewing him at his home near New York when, fairly early, Wodehouse switched the conversation from himself and his literary achievements to Robinson's early university novel, *Landscape With Dead Dons*, admiring its technique.

The novel, explosively funny in parts, was indeed worthy of praise from a master. Wodehouse was probably not being hypocritical. What he *was* being was deviously evasive. Robinson, normally not reluctant to talk about himself but aware that an interviewer must keep an interview on the right lines, didn't let him get away with it. He quickly cut in: 'But I mustn't allow you to talk about me, I have come here to talk about you. Would you . . .' And the interview was back on to its proper subject – the interviewee.

A newspaper or magazine interviewer may reason that, as he is not on air, it will do no harm to let an interview wander a little off-course as a courtesy to the interviewee. It is dangerously lazy and more often than not a mistake. Once the interviewer has lost control of the interview, for whatever reason (and talking about himself is one of the most attractive) it will be difficult for him to reassert that initiative. Having seized the reins the interviewee is quite likely to keep them, while the interviewer sits there impotently cursing his own mistake but unable to see how he can now correct it without jarring impoliteness.

Here is a maxim to write, if you have an unreliable memory, on the inside of your wrist with a ballpoint pen before every interview: talk about yourself volubly to your mother, sparingly to your wife or partner, and not at all (save in exceptional circumstances) to men or women you are interviewing.

There are exceptional circumstances but even these need to be watched. If you are interviewing a person about his cardiac arrest and you have had a cardiac arrest yourself, you may choose to mention this fact as a means of getting him to agree to the interview. It may promote fellow feeling. You are a fellow sufferer, not a mere rubberneck. But you should not mention it again during the interview itself, confining the talk to the interviewee's own experiences. By all means use your own experience to give depth to your questions, but let them always be questions about *him*. Do not mention your own experience again until you are shaking hands at the end of the interview, if then. You will have neither bored the interviewee nor, later, the reader, listener or viewer.

In an interview for print, you may be able to cut out more easily any digressions about yourself. But the fact remains that time spent in talking about yourself is time you cannot spend talking about the interviewee. Time is important. Most interviews have a time limit. It is true that most will overrun that limit, but only if the interviewee is by then interested and thoroughly involved. He is most likely to be interested and involved if he is talking about himself, not you.

If you waste time, even if you ultimately succeed in getting the interview back on to its proper path, you may find that time is now short and that essential questions have to be asked in a short, almost curt, way. In this case, they may well be answered in an equally short – and unrevealing – way.

Allowing the interviewee to talk about you as the interviewer may have a worse effect than simple boredom on a radio or television audience if the interview is not strictly edited, which of course it cannot be if live. It can show the interviewee, even if he is, say, a crafty type of politician who always puts himself first, as agreeably self-effacing and generous. Why, he doesn't want to talk about himself, he wants to talk about you! He must be a nice chap, well worth voting for! Nero, Hitler, Stalin, the Borgias and Ebenezer Scrooge could have pulled off this trick, if an interviewer had let them.

From this point of view as well as the others I have mentioned, always talk about the interviewee, not about yourself. Do not allow the interviewee to reverse this self-denying ordinance, and correct him politely immediately he tries.

Chapter 32

Preconceived

INTERVIEWER: Suzanna Portable, when you both started acting you as the elder were the better known one, you got the better roles and your sister very much the walk on parts. But now Henrietta has had two West End successes in *Mostly Murder* and *The Milkman Cometh* and one on Broadway, *Dancing On Nothing*, apart from her film work. Aren't you terrifically jealous of her?

SUZANNA PORTABLE: Not at all. When we were girls at school we were very competitive and I remember Henrietta pulling my hair on the playing field and I hit her with a hockey stick. But we were both in our early teens then. Since we've been adults we've developed great sympathy with one another's problems, especially the really bad ones.

INTERVIEWER: But one of the reviewers said of her in *The Milkman Cometh*, 'Henrietta Portable dominates this scatter-brained farce in a way her older sister Suzanna could never do.'

SUZANNA PORTABLE: Not surprising, really, since farce has never been my thing. Good luck to her. I have gone largely on the classical course, with the Royal National Theatre and the Royal Shakespeare Theatre. As a matter of fact, I remember reading that review over the phone to Henrietta, who hadn't spotted it, because she doesn't usually read reviews and neither do I, and we both fell about laughing. The reviewers like nothing better than to stir up a bit of trouble, but Henrietta and I think it's all a great joke.

INTERVIEWER: But you must have wanted to kill her when she got the same role in the Hollywood film version of the play.

SUZANNA PORTABLE: Not at all. She rang me up the day before it was announced and said she was certain they'd want a bankable Californian actress for the role, not her, and she was losing confidence in her ability to support a Hollywood film as the star. I told her she was talking nonsense, she would be great for the role, which she'd already proved, far better than anyone else I could think of, and they were idiots if they couldn't see it. The next day they offered her the role.

INTERVIEWER: But there must have been a time you were spitting blood after they'd announced they were giving her two million dollars for the role and you were still in the *Midsummer Night's Dream* tour – in Newcastle, wasn't it?

SUZANNA PORTABLE: Not at all. I rang her again to congratulate her and she said the money was a great joke, because no actress was worth that, and that she'd nearly fainted when her agent asked for it and got it; and she asked whether it was true that I'd be playing in *Cymbeline* at the National opposite a very big name indeed. She was tremendously thrilled when I said I was.

INTERVIEWER: Oh, come on! You must have been a tiny bit jealous at the thought of her making two million dollars and being in Hollywood and everything. In fact you must have been hopping mad. You must have been *seething*!

SUZANNA PORTABLE: Not in the least, actually. I didn't tell her this, of course, but I can think of nothing worse than being in Los Angeles, where they can't talk about anything except money – not even films these days, just money – or do anything except sniff coke up their noses by the handful. Not for me, thank you. I've been approached myself and I've always said no. Henrietta simply doesn't notice that sort of thing; give her a good role and she'd be happy anywhere.

INTERVIEWER: Come on, now, think back to that time when she pulled your hair and you hit her with a hockey stick. Are you saying that you're both completely different now?

SUZANNA PORTABLE: That's just what I'm saying. I'm rather sorry I ever told that story to some paper all that time ago; it's dogged us for twenty years. I wish you'd throw out some of your old press cuttings.

INTERVIEWER: But surely—

SUZANNA PORTABLE: Look. If you want the absolute truth, it never happened. I made it up because the press agent said it would be good copy and of course it was. What he didn't tell me was that it was going to carry on being good copy for the next twenty years and every journalist who interviewed either of us would do scales on that bloody hockey stick that never existed. Very boring. My sister and I have a laugh about it every time we meet. No, it was complete invention.

INTERVIEWER: But when she announced her engagement to Hollywood's hottest property, Hunk Buzzard, you must have been green with jealousy.

SUZANNA PORTABLE: Why? Not my type at all. She always did go for six foot four muscular types whereas I'm rather more interested in what they have between the ears. But I gather he's quite a nice man, actually, and quite intelligent. I and my partner will definitely be going to their wedding.

INTERVIEWER: But when you're in Los Angeles, looking at all those multimillionaire stars turn up for her wedding, won't you feel absolutely livid with rage . . .

Analysis

This was a classic example of an interviewer with one (fairly hackneyed) question in her mind, who kept blindly thrusting it, in only slightly different words, at the interviewee. Disregarding the fact that it was getting nowhere, she nevertheless ignored the potentially promising leads that were fed to her by the interviewee.

Some lazy interviewers do this for too much of the time. If the interviewee loses her patience and temper with the one track mind of the interviewer, this may be thought 'good television' or 'good copy' whether or not anything of substance has emerged.

Could it have been that the interview was a dead loss from the start, because the interviewee did not have anything very interesting to impart? Not necessarily. The interviewee sounded like an intelligent and sensible woman. She might have had things to impart, but the interviewer with her one persistent (and misconceived) question was not the person most likely to get her to impart them. The interviewer appeared to be less intelligent than her interviewee, which is not the right way round.

Had she been more intelligent and less obsessed with one question, about the alleged mutual antagonism between the two sisters, she could have followed up a number of interesting leads. The interviewee said that she and her sister always talked if they had 'really bad problems'. The interviewer could have asked for examples of problems which they talked over in this way. The interviewee said she and her sister regarded critics as 'a joke'. Why was that? Then there was the interviewee's statement that the up-and-coming Henrietta had 'lost confidence in herself' over her part in the big movie. Did she often appeal to her elder sister when she lost confidence?

The interviewee let slip that she was to play in *Cymbeline* opposite the 'big name'. How did that come about? She referred to approaches from Hollywood she herself had had. She could have been asked for examples. Then there was her admission that the story that she had once told about hitting her younger sister with a hockey stick was invented at the suggestion of a press agent. Were any other parts of the sisters' legend similarly flamboyant inventions? Finally, her impression that the Hollywood star Hunk Buzzard, who was about to marry her sister, was 'a nice man'. Why did she think that when he was obviously not her type?

Any moderately competent interviewer from a local weekly newspaper should have been able to detect things in the course of the interview which could have been followed up and developed. But this interviewer tried, as it were, to compose a symphony consisting of only one note. Once it became obvious that the notion of ill-feeling between the sisters was ill-conceived, it should have been abandoned in favour of other lines of questioning long before the interviewee became irritated.

A one-question interview is usually a sign not of determination and persistence but of a lack of empathetic imagination or of homework by the interviewer. Any interviewer should always have more than one shot in his or her locker. A more than superficial interest in human nature, plus homework, is the way to achieve that.

Chapter 33

The Price of Rudeness

INTERVIEWER: Prime Minister, you have said that you would not accept any more European Union regulations affecting the way in which British cheeses could be made, but no one believes you, do they, or else your government wouldn't be slipping in the opinion polls.

PRIME MINISTER: Who are these people who don't believe me? Name one.

INTERVIEWER: Well, I for one, Prime Minister, remember you saying you would not tolerate other European Union restrictions, such as on the size and shape of cucumbers, but after a while you accepted such regulations; so, no, I don't believe you would in fact veto regulations on British cheeses. Why should I?

PRIME MINISTER: I have said I shall veto such regulations. If you are going to call me a liar, there is no point in this interview.

INTERVIEWER: I am merely drawing attention, Prime Minister – as many members of the public would if they were in my place – to the reasons why people evidently don't believe your promises.

PRIME MINISTER: Look, I have made a statement, I stand by it, no one can say that I haven't kept all my promises in the past, so I demand an apology—

INTERVIEWER: Oh, chuck it, Prime Minister! We all know what politicians' promises are worth, and we all know that neither you nor any other politician has kept all of them, so why get on your high horse about it?

PRIME MINISTER: Are you going to apologize, or do I terminate this interview? I do not believe the people wish their Prime Minister to waste time consenting to an interview in which what he has to say is not believed, and he is called a liar.

INTERVIEWER: Forget these shifty tactics that anyone can see through, Prime Minister, and just answer the question. Why should I or anyone else believe you are not going to accept European Union regulations on the making of British cheeses when you have accepted other regulations after promising not to?

PRIME MINISTER: I cannot talk to anyone who questions my word. What point is there in my saying anything, if you believe that I am a liar? I will not be called a liar when, as a guest in your television studio, I am surely entitled to the common civilities. In the House of Commons, had you called me a liar you would have been forced to withdraw.

INTERVIEWER: Perhaps that is why your government has got away with as much as it has, Prime Minister – except, that is, in the country as reflected in the opinion polls, where plainly you are shown with clarity to be increasingly unpopular?

PRIME MINISTER: That is enough! Do I receive an apology for an unwarranted insult that would not be tolerated in the Chamber of the House, or do I not?

INTERVIEWER: Prime Minister, why are you deliberately trying to—

PRIME MINISTER (*gets to his feet, tears microphone from jacket lapel*): The bad manners of certain sections of the media has become a national disgrace. I do not believe there is one person in a million watching this interview who believes that I could be expected to carry on in the circumstances. This is entirely deplorable and absolutely pointless. Goodnight.

Analysis

There are bad interviews and there are those that don't really exist at all. This was one of the latter.

The interviewee was able to use the interviewer's rudeness, or alleged rudeness, to abort a potentially informative but (for him) potentially dangerous interview.

It is rarely helpful publicly to attribute dishonest tactics to an interviewee, even if he is plainly employing them. It enables the interviewee to make *your* manners rather than *his* handling of delicate issues the centrepiece of the interview. By the law of averages, roughly half your audience will politically support the interviewee, and will therefore tend to agree with him about your manners, whether that view is objectively justified or not. You certainly cannot afford to assume that your audience as a whole will necessarily see things from your point of view.

It may be argued that politicians and other public figures should be told they are not to be trusted because they have lied before. It is a flawed argument. It is perfectly acceptable to say, 'Prime Minister, there have been occasions in the past when you have promised not to accept European Union regulations and then have accepted them?' This does not directly impute dishonest motives. Unlike a direct insult, it enables the interviewee to make a reply. That reply might be something like: 'The government has had to adapt its policies to changed conditions. When I said I would not accept European Union regulations on the size and shape of British cucumbers, that was the government's intention at that time. But then Spain and Greece, which had said they would also resist such regulations, came into line with them and we had to face the fact that if we continued to resist, the competitive position of the British cucumber in Europe would be gravely affected.'

This answer may or not convince the public, but it is at least some sort of case and is more worth public attention than are wrangles about who is lying and who isn't. In a *New Statesman* interview, the formidable television interviewer Jeremy Paxman, this time in the role of interviewee with Mary Riddell as interviewer, said that it was very difficult to remain calm when listening to someone talk 'complete bollocks'. There were so many of them now, not just politicians, but captains of industry, union leaders, people speaking for one vested interest or another. The interviewer owed it to the electorate, the viewers and the people who paid the licence fees to try to 'get through that'.

It is certainly true that there has been a nose-dive in the candour of interviewees, coupled with an increased aggressiveness in interviewers, with each side disagreeing about which is the chicken and which the egg. I sometimes think that every media interview should be more like a House of Commons Select Committee hearing. Members of such committees are allowed and expected to ask ministers penetrating questions, but with the utmost politeness; and ministers are expected to give factually correct answers which do not insult the intelligence of those asking the questions. To expect that degree of gravitas and mutual respect in media interviews may be Utopian, but some degree of it would be welcome.

In the meantime, an interviewer is wise, in his own interests, to mind his manners, to give the interviewee no opportunity to sideline the real subject of the interview in favour of subject of the interviewer's manners, and to remember that one man's 'bollocks' may be another man's idea of wisdom.

If the interviewee's case is ridiculously weak, the interviewer is perfectly entitled to put questions that may reveal how weak the case is. He may quote another 'player' in the political, commercial or social game who has described the case as nonsense and ask the interviewee how he reacts to that. But the interviewer should not take it upon himself to be overtly the final judge of whether the interviewee is talking honest sense, honest rubbish or dishonest rubbish. The interviewer is not a god, nor a player in the game: he should be an honest spectator.

The more he allows himself to become partisan the nearer he is to losing control of the interview – and perhaps of the interviewee, who may walk out, with half the viewers (certainly those who agree with his basic position) sympathizing with him.

Chapter 34

You Must Be Joking

INTERVIEWER: Sir Evelyn, you are widely recognized as the doyen of art collectors. Your palatial home here on the Côte d'Azur, crammed with paintings, antiques and *objets d'art*, has been the refuge of artists and aesthetes for over a century, during your own lifetime and that of your equally distinguished father Sir Cecil Airy.

SIR EVELYN AIRY: Most kind, dear boy, most kind. But you really mustn't call me a doyen, you know. In my dictionary 'doyen' means 'old bore'. What?

INTERVIEWER: You are too modest, Sir Evelyn.

SIR EVELYN: I have much to be modest about! My father, as you may know, was a famous sportsman of his day. I was absolutely no good at it; one had only to show me a cricket ball and I fainted. And as for rugby – he was a Blue, you know – I only kicked a rugger ball once and that landed up in my eye. Whenever he wanted me to go with him to watch any sport, I used to go and hide in the servants' quarters. That is how the ugly rumours sprang up about me and the housekeeper's daughter. Actually I was only helping her to make a bed.

INTERVIEWER: Is that a fact?

SIR EVELYN: No, I made that anecdote up at Balliol to make myself appear more interesting. What? But I did hide when my father tried to take me to sporting events. The one time I couldn't avoid him was the Olympic Games in Berlin just before the war. He got hold of me by the ear and didn't let go until he had me in Berlin, with my dear sainted mother following up weeping until we got safely back to London and he finally released his grip. As it were.

INTERVIEWER: You must remember that occasion very vividly.

SIR EVELYN: Oh, absolutely. Hitler turned up in a ghastly vulgar great Mercedes and left in a huff because a black fellow had won some race or other, or was about to win some race or other. Bit of a racist, you know, Hitler. I started to shout a few well chosen *bon mots* at Hitler's back as he walked out – I rather liked the look of the black fellow – and my father hustled me out of the Stadium, still holding me by the ear. It was quite an event. My dear friend the painter Francis Brisket, who of course was frightfully Left, much later painted a picture of Hitler leaving the Stadium, showing him with three heads and with an elephant's trunk sticking out of his derrière, which was quite fun. No one would buy it and in the end I bought it for nine pounds ten, offered it to the National Gallery and when they wouldn't touch it, pack of cowards, I put it in the lavatory where everybody could see it. If Hitler had still been around I might have crated up the picture and sent it to him to drive the silly man more barking mad than he was already, but there you are.

INTERVIEWER: Was your friendship with Francis Brisket always a close one?

SIR EVELYN: He was the last of the modern British artists I can find it in myself to admire. Oh, very, very close, ever since we met in that frightful pub in Soho where we all used to go in those days. Millionaires could rub shoulders with barrow boys and all that sort of thing. He was brought in by Lord— I'd better just say he was brought in by the scion of one of our oldest families, and tried to charge people a fiver for drawing them. He had long black wavy hair, a cleft chin, and he was very muscular; everyone was after him, even the women. Well, I joined him and asked what he would do for a tenner and he said he'd draw me like I really was. He was using that quaint accent of his – Bermondsey with a charming touch of Birmingham, you know. Definitely below stairs. So I gave him a tenner – quite a lot of money in those days – and asked him to draw me as I really was and you know what, he had such wit in those days before he experimented with the meths, he drew me as a great fat pink pig with four eyes, three feet and two stomachs, each hanging down to the ground. A lad of spirit. We were great friends from that moment.

INTERVIEWER: And you remained friends?

SIR EVELYN: Absolutely, except that he had this frightful habit of borrowing money from all his many friends. On one occasion just after the war I gave him fifteen pounds – quite a lot of money in those days – for paints. Two hours later he turned up at my parents' home in Chelsea having spent it all on champagne and a stuffed boar's head which he had with him and which he wanted to paint, and asked for another fifteen pounds. On that occasion I wasn't at home and Frampton, the butler, who then didn't know who he was, positively threw him down the steps. But usually people let him get away with a lot, often including the family silver in large quantities. He had such lovely eyes. His *Christ Selling Bananas at Covent Garden* – the one showing him with two wooden legs, three arms and wearing a feather boa hat – will be the supreme masterpiece of the twentieth century, I am absolutely convinced. That was the *pièce de résistance* of my Chelsea home for many years until eventually I got out.

INTERVIEWER: Yes, Sir Evelyn, why did you decide to leave Britain?

SIR EVELYN: I thought the place was getting decidedly mediocre as well as decidedly rough. One day in the 1970s, when I was wearing my usual purple-lined cloak and white panama hat and carrying my silver-topped cane, I was actually pursued down the Kings Road by a gang of young persons of indeterminate sex chanting' 'Get 'em off!' until I came across a constable who took one look at me and virtually chased me back up the Kings Road in the other direction. Very tiresome. England, I saw, was no place for the aesthete. I sold the place that had been the family's London home for generations to a charming American for simply fistfuls of dollars, and moved entirely to the Côte d'Azur château from where I can observe what remains of what was once my nation at a safe distance. I pride myself that I have never set eyes on a Briton of the unwashed tendency ever since.

INTERVIEWER: That must have been difficult to arrange.

SIR EVELYN: Oh, you mean tourists? During the tourist season, when we do see some British citizens of the lower orders, I say a little prayer every night before pulling the thick shutters – Frampton passed away a long time ago, poor fellow (why I say poor fellow I don't know, I think he ended up richer than I was) – and one can't get the required standard of butler these days unless one is an American – charming, charming people nevertheless, the Americans. I discuss investments with them from time to time. They come here in their tight double-breasted suits and tell me what to do with the fiver or tenner I have left. One of them last month was rather a dear, nice eyes, he stayed a few days longer than the rest. Have another glass of port. Where was I?

INTERVIEWER: We had got to the point where you decided to leave England for good. It must have been a wrench.

SIR EVELYN: Never seriously missed anything except *The Times* and the Royal Ballet. Never much regretted not seeing the Royal Academy Summer show because that was always stuffed with dreary mediocrities – almost as bad as those half-witted farts at that cesspit of trash the Tate, who nowadays seem to think a pile of used French letters is Art provided the artist can get himself written up in the gossip columns. I seriously considered sending the chap who did that one a ton of pig manure and desisted only because I didn't see why I should give the fellow something far more valuable than his bloody used French letters. I hereby offer £50,000 to anyone who murders the director of the Tate in the most painful and public way possible. Cheap at the price. How's your glass, my dear fellow? I see mine's empty again. Where does the stuff go?

INTERVIEWER: There were recent reports that you would never return to England until there was an Old Etonian in Number 10 again.

SIR EVELYN: Pretty safe promise to make, don't you think? Not much chance of that if things go on as they are. Wilson, Heath, Callaghan, Thatcher, Major – none of them even cleaned the windows of Eton or delivered milk there. Blair's rather sweet, but he went to some Scottish public school, didn't he? All of them, except perhaps Heath, wouldn't know a Titian from a tit. What do I have in common with such frightful people? You see, you can't answer.

INTERVIEWER: There have also been suggestions that you are changing your intention of leaving this magnificent château to the British nation as a place where British art could be displayed, built round your collection as a nucleus, and to which impoverished young men interested in art would be admitted free.

SIR EVELYN: I will go further. I will set fire to the place rather than have it become British property. If I feel myself slipping away, I will set fire to the place myself. Excuse me. I must have a pee.

Beginning of *Sunday Defender Magazine* interview as it appeared:

Sir Evelyn Airy, the aesthete, art collector and well known grand seigneur and socialite of the Château Morte in the Côte d'Azur, has offered £50,000 to anyone who will murder the director of the Tate Gallery, and has declared that he will burn his two hundred year-old home to the ground rather than see it used as a museum for British art after his death. This would reverse his promise to turn it over to the British nation for such a museum, to which impoverished young men interested in art would be admitted free.

He has also threatened to send a ton of pig manure to any artist shown at the Tate gallery who offends his own more traditional views on art, and has said he will not set foot again in Britain until it has a prime minister who went to Eton.

Wearing his characteristic purple-lined cloak, white panama hat and resting his well manicured hands on an equally characteristic silver-topped stick, Sir Evelyn reminisced about his long-long friendship with the controversial painter Francis Brisket, who he described as the last British artist he could admire, explained his reasons for leaving Britain and revealed that during the tourist season in the Côte d'Azur he always prayed for divine protection from English thugs before putting up the heavy wooden shutters . . .

Analysis

The interviewer encouraged a natural talker to talk, which was the right thing to do. But the published result was mistaken and dangerous because it presented as hard fact the 'intentions' of a man who was obviously an habitual tease, given to over-the-top statements and declarations that could, as in this case, have been no more than a colourful fantasy.

The port decanter never seemed to stop being passed round. This should have been made clear early in the story. It would have been a hint not to take too literally anything Sir Evelyn said. A more suitable intro might have been:

> Sir Evelyn Airy, the aesthete, art collector and celebrated host of the Château Morte, was in fine form over the vintage port at his beautiful Côte d'Azur home. Among his targets this time were the modern British, modern art and prime ministers who hadn't gone to Eton.
>
> He has made many threats in the past – usually withdrawn in the cold light of dawn – about whether or not he would leave his home to the British nation as a museum of British art on the Continent. This time, as the port flowed, he threatened to burn the place down rather than let it be used as a 'cesspit of trash' like the loathed Tate gallery, and facetiously offered £50,000 to anyone who would murder its director 'in the most painful and public way possible'.

This version is certainly less obviously dramatic. If the interviewer felt that the loss of the greater drama was too great for him to bear, he could and should have asked Sir Evelyn directly, at various times in the interview, whether he meant his threats to be taken literally.

Plying an interviewee with drink may be a valid way of getting him to talk. In this interview, the interviewee plied *himself* with drink and so could not complain. But it is not valid to take literally what may be merely wine – and a tendency to flamboyant hyperbole – talking. Sir Evelyn should have been given several chances to make clear whether he was joking or not. If he was not given such chances, taking what he said literally was unfair and potentially dangerous.

Some might argue that a sophisticated man of the world like Sir Evelyn should not make the mistake of saying things in his cups that he does not literally mean, especially when talking to a journalist he has not met before and who does not therefore necessarily know that Sir Evelyn habitually talks wildly for flamboyant emphasis. But Sir Evelyn's lawyers might argue that, as a man of the world himself, any journalist should be able to tell whether an interviewee is joking or not, and that therefore in this case Sir Evelyn had been damagingly misrepresented.

Whether or not the result makes such a good story in hard news terms, jokes should always be carefully checked out and, if necessary, clearly reported as jokes.

Chapter 35

Degrees of Deference . . . 1

INTERVIEWER: Henry Sherbert, your first novel which has just been published has been described as 'startlingly new, fresh and original' by no less a critic than Alan Rake. How did you manage to produce a work of such genius, given all your fine medical work as a doctor?

INTERVIEWEE: Well, I don't think they actually used the word genius . . .

INTERVIEWER: That's really typical of you, sir, so modest as well as talented. But producing your first novel at the age of fifty, about the same age as my own father, after a lifetime devoted to healing the sick as a doctor must prove that you had it in you all the time. Why was it that it took you so long to produce what Albert Creeper called the best book of the decade?

INTERVIEWEE: He said *one* of the best books of the decade, actually, which is a rather important distinction. You must also remember that Joan Boggis called it disgusting in its subject matter; she thought the leading character, a surgeon who could operate successfully only when drunk, was not a fit subject for comedy—

INTERVIEWER: But Anna Cropper called its humour sly and arresting, and rightly compared you with such towering classics as Mark Twain. Are you like Mark Twain?

INTERVIEWEE: No, I'm still alive, unlike Mark Twain.

INTERVIEWER: But seriously—

INTERVIEWEE: Perhaps there's something of Twain in my leading character who, if you remember, committed suicide after he operated on the Prime Minister when sober and yet somehow succeeded in saving his life.

INTERVIEWER: That was a masterly touch, as Maurice Binns pointed out in his review, in which he accurately called you a master stylist on a par with Evelyn Waugh.

INTERVIEWEE: He said in the same style as Evelyn Waugh, if I remember, which is not precisely the same thing.

INTERVIEWER: Sir, will you go on with being a doctor now that you have written what Alan Rake called a novel that will become a classic . . .

INTERVIEWEE: He said that the novel 'deserved' to become a classic, which is rather different, given the reading taste of today's and possibly, even more, tomorrow's reading public.

INTERVIEWER: Was anything in the marvellous story based on your own experience as a doctor?

INTERVIEWEE: I think all that occurs between me and my patients and my professional colleagues must remain confidential. Sorry, my receptionist is not here and I simply must answer that telephone. . . .

Analysis

Here the interviewer displayed too much deference, possibly because the interviewee was so much older than he was. The result was that he was so busy minding his manners and being intimidated by a (possibly genuine) admiration of the interviewee that he failed to press home his own questions and failed to initiate new questions when the interviewee himself volunteered points which needed following up.

Up to a point, it was legitimate of the interviewer to ingratiate himself by reciting praises of the novel – that is to say, if he had reported the praise accurately. As it was, time was wasted because the interviewee felt compelled to keep correcting the interviewer's inflated version of the praise. Even vain people, perhaps especially vain people, must always be praised discriminately, or they will feel that their intelligence is being insulted.

The interviewer first asked the interviewee about how he had managed, with all his medical work, to produce a novel. That question did not get answered, then or later.

Then the interviewer asked the interviewee how long it had taken him to write the book. That question, too, got lost as the interviewee felt bound to correct the interviewer's suggestion that his book had been called the best book of the decade as distinct from 'one of' the best.

In pointing out this distinction, the interviewee brought up a good point – that the book had been criticized as disgusting in its subject matter, because it was about a surgeon who could operate successfully only when drunk. But the interviewer not only failed to press his original question, he also failed to latch on to this point and to question the author about the validity of making such matters the subject of humour. He gave the impression throughout of being too much in awe of the interviewee.

The interviewer made no attempt to follow up the comparison with Mark Twain by asking what particular qualities the interviewee felt he had in common with the great American humourist. He allowed the praise of him by a critic to stand as mere hyperbole. He also failed to follow up when the interviewee recalled the incident in which the leading character, the surgeon who could not operate successfully when sober, operated on the Prime Minister when sober, unexpectedly saved his life and then took his own. Was that satire aimed at a particular politician or at politicians in general? The question was never asked, because the interviewer was too busy finding ways to gush over the interviewee.

The question of whether the doctor would continue practising now that he had had a literary success was asked, but got lost in the argument about whether a reviewer had said the book would be a classic or that the book deserved to be a classic – not a distinction of great moment, especially as only posterity could judge. As a result, the question of whether the author was similar to Evelyn Waugh got lost, and the oblique comment volunteered by the interviewee about the taste of the reading public was not followed up.

Finally, the interviewer allowed his question about whether incidents had been based on the author's own medical experience to be brushed aside.

Obviously a doctor would be wise to answer all incoming telephone calls at once. The interviewer, nevertheless, should simply have hung on and quickly pressed the question again before being shown out. But he was too much restricted by deference. Studious politeness is one thing and should almost always be maintained; subservience quite another.

The degree of deference which is suitable is roughly that which would operate if you asked a man in the street the time. You would be polite, but you wouldn't bow low or fall to your knees in front of him. Nor would you be too much in awe of him to listen to what he was saying, or to ask him again if he didn't reply or you didn't understand his answer.

Chapter 36
Degrees of Deference . . . 2

INTERVIEWER: Derek Bull, having a first novel out is always an exciting experience for any writer, even when it is greeted with the sort of criticism launched at it by the critics Joan Gasser and Osbert Nill, but I imagine that because you are fifty years old rather than just out of medical school you took it more calmly than most.

INTERVIEWEE: Really? How can a journalist know what a novelist feels when his first book comes out? How many novels have you had published?

INTERVIEWER: Well, three actually. The first was thirty years ago, when I was thirty.

INTERVIEWEE: Oh.

INTERVIEWER: What do you feel about the controversy the book has stirred up? Are you surprised, pleased, or just indifferent?

INTERVIEWEE: Well, you'll probably know more about that than I do.

INTERVIEWER: At first I found it exciting, then it began to pall, and then I discovered that the sales were not keeping pace with all the controversy, so I formed a scepticism about the selling power of controversy where books are concerned, and that's never left me. People talk about 'buzz' books but don't necessarily buy them. Do you agree?

INTERVIEWEE: Well, it's still early days for me.

INTERVIEWER: I can sympathize with you about what Joan Gasser said about the 'disgusting' portrayal of the architect dying of cancer whose great secret ambition was to design gas chambers on the lines of Nazi death camps, for the unemployed. The leading character of my first novel was a politician who survives an air crash marooned on top of the snow-covered Alps and ends up by eating a constituent who was also on the plane, and some readers didn't understand the satire.

INTERVIEWEE: Yes.

INTERVIEWER: Do you consider the use of humour in your novel about the architect valid?

INTERVIEWEE: Of course, otherwise I wouldn't have used it. You'll know all about that.

INTERVIEWER: But it's your reactions I'm after. I remember being discour-

aged by the first critical review I read and then discovering that all the criticisms were cancelled out by other critics who praised it, and vice versa. For
instance, one reviewer said the dialogue was stilted and lifeless while
another said it was pacy and crackling with life. Have you found that?

INTERVIEWEE: More or less. Actually, I haven't read many reviews. My wife
has managed to keep a lot of them away from me.

INTERVIEWER: Well done, I wish mine had been as thoughtful. I must
remember that for next time. Will you go on writing now that you've had
this first success?

INTERVIEWEE: I hope to, but I don't want to talk about my next novel.
That's supposed to be bad luck, isn't it?

INTERVIEWER: Or bad policy. If you let all the air out of the tyre by talking
about it, there's no more left to do the writing.

INTERVIEWEE: I couldn't have put it better.

INTERVIEWER: I know it's an irritating question for any novelist to face,
because it implies that he lacks the novelists' imagination, but was any of
the novel based on real incidents in your life as a doctor?

INTERVIEWEE: You're right. It was all imagination. Real life wouldn't have
produced dramatic enough situations to sell the book, let alone the film
rights.

INTERVIEWER: Ah, I remember the thrill when I sold the film rights of my
first novel . . .

INTERVIEWEE: Well, I've only sold a six month option, actually. . . . Would
you excuse me now? I have another interview appointment in one minute's
time . . .

Analysis

Those beginning to conduct interviews may think their youth is an
unmixed disadvantage. Not so. As one gets older, deferring to interviewees may become more difficult rather than more easy.

Of course one has no difficulty in being polite as an interviewer, even
if one has little respect for the interviewee: but flatteringly behaving as
if the interviewee were some sort of god becomes more difficult. One
can no longer look gooey-eyed and upwards; sometimes one has to stop
onself looking hard-eyed and downwards. Especially with politicians
and other hucksters, one has heard too much of the patter before.

Even in the case of interviewees one respects, one may have to
evolve a persona to cope with this situation. I might never have realized I had done so but for an interview I did with the playwright
Arnold Wesker late in my career. I had written about him and his
projects several times before and we were both over sixty.

At the end of the interview he said: 'You know, I've been trying to analyse your manner all through this interview, and at last I've got it. You come across as a very understanding family doctor.' I realized then that that had become my method of putting a friendly, encouraging face on the fact that I had seen and heard so many things so many times before.

It may be essential, as you become more experienced, to evolve a face or persona that serves the same purpose. It must be a congenial, if sometimes firm, one. Experience must not be allowed to lead to outward or inward arrogance, which can so easily happen. I was for a lengthy period a regular guest on Robert Robinson's *Stop the Week* BBC Radio 4 programme. The electronic aura of celebrity was inevitably more potent than my appearances in print. Once when I started conducting a routine newspaper interview on the telephone, the interviewee, catching my name, said, 'Do you mean *the* Dennis Barker?' I realized then that it was time for my radio celebrity, such as it was, to peter out: it would tend to get between me and anyone I was trying to interview as a working journalist.

The truth is that every interviewer has to devise, consciously or unconsciously, a manner which can do two things: facilitate efficient interrogation and, at the same time, imply the sort of deference necessary to free the interviewee's ego, so that he can make or break himself. The interviewee, even if he is going to be debunked, must always feel, for the purposes of the interview, that he is without doubt the most important person present. And he must feel that you feel it too. Difficulty can exist for many reasons other than the age and experience of the interviewer. If as a media interviewer you are the Hon. Nigel Double-Barrel (and you are increasingly likely to be now that Britain no longer has an empire you can govern) you may have a problem convincing a 70-year-old Doncaster retired nurse that you are treating her seriously. If, on the other hand, you have a Doncaster accent, you may have difficulty in persuading the father of the Hon. Nigel Double-Barrel that you are not laughing up your sleeve at him. If you are a black interviewer you may still alas have novelty value, but you may find it difficult to convince a spokesman of the South African National Party that you are treating him with deference and not frigid hostility. If you are built like a double-decker bus and play rugby in your spare time, you may have difficulty in persuading the Chairperson of the South London Feminist Collective Workshop and Therapy Unit that you are not an arrogant bastard, or a five-feet-two professor of nuclear physics that you are not an overblown ignoramus who is patronizing him as a midget.

It can be, in fact, far more difficult deferentially to efface yourself than to assert yourself for the purpose of conducting an interview.

It was possible for that great interviewer Sir Robin Day to have more flamboyant neckwear and a more heavyweight manner than those he was interviewing only because they were chiefly politicians: that is to say, people of oversized ego, used to having verbal duels in public and trained to give as good as they got. Whether Sir Robin would have been quite as effective if he had specialized in interviewing, let us say, poets or painters, or for that matter nurses and unmarried mothers, is an open question.

In the case of the fictitious interview we are now considering, the interviewer made several mistakes because he found deference difficult. Seniority in age is not an advantage to an interviewer and this one should not have called it to the attention of the interviewee. He should not have trotted out the fact that he had had his first novel published thirty years previously at the age of thirty. It only served as a sort of reproach to the interviewee, whose first novel was now being published when he was fifty.

It was also a mistake for the interviewer to describe how he had felt about the controversy over *his* first novel; he should have stuck to asking the interviewee about his feelings in a similar situation. In that way, deference would have been maintained better than it was here. The conversation continued amiably enough – but that was what it was: a conversation which was rambling rather than revealing.

The interviewer was altogether too articulate. He constantly made the mistake of expressing things better than the interviewee could, thus preventing the interviewee seeing himself encouragingly as a talker and oracle. Though he should have been deferentially conscious that the interviewee's answers were getting shorter and shorter, he merely took advantage of that to talk more himself. Why mention that he had sold film rights when the interviewee had only sold an option, usually amounting to about a tenth of the rights? It was an unpolitic lapse in deference. And so on. This interviewer had the burden of age, but did not take steps to safeguard an air of necessary deference.

It is not a question of being servile: even if an interview is searching or hostile, the interviewee must still feel that he is the important part of it. The interviewer should always come across not as inferior but in some way or another as deferential: subordinate to the interviewee. The reverse is unlikely to be satisfactory to the reader, listener or viewer.

If you doubt this, try to find an example of an interview which disproves the assertion. You will need plenty of time.

Chapter 37

Don't State

HOME SECRETARY: Our policy to prevent more escapes from prisons is two-fold, firstly to increase security in prisons by the use of modern security techniques, and secondly to improve conditions in prisons for the entire prison population, inmates and staff alike, so that there will no longer be such a strong temptation to escape.

INTERVIEWER: That policy is already in rags and tatters.

HOME SECRETARY: It is not yet as successful as we would wish—

INTERVIEWER: It's not successful at all, when you bear in mind that the number of escapes went up this year by three per cent.

HOME SECRETARY: In previous years, the increases were five per cent and four per cent—

INTERVIEWER: That's a quibble. What the public wants to know is how so many men are able to break out of prison despite the security techniques which you claimed would cure the problem.

HOME SECRETARY: In previous years, I repeat, the increases were five per cent and four per cent, so it is quite clear that the variation is in the right direction.

INTERVIEWER: That's playing with figures. When new security methods have been introduced, the figures should be much lower than they are. You can't possibly say your policy has been a success when the number of prison escapes keeps going up.

HOME SECRETARY: We are not complacent, but even you must concede that conditions in prisons have been improving . . .

INTERVIEWER: The report by Mr Justice Cribbage gave the lie to that when he said that some prisoners had to share three to a cell.

HOME SECRETARY: That was a year ago, since when—

INTERVIEWER: Since when conditions have got even worse, if we are to believe the Prison Officers Association, which said their members feared more physical attacks on them if security precautions were not tightened up.

HOME SECRETARY: Physical attacks on prison staff were going down when

217

the spate of riots broke out and prisoners were locked up in their cells for safety's sake until the causes had been investigated—

INTERVIEWER: In other words, the failure of your policy is someone else's fault.

HOME SECRETARY: For the third time, I do not concede that our policy has failed. The question of physical attacks is a different one. We are trying to reduce the amount of anger inside prison walls. We had virtually ended the dreadful practice of inmates having to slop out their own excreta at various times of day. We are well on the way to having flush lavatories in all cells—

INTERVIEWER: That's not true.

HOME SECRETARY: I repeat, we are well on the way to having working flush lavatories in all cells, and we are confident that, despite recent set-backs, we will achieve our aim in this Parliament.

INTERVIEWER: But, Home Secretary, that's pure moonshine. The fact is that in every respect conditions in prisons are now worse and are deteriorating further still, that the staff are demoralized and that this is causing the recent increase in the number of escapes.

HOME SECRETARY: Are you asking me or telling me?

Analysis

The Home Secretary's final remark was an instructive one. The basic mistake of the interviewer in this interview (involving quite fictitious 'facts') was to make statements rather than ask questions. When these statements took the form of vilification – justified or not – they slowed up the interview by enabling the interviewee constantly to reiterate what he had already said. This enabled him to hammer home his points while, in the process, possibly enjoying more public sympathy than he was entitled to.

A forceful interviewing style can be successful, if it does not give the impression that it is designed to trash the interviewee whatever he says. A statement like, 'Your policy is a hopeless failure', even if directly followed (as it was *not* here) with a nominal question like, 'Isn't it?' is a naïve one. Would you expect any interviewee to agree?

Such question/statements were pioneered in the 1940s and 1950s by a newspaper journalist called Douglas Warth, who made a reputation by asking rude questions on television, sometimes after generous liquid refreshment. It had novelty value in those more formal and polite times. It has none now. If scepticism is to be indicated by the interviewer, it is more likely to work if it takes the form of sentiments such as, 'There are many people who might claim your policy is in rags and tatters'. Or, 'But those who recall that the number of escapes went up this year may well ask whether your policy has had any success at all'. Or, 'Isn't it a quibble to bandy figures about when the simple fact is that the rate of escapes is getting worse?'

In other words, the interviewer represents the prosecution witness who is not in the studio, but is not himself the prosecution witness. Apart from making for a smoother interview, with less time wasted on slanging one another, keeping this in mind will not force – or allow – the interviewee to make his points more than once. It does not place public sympathy on the side of the interviewee rather than that of the interviewer.

It is sometimes argued that an experienced interviewee like a politician or actor can be stimulated by having hostile statements hurled at him. Sometimes, but less and less so. Most politicians have already decided what they are and are not going to say. Certainly the interviewer should try to get through the defences of this pre-planned essay, but stridently hostile statements are not likely to help that process. They are more likely to make the interviewee more cautious or more repetitively assertive.

Brief yourself with as many unfavourable facts as possible and do not hesitate to put them to the interviewee more than once if he tries to evade them. But do it in the form of questions, not statements.

Chapter 38

Showing the Flag

SIR WALTER HOITY: Are you the music critic of the *Daily News*?

INTERVIEWER: *Daily Gazette*. No, I'm not the music critic, I'm a feature writer. I hope your fiftieth birthday will be a happy one. What was the first symphony you ever conducted?

SIR WALTER HOITY: Hm. . . . Will you have anything to drink? Sorry, nothing stronger than coffee here in my office.

INTERVIEWER: Coffee would be fine, I wouldn't touch anything stronger at eleven in the morning.

SIR WALTER HOITY: Hm. . . . The first symphony I had to conduct was Bruckner's Fourth – you've heard of it? – and I was only twenty-three at the time. It was a monumental challenge. Sir Malcolm Crump – you've heard of him? – had to fall out because of illness and I had to take over at twenty-four hours notice. He had also agreed to conduct Boulez's *Pli Selon Pli* – I'll spell it for you, P-L-I S-E-L-O-N P-L-I by Pierre Boulez, P-I-E-R-R-E B-O-U-L-E-Z, at the same concert at the RFH, I beg your pardon, the Royal Festival Hall.

INTERVIEWER: But you didn't conduct the Boulez?

SIR WALTER HOITY: It was entirely new to me, it incorporated all sorts of weird instruments which I won't attempt to describe to you, and as music it wasn't for me, though I'm not against the moderns *en bloc* – that means as a whole. Instead I said I would conduct William Alwyn's *Lyra Angelica*, which is a concerto for harp and string orchestra – you probably haven't heard of it – because I thought if they could assemble all these weird instruments for the French Boulez, they should certainly be able to procure a harp for a British composer, one of the Romantics you may not have come across, A-L-W-Y-N.

INTERVIEWER: What was your very first experience of music?

SIR WALTER HOITY: This is a story that may appeal to you. One night my mother was bathing me when the radio was on to the Third Programme. I must have been about four. I farted in the bath and five minutes later there was the sound of a bassoon from the radio and I said to my mother, 'Farting!' That appeal to you?

INTERVIEWER: Do you remember what they were playing?

SIR WALTER HOITY: I don't remember, but my mother told me later it was the Mozart Bassoon Concerto. I played it at my very first concert and did a programme note about why. That amused a lot of people.

INTERVIEWER: You have always refused to play Strauss. Why?

SIR WALTER HOITY: That story's reached you, has it? Oh well, I suppose I shall have to do a rerun. Not Johann Senior, Johann Junior or Josef or Eduard, you understand – I'll spell their names if you like. No, Richard Strauss. Let me fill you in with some history. Some German musicians went along with Hitler and some didn't. Richard Strauss thrived under Hitler, went along with Hitler, offered no resistance to Hitler, said not a word publicly against the extermination of the Jews. . . . Is that enough for you?

INTERVIEWER: But didn't he also help a lot of Jewish friends and in any case, shouldn't music be separate from politics?

SIR WALTER HOITY: You have mugged up something about him, haven't you? If you've got it in the cuttings, you don't really need me to go through it all again, do you?

(*And more in similar vein.*)

Analysis

Almost at the outset, the interviewer should have put up a polite, perhaps humorous but quite unmistakable invisible flag bearing the words, 'I am not the sort of interviewer you need patronize!' He didn't. He let the interview creak not very productively on, with the interviewee clearly dismissing him with the tone of his answers. Let us imagine how the interview might have gone if the interviewer had shown the flag:

SIR WALTER HOITY: Are you the music critic of the *Daily News*?

INTERVIEWER: *Daily Gazette*. No, I'm not the music critic, Sir Walter, I'm a feature writer who tends to specialize in cultural subjects and as far as music is concerned my record collection runs into thousands rather than hundreds. Your first version of the Mahler Seventh is one of the most often played. I hope your fiftieth birthday next week, which I've come to see you about, is a happy one. You've been called 'the Handyman of the Symphony' because people say you are almost as happy with one composer's symphony as any other's. Is that really true?

SIR WALTER HOITY: As true as I can make it. . . . Will you have something to drink? Nothing stronger than coffee in my office, I'm afraid.

INTERVIEWER: Coffee would be fine. Even if you were to promise me that I could hear your latest recording of the Mozart *Requiem* which is due out next month, I wouldn't touch anything stronger at this hour of day. Are you really saying that you like doing Stockhausen or Tavener as much as Mozart?

SIR WALTER HOITY: Hm. . . . 'Like' is not perhaps the right word, but I have always responded to a challenge. The very first symphony I ever recorded was Bruckner's Fourth – is that on your shelves?

INTERVIEWER: Your Romantic certainly is. Was that the Haas, the Nowak or the original 1874 edition?

SIR WALTER HOITY: Ah, my dear chap, in those days we didn't hear so much about the 1874 original edition, it was all Haas or Nowak. I conducted the Nowak, which is arguably the most poetic of all the versions. Sir Malcolm Crump was going to conduct it but he had to fall out because of 'illness', as it was reported at the time. Actually he was after a girl in the second violins, and she refused to play if he appeared, giving as her reason the fact that she was pregnant. Oh dear, how indiscreet of me, just as well he's now dead, isn't it? Anyway I had to take over at twenty-four hours notice, so I had to get my skates on. I insisted on double the scheduled rehearsal time and . . .

(*And much more of the same, including readily volunteered information and anecdotes about why he disliked conducting Richard Strauss.*)

It is easy to see that this interview is the more promising. The interviewer took the trouble to signal both his intelligence and his (albeit amateur) musical knowledge and appreciation.

The interviewee responded, as many in such circumstances will do, by relaxing and giving the interviewer his friendly and serious, if not solemn, attention. He did not continue to have the sensation that he was locked in the same prison cell as an unintelligent, vulgar hack with no interest in his life's work, a hack likely to respond only to scatological jokes about farting in the bath.

The amiable signal, 'I'm not a fool!' is invaluable to an interviewer. It should always be oblique, never overt. It should suggest amusement rather than resentment at any misunderstanding. The manner in which you inflect the conversation, dropping in a plainly intelligent and knowledgeable response at the right moment, can amount to a polite request for serious treatment without the risk of giving offence or being thought hoity-toity yourself.

As in so much else concerned with interviewing, putting yourself in the interviewee's place and then trying to reach him there is likely to produce the best results, whether you are dealing with a saint or a villain. If you come over as an ignoramus, that is your fault. Assert yourself and your claim to be taken seriously, but in the most friendly and knowledgeable way possible.

Part Four:
In Conclusion

Chapter 39

Rules and Roles

Journalists and the public people they interview both proceed according to the rules of the game as they perceive them. Troubles occur when these two sets of rules are incompatible. The point is a practical as well as theoretical one: it directly affects the work of the interviewer and the atmosphere in which he tries to do it.

When I began in journalism, half a century ago in chronological time and several million light-years away in terms of official, public and journalistic mood, journalists and politicians in particular were by and large agreed on the rules, though not necessarily on what was said in interviews. Most statements of intent and counter-statements on that intent were made in the House of Commons rather than in the media direct. Asked a question outside the House, politicians would give the brief structured answer they had made up their minds to give, and that was that. Newspapers – the media usually meant newspapers at that time a million light-years ago – were grateful for these morsels, printed them in their news columns and commented on them only in their leader columns.

Both parties respected the rules and at least pretended to respect each other; very little time was wasted in arguing about the rules, certainly not in public.

The essential point is not whether those rules were good or bad; the central point is that they were mutually accepted. When politicians spoke first in the House of Commons and only secondarily in the media, the rules and the roles on which they were based were clear: the politicians were the players and what would now be called the media were the spectators.

In the second half of the twentieth century this clear division of the roles and the rules that went with them began progressively to break down. In the television studio, a politician and an interviewer may appear to be of equal weight, a fact bound to have an effect on the psychology of both. The interviewer in studio or print may even come to believe that he and his affairs are as important as the interviewee and his affairs.

A clear indication of this breakdown was when Peter Mandelson, Minister Without Portfolio in the Labour government elected 100 days previously in 1997, the man described in the media as the Prime Minister Tony Blair's 'fixer', and the man credited with masterminding the party's victory by shrewd presentation for the benefit of the media, clashed with that self-same media when presenting the 'First 100 Days' report.

The clash took place on BBC Radio 4's *The World At One* programme, on which he was being interviewed by Martha Kearney, who was presenting the programme for the second time. The day previously the Minister Without Portfolio had said that he and John Prescott, the Deputy Prime Minister, were 'running the shop' while the Prime Minister Tony Blair was away on holiday. Earlier in the week, the same programme had used reports suggesting that Peter Mandelson had manipulated the news the previous weekend to downpage the story of the break-up of the marriage of the Foreign Secretary Robin Cook.

In the interview with Martha Kearney, Peter Mandelson was asked a series of questions about the statement that he was 'running the shop' with John Prescott, and why he, a minister without departmental responsibility and not a member of the Cabinet, was doing so. The implication was that he was trying to manage the news.

Peter Mandelson said: 'I think the reason why media people like you like talking about news management is because you really rather prefer talking about yourselves and your work and your lives in the media than talking about things that interest the bulk of the population. I'm talking about their schools and their health service. I'm talking about their fear of crime. I'm talking about unemployment and poverty in this country. This week we've had day in and day out a preoccupation with yourselves. I think it's become very boring and tedious.'

He went on: 'I've never heard such a stream of vainglorious, self-indulgent questions from members of the media about how they are allegedly managed by me. I'm sorry if you're not doing your job properly, such as you have to have me write your scripts and fix your headlines.'

As they say in examination papers: Discuss.

Such an overt and specific critique from a politician, who would have everything to gain by keeping on the right side of the media, merits attention.

For a start, how can a politician 'manipulate' the media? By leaking a story that he hopes will overshadow and relegate another story he wants buried? But a newspaper with firm intentions will itself decide on what prominence to give to any particular story. If a medium is so terrified of the opposition that it feels it must give prominence to a story just because other media are likely to do so, that is the medium's fault, not the politician's. There are many praiseworthy cases where a newspaper or a radio or television channel has stuck to its own view of what is important, whatever competing media may be doing. Even more would be welcome. An editor, even one more concerned with keeping his place on the greasy pole than doing his job immaculately, should at least make an attempt to edit from *his* chair, not from somebody else's.

An interviewer or editor who is not afraid of criticism ('Why didn't you go bigger on this story, Braithwaite?') and is not overwhelmed by the promise of bribes ('We can drop a few future exclusives your way, you know') is not easily manipulated. Manipulation is as old as the hills. It thrives on gutlessness and its every success further weakens the position of the honest practitioner. Someone who claims raucously that he has just been bribed or bullied is not in the strongest of moral positions.

The undeniable fact is that in recent years the balance of power between politicians and the media has shifted substantially in favour of the media. The media is now markedly different in its attitudes and practices from the days when my first news editor told me that no one was interested in a reporter, or what he thought, and that I should report accurately what other people said and leave it at that.

For the media, consciously or unconsciously, to seek a more direct role is perhaps predictable: its mechanics and electronics now make it almost omnipresent; and, at the human level, it is certainly human nature to advance as far as possible and pick up such additional powers as possible, until directly challenged. But does sophistication of means justify each and every end the media may desire? Should any limits be set on an unelected media in the face of democratically elected politicians – even the limitation of good and deferential manners? In treating politicians with contempt, is the media treating with contempt the public which elected them?

The implications of the increased technological power of the media have not yet been addressed; and though the old rules have been discarded (often with good results, sometimes with bad), no foolproof new ones have yet evolved. It should not be beyond the power of human intelligence to find new rules and roles, and it is perfectly possible that before another half-century is out the public spats between the media and public figures about roles and rules will strike contemporary journalists and public figures as being as risible as the nineteenth century controversy over the law obliging motor cars to be preceded by a man waving a red flag. 'The international media "impossible to control" because of satellite and other technologies? How quaint! How could anybody have ever thought that?' That is what people may well be saying in fifty years' time. Eventually a highway code to cover the real problems of motor cars grew up; perhaps a non-statutory international highway code of powerbroker/media relations to fit modern needs is overdue.

Rules, mutually acceptable even if unwritten, are necessary in any enterprise. Anarchy has its dangers, including the risk of the emergence of dictatorial 'saviours' promising to end the bedlam by strongarm methods such as governmental media control.

It is certainly the case that the media now talks about itself more than ever before and that this has psychological dangers. Peter Fiddick created the first newspaper media page, for *The Guardian*, in the 1980s, and now many sections of the media run sections on the media. Journalists of great energy and expertise like Raymond Snoddy, who made his reputation as a writer on the media for the *Financial Times* and further developed it on *The Times*, are now media stars in their own right. It is good that the media can examine and criticize itself in this way. The downside is that self-absorption may create not self-criticism but self-importance, and that this will be reflected in the way the media does its job, especially in how its interviewers approach interviewees. As the cynical newspaper proprietor Lord Beaverbrook once told one of his editors, Beverley Baxter, when he was due to go to dinner with the Prime Minister of the day: 'Baxter, do not patronize the Prime Minister. I know you patronize me, but I am but a poor peasant. If you patronize the Prime Minister, he may not like it.'

The 'media', long before it was given that dangerously monolithic title not entirely devoid of self-importance, used to consist of a man with a little notebook who observed and wrote about as much as he was able. It has ballooned into a sort of floodlit circus ring in which interviewees are 'allowed' to perform their soundbites under rules laid down by the ringmaster. There is an obvious danger of hubris on the part of the media and of vengeful resentment on the part of public figures or of private figures who have suddenly found themselves spotlighted. If a government wanted to limit the powers of the media, would there be a great public outcry of protest from the intelligentsia or the common people? Or would they on balance side with the government which wanted to clip the media's wings by law? It is a sobering question that should be in the mind of every interviewer as he goes about his day-to-day work, for he inevitably contributes, positively or negatively, to public perception of the media.

To some perplexed observers it may occasionally seem as if the media were locked in a private battle for surpremacy with an 'establishment' consisting not merely of antisocial fat cats but of anyone at all who has done anything in life, from being elected to some office to writing or acting in a play. The impression might appear to be confirmed if a newspaper described the Prime Minister as the prime minister while describing its own editorial head as the Editor. The unique function of the media (which is also its social value) is not to inflate or deflate (that is the function of the lobbyist); it is essentially to report. Once that is understood, the work of the interviewer will not be bedevilled by excessive self-importance, by a feeling that even a Mother Teresa must be brought low if the interviewer is to deserve his professional spurs.

Tendencies towards self-importance in media folk are perhaps part of a general fashion away from self-deprecation and towards self-aggrandizement. Self-deprecation is possible only in those whose position in life is secure. In a society in which old social barriers are breaking down but no one is truly secure, there is an inevitable tendency competitively to puff oneself up rather than drily to admit to human shortcomings. As some politicians certainly suffer from this, it would be odd if the media entirely escaped the danger. The old-fashioned reporter in the dirty raincoat may have had limitations but he had one great advantage: he may have taken his work seriously, but he did not take himself seriously.

Such is the larger sombre social backcloth against which interviewers have to do their job in the present day. It darkened even further, and in a way which may linger for decades, when Diana, Princess of Wales, was killed in a high speed car crash in Paris on August 31, 1997, while being pursued at a distance by paparazzi on motor cycles through a tunnel near the Seine. Allegedly taking pictures of the Princess as she lay trapped and fatally injured, though not yet dead, in the mangled wreck of the Mercedes – especially when in one case it apparently entailed opening the door of the car to get a better shot – showed an extreme manifestation of what some sections of the media increasingly display and can decreasingly afford: an arrogant unaccountability to any set of rules, moral precepts, simple humanity or 'professional' justification. Afterwards they were put under investigation for, among other things, manslaughter and not rendering help at the scene of the accident, an offence in France punishable by fines or imprisonment.

Some critics of the media will inevitably continue to see such alleged behaviour as arrogance bordering on the psychotic. It is always a mistake to think oneself untouchable. Such hubris has a habit of conjuring up its own Nemesis. The arrogance of printing-union militants, and their conviction that they could impose terms because the newspaper industry could be brought to a halt if they simply took their finger off a printing button, arguably produced Rupert Murdoch and a new technology that bypassed them.

In Paris, some of the paparazzi were set upon by passers-by. The day after the paparazzi had followed Diana, Princess of Wales, to her death, one cloth-capped worker appeared on British television saying to the cameraman: 'You are still here, aren't you? Why don't you piss off and leave us alone?' Us? When the public instinctively feels it has more in common with the famous than with the media reporting on the doings of the famous, supposedly on its behalf, the task of interviewers as a whole will inevitably grow more difficult and even dangerous.

Media reaction itself showed where sympathy lay and did not lay. An Independent Television News reporter spoke of the plight of the two bereaved young sons, Prince William and Prince Harry, and of the implications of possibly having a future monarch who mistrusted the media for what seeemed to him to be good reasons.

Max Hastings, editor of the *Evening Standard*, spoke of the necessity for the media behaving 'with humility' in the circumstances. In *The Guardian*, John Ezard wrote about how Diana had 'flinched and quailed in shock outside her London nursery school as the media discovered that almost any cobbled-up material about her raised newspaper sales and TV audiences. The same look of stress – the look of a highly vulnerable woman steeling herself before a firing squad – was there a few months later on her first Welsh tour as princess and later in the 1980s during the tours of the Gulf and Hong Kong.' The paper's editor Alan Rusbridger, who on radio had warned of a 'terrible backlash' against the press, wrote of the necessity for practical steps: 'The press in this country, and elsewhere, must take part in a soul-searching public debate about the dividing lines between the private and the public ... the Government should engage in a quiet and reasoned discussion – no panic handgun or dangerous dogs ban here – about sensible reforms affecting all the laws relating to information, including privacy, libel, data protection and Freedom of Information.' The former editor Peter Preston wrote about the ultimate responsibility: 'The true question, alas, is whether we can change a little; whether – in our interests, our human interests – we can become a touch more civilized. If we can, then many acts that are committed in our name (the right to goggle and gawp as well as to know) will gradually fall from fashion, and we may come to live in kindlier times.'

The satirical magazine *Private Eye* underlined his point with brutal clarity on its front cover where a spoof photograph of the crowd outside Buckingham Palace under the heading 'Media To Blame', had one of the crowd saying, 'The papers are a disgrace', another one saying, 'Yes. I couldn't get one anywhere', and a third saying, 'Borrow mine. It's got a picture of the car'.

Quite. Human nature being what it is, the public as ultimate paymaster is much less likely to blame itself than on-the-spot journalists for media excesses. It is likely to hold a grudge against all journalists for the excesses of a few and perhaps to be hostile to them as they try to do their jobs. Realism insists that interviewers accept this as at least a possibility.

The coverage of the death of Diana contained a cause for reflection which bordered on this point. At her funeral service in Westminster Abbey, Lord Spencer, her brother Charles, said his sister had goodness and attacked the press as being at the 'other end of the moral spectrum'. This was a remarkable attack to mount at a funeral service in a cathedral. What was even more remarkable in a cathedral was that, at the end of his speech, the congregation burst spontaneously into thunderous applause. Everyone concerned with dealing with the public on behalf of the media, and justly priding themselves on possessing some shrewdness, should have felt a slight chill down the spine. Such mass moral scorn, if not addressed, is a menace to every interviewer trying to do his job. The day after, Sir David English, chairman of the Code of Practice Committee of the Press Complaints Commission, a former editor of the *Daily Mail*, said the matter would have to be considered by the Commission. The veteran broadcaster Alistair Cooke, in his BBC Radio 4 *Letter From America*, attacked 'speculation masquerading as news' and repeated the saying of a French sage: 'Freedom is the luxury of self-discipline.'

It became obvious, as investigations into the death of Diana continued, that several other factors besides the behaviour of the media were crucial to the tragedy. But the media were a convenient scapegoat for members of the public who preferred not to think too analytically and blame themselves as customers of that media. As the media will always be a convenient scapegoat, it might be wise for it as a whole not to give too many hostages to fortune, too many excuses that could be used by those who for their own reasons would like to silence or castrate it.

Some months before the death of the Princess, Martyn Lewis, the BBC TV newsreader and presenter was attacked when he said that newsmen and women were too interested in finding negative angles to stories. He was immediately and unfairly lampooned by some other media people as a sycophantic ass who had suggested that the media should report only good news – a fatuous suggestion that no one in his right mind would make and which Martyn Lewis did not make. What he was against was the distortion of all news into some sort of negative story. He was treated as if he had tried to limit the power of the media, as if he were some sort of mock-humble Uriah Heep.

Immediately after the death of Diana, Princess of Wales, it was visible and audible that whereas some other interviewers had to change gear in their manner, sometimes unconvincingly so, somehow to fit the needs of a very real human tragedy of universal concern, Martyn Lewis's style needed little alteration: it was polite, modulated and non-inflammatory – as usual. This fact revealed that for all the attacks on him, for all his alleged limitations, his questioning had always been conducted as an exchange between two fellow humans, not as a verbal version of the paparazzi's attentions. It was evidently a style, whatever might be said of it, that could take and survive all weathers. I would not necessarily have expected to find myself in the same camp as Martyn Lewis, but here I did.

If a government is ever mistakenly to be pushed by public demand into legislation restricting the freedom of the media in general and interviewers in particular, it will not be because of the Martyn Lewis brand of interviewing but because of insensitive and arrogant intrusiveness with camera or notebook, a forgetfulness of the fact that the media are dealing with animate people, not inanimate 'images', and that it is not 'professional' to be so forgetful.

At street level, as it were, with few rules mutually accepted and watertight, perhaps it would be at least a small first step towards a mutual improvement if a degree of now unfashionable formality could re-emerge and be mutually accepted by interviewers and interviewed. My experience as a journalist and as a human being does not support the notion that contrived mateyness or familiarity is helpful in any calling or situation. It usually leads first to slovenly language and then to slovenly or disputatious behaviour.

An indication of how blurred the necessary distinction between players and spectators had become, and how suspect necessary formality had become, came in the Tatton constituency of Derbyshire when Martin Bell, the distinguished ex-foreign reporter of the BBC, stood as an independent candidate against alleged corruption.

Immediately after his candidature had been announced, an ex-colleague on the BBC, with whom he had been on first name terms, addressed him in public as 'Mr Bell'. Martin Bell was surprised, and apparently continued to be so. It is arguable that he should not have been surprised; that his surprise was an indication of the confusions which have multiplied as the distinction between players and spectators has blurred. The ex-colleague who addressed him politely as he would have done any other political candidate was doing something perfectly proper and desirable. It was a signal that the interviewer would regard him with the objective respect due to a candidate. To have gone on addressing him as 'Martin' while he addressed other candidates as 'Mr So-and-So', would have suggested a not impartial mateyness inappropriate between contending politicians and the media interviewers.

From the moment he declared himself as a candidate and sought people's votes, Martin Bell was willy-nilly a politician. It was right that he be addressed and treated as a politician.

Of course, if there was any personal frostiness in the use of his surname, that was not praiseworthy. In such a case (I am not suggesting it happened here) there could have been a feeling that Martin Bell was 'getting above himself', a state of affairs much deplored by the British who (unlike the Americans) regard 'counter-jumping' as bad form rather than an indication of enterprise. But even such a grudging envy would not invalidate the central point: that it is perfectly proper in an interview for the interviewer to have one status and the interviewee another, and that the point should be made by a certain degree of formality.

Should not the interviewer always be subordinate to the interviewee, politician or other, potentate or pauper? On what basis can the interviewer claim otherwise? Certainly not democratic election: the media is self-appointed, not democratically appointed, and long may it remain so; a Soviet system would in practice have more oppressions than benefits.

The media, because of electronic developments, has undoubtedly become much more powerful: politicans and other interviewees can get their points across only with its help, while their reputations are largely made and unmade by the selfsame media's editorializing in some shape or form. The days when a solitary individual could make an impression by getting on a soapbox (except on television) are long gone, yet no counter-balance to the sometimes capricious power of the media that would not entail totalitarian control has been found. Perhaps eventually some will be. In the meantime, conscientious interviewers may profitably remember that they are not important in themselves, only in their function as a servant of the public, and may wisely tailor their methods of working accordingly.

Some people employed in the media may think I have overdone my emphasis on the need for humility in interviewers. If so, it emerged perhaps as a corrective to some present trends. But the central point would remain whatever the period in which we lived: inevitable self-assertion in getting the interview, but deferential good manners in conducting it. Don't worry that following my advice might blunt too much the underlying arrogance any human being needs to survive in a hard world: that arrogance is well able to take care of itself. Just don't flaunt it; diplomatically play against it for the purposes of the craft.

Perhaps, when working at street level against the broad social back-cloth I have described, with the dangers of provoking a legislative backlash providing the most dramatic colours, the following profile of suitable underlying attitudes for interviewers may have some practical value.

Minister/Your Royal Highness/Your Eminence:
(1) Get on your pedestal.
(2) Stay on your pedestal – mutual rubbishing is more suited to closing time in the pub or wine bar than to public debate.
(3) I will respect that pedestal, and will not automatically assume you are unworthy of it, though I reserve the right to see the pedestal and you as two separate entities.
(4) You must justify your being on that pedestal, to which justification I will listen politely.
(5) I have the right to ask you any supplementary questions I choose, provided they are framed with good manners rather than vainglory.
(6) I will always remember that I am a spectator, not a player; and recognize that the moment I try to be a player, you are justified in denigrating me, outsmarting me and belabouring me as you would do any other player.
(7) I will always remember that, whatever your faults, you are a human being and that, whatever my virtues, I am only a human being too.
(8) If I observe the rules, you will not waste the time of both of us and insult my intelligence and that of the public by talking patently glib rubbish; and if you do, you will have to accept the penalty of being quoted, as in every other respect, absolutely accurately.

Perception and accuracy, the attributes of the honest witness, not self-importance, insensitivity or distortion, remain the interviewer's most formidable long-term weapons.

Chapter 40

Remember . . .

It is *not* just about making your reputation and a quick buck by denigrating or hyping inflated 'celebrities', or about filling comparatively cheaply the space between the advertisements.

The published interview can condition the way we lead our lives. It can do this by influencing the way we regard our fellow human beings and ultimately the way we regard life in general. It can help determine whether we think of ourselves as worthwhile creatures, who can sometimes see the stars as well as the mud, or degraded creatures capable only of base motives.

These are sobering facts. They *are* facts. Those who dismiss them as merely fanciful or piously high-minded should reconcile themselves to living in a moral and aesthetic pigsty, for that is where they will in effect have chosen to live. If one lives in a pigsty, it is a mistake to think that only other people, not oneself, will be blighted by the smell.

Let us blow away any suggestions of fancifulness with a piece of stark realism. Sensitivity, intelligence and perception can sometimes be highly uncomfortable qualities to those who possess them: at worst they merely give their possessors front stalls seats in the theatre of their own powerlessness. They do not of themselves enable their possessors to be effective in managing the world as distinct from letting the world manage them.

But they are qualities which can be used to highly positive effect by the media interviewer. They increase the interviewer's ability to remain a keenly perceptive *observer* as distinct from participant. They provide clues about what questions to ask. They enable better understanding of the answers, even if more assertive and less sensitive qualities may be necessary to get the interview in the first place.

Take a coarse and degraded view of your fellow human beings – your interviewees – and you will ultimately coarsen and degrade yourself. The worst interviewee imaginable deserves justice, and, if you think about it, should have precisely that. The best, if still not perfect, interviewee deserves the ungrudging if not blind respect due from one fallible human being to another. No doubt even Mother Teresa was imperfect. She was still preferable to Jack the Ripper.

Technical tricks to get the interviewee to talk are justified only if the results are treated with accuracy and honesty. The interviewer should at all costs avoid the kind of fat-cat posturing that could, and sometimes does, make the media as distrusted and even detested as the 'establishment' from which the media is supposed to protect the ordinary person.

Try always to think of the interviewee as another three-dimensional human being. Is he (or she) honourable? Is he kind? Is he generous? Is he original? Is he capable of humour? Is he talented? Is he a genius? Is he practical? Is he conscientious? Is he understanding? Is he a survivor? Is he sensitive to others or only to himself? Does he have a strong character (not always easy to discover on brief acquaintance) or only a strong personality (all too easy to discover)?

Is he an opportunist? Is he mean-spirited? Is he a humanly empty careerist? Is he a mediocrity? Is he a prisoner to ideas which have no relation to the real needs of human beings? Is he an instinctive exploiter who gives nothing back? Is he always a prisoner of the herd?

Contemporary life, infatuated with and intimidated by what for the time being are still novel technologies, has perhaps partly lost sight of those sorts of words and phrases, and their meanings, as criteria for human assessment. If interviewers would try to write of people in relation to these things, as well as the more easily visible tinsel criteria of money and position, the interview might have an enhanced significance and so, as life sometimes follows art, might human beings.

No, it is *not* just about making your reputation and a quick buck by denigrating or hyping inflated 'celebrities' or filling comparatively cheaply the space between the advertisements.

It is a complex, subtle, demanding craft requiring both guts and sensitivity, and capable not only of exposing human fallibility but also, no less importantly, of honouring human potential in all its rich warmth, humour, integrity, compassion and strength.

Index